Mythos and Logos in the Thought of Carl Jung

Mythos and Logos in the Thought of Carl Jung

The Theory of the Collective Unconscious in Scientific Perspective

Walter A. Shelburne

State University of New York Press

Published by
State University of New York Press, Albany

For information, address State University of New York
Press, State University Plaza, Albany, N.Y., 12246

Library of Congress Cataloging-in-Publication Data

Shelburne, Walter A., 1946-
  Mythos and logos in the thought of Carl Jung.

  Bibliography: p.
  Includes index.
  1. Archetype (Psychology)   2. Jung, C. G. (Carl
Gustav), 1875-1961. I. Title.
BF175.5.A72S54   1988   150.19'54   87-10210
ISBN 0-88706-693-3
ISBN 0-88706-695-X (pbk.)

10   9   8   7   6   5   4   3   2

To Marilyn Holly with gratitude, admiration, and love.

Contents

Acknowledgments

I would like to thank the following publishers for permission to quote from various works to which they have rights:

J. G. Ferguson Publishing Company for permission to quote from *Man and His Symbols,* by Carl G. Jung, et. al. Copyright © 1964 J. G. Ferguson Publishing Company.

Harper and Row for permission to quote from *Re-Visioning Psychology* by James Hillman. Copyright © 1975 by James Hillman. Reprinted by permission of Harper and Row, Publishers, Inc.

Pantheon Books for permission to quote from *Memories, Dreams, Reflections* by C. G. Jung, recorded and edited by Aniela Jaffé, translated by Richard and Clara Winston. Copyright © 1962, 1963 by Random House, Inc. Reprinted by permission of Pantheon Books, a division of Random House, Inc.

Princeton University Press for permission to quote from C. G. Jung, *Letters,* ed. Gerhard Adler and Aniela Jaffé, trans. R. F. C. Hull, Bollingen Series XCV, Vol. I: *1906-1950. Copyright* © 1971, 1973 by Princeton University Press. Excerpts reprinted with permission of Princeton University Press. C. G. Jung, *Letters,* ed. Gerhard Adler and Aniela Jaffé, trans. R. F. C. Hull, Bollingen Series XCV, Vol. II: *1951-1961.* Copyright 1953, 1955, © 1961, 1963, 1968, 1971, 1972, 1974, 1975 by Princeton University Press. Excerpts reprinted with permission of Princeton University Press.

Princeton University Press for permission to quote from *The Collected Works of C. G. Jung,* ed. Gerhard Adler, Michael Fordham, William McGuire, and Herbert Read, trans. R. F. C. Hull, Bollingen Series XX. Excerpts reprinted with permission of Princeton University Press. Quotes from:

The Collected Works of C. G. Jung, trans. R. F. C. Hull, Bollingen Series XX. Vol 2: *Experimental Researches,* copyright © 1973 by Princeton University Press.

The journey which the undertaking of this project has represented for me has been a long, arduous, and interesting one. In many ways it has been truly the *longissima via.* Along the way I owe debts of gratitude to many who have assisted me and given generously of the resources of their time and energy. I would like to thank Tom Auxter, Franz Epting, Richard Haynes, Marilyn Holly, and Tom Simon who were actively involved in the formative first stage of this work and especially Marilyn and Tom for their substantive and helpful criticism.

I would also like to acknowledge Ira Progoff for the inspirational example of his life and for his personal encouragement very early in the process.

Tom Hanna and Jimmy Millikan have greatly assisted this work by being my teachers and role models in wholistic philosophy.

Thanks are due George Clough for the contribution of his personal dream material and Joan Alpert for her help at the library of the C. G. Jung Institute in San Francisco.

Joan Palatine of Princeton University Press and Carola Sautter and Marilyn Semerad of State University of New York Press have rendered friendly encouragement along with their indispensable editorial expertise.

Most of all I would like to thank Carl Jung, whose boundless passion for understanding inspired this book.

Introduction

JUNG'S writings concerning his notion of the collective unconscious confound the reader with many perplexities. Not the least of these is Jung's claim that his theory falls within the domain of the scientific method.[1] However, on account of the many obviously extrascientific aspects of Jung's work, we are led to wonder how the scientific elements of his writings can be reconciled with the extrascientific aspects. Is there in fact a viable scientific theory reconstructable out of Jung's views? What would be the significance of such a scientifically defensible theory of the collective unconscious? Would it be intelligible? Would it really be compatible with present scientific knowledge? And is there any compelling evidence to suggest that such a theory is in fact true?

The present work offers itself as an attempt to answer the questions above. In order to have any success, it is clear that such a task must begin with a rational reconstruction of Jung's views of the collective unconscious. A rational reconstruction would attempt to clarify the meaning and interrelationships of the basic concepts of Jung's theory so that it could be shown to be coherent and consistent. In Jung's style of theorizing, clarity and precision of basic concepts are much less important than fullness of meaning and phenomenologically accurate characterization of phenomena. As a consequence many of Jung's ideas are as vague and ambiguous as they are fascinating and insightful. However, the purpose of a rational reconstruction, as it is understood here, is not to oppose the spontaneity and richness of creativity with a narrow desire for order and clarity. Rather the aim of such a task is the transformation of the untidy richness of creativity into a more directly useable form. In Jung's case this transformation amounts in large measure to a sort of translation from a symbolic and metaphorical mode of expression into a simpler and more linear mode. In this regard we have endeavored to make sense of what Jung is saying without losing sight of what he actually does say. Jung was himself the first to acknowledge the value and necessity of such reconstruction of his views.[2]

In order to demonstrate the possibility of a scientifically accountable theory of the collective unconscious, we will need to approach the reconstruction from a naturalistic point of view. This naturalistic viewpoint will be one which emphasizes the continuity between the world of ordinary experience and the reality of archetypes rather than appealing to a radical discontinuity where the latter are centered in a supernatural or transempirical realm transcending space and time. Looking at the archetypes from a naturalistic perspective then would mean assuming that archetypes can be fully accounted for within the world rather than having to appeal to what lies beyond the range of our possible experience.

In spite of his speculations concerning what lies beyond space, time, and causality, it is clear that Jung's work as a whole lies already within this naturalistic attitude. This is evident from the centrality of the idea of the *unus mundus* in Jung's thought as a unified world scheme embracing both material and spiritual phenomena. Thus, although Jung believed in the existence of God and the prospect of a spirit world, these beliefs are not incompatible with a naturalistic outlook. For naturalism as meant here does not have to entail materialism or the denial of any reality outside of space and time or anything not subject to causality in the ordinary sense. There may well be more to reality than what we see manifested in time, space, and causality. A naturalistic perspective simply assumes that nature will eventually yield to an intelligibility which will not need to appeal to what may exist completely outside of itself.

However, the sort of reconstruction we are attempting in the following will necessarily be more narrow in its focus than the full range of Jung's thought. In order to argue for the scientific credibility of his theory of archetypes, we must show not only that Jung's theory is a naturalistic one, in the most general meaning of that term, but also that the theory is compatible in principle with standard, scientifically informed understandings of nature. Thus, we will have to show how the essential features of the theory can be understood without having to rely on aspects that go beyond the scope of science or that are incompatible with chief tenets of current scientific knowledge. In concrete terms this will mean bracketing away from consideration the notion of synchronicity as an essential and intrinsic part of the archetypal theory. In addition it will mean understanding the archetypal theory in such a way that the possibility, sometimes hinted at by Jung, that archetypes might subsist separate and independent of human consciousness, and that the collective unconscious might thus be a superindividual entity, is clearly denied. Lastly the archetypes per se will have to be understood as hypothetical constructs rather than as "irrepresentable" transcendent entities.[3]

The intent of the sort of naturalistic reconstruction we are attempting here is to show how a theory of the collective unconscious does not have to clash with a world outlook conditioned by an assimilation of scientific knowledge. But what is really at stake in this issue? Why is it so important to show that the theory can be construed as compatible with a scientifi-cally informed perspective?

In looking further at this question of the relevance of scientific compat-ability, it is important to remember that this was a concern which Jung himself shared and which he attempted to address, if even in a highly idiosyncratic fashion. Our concern with this issue is motivated by what we perceive to be an essential guiding theme in Jung's thought. For Jung was trying to interpret the phenomena of the archetypes in such a way that these experiences could be assimilated by the scientifically influenced modern intellect. By framing his theory in a way that he thought would be compatible with a scientific perspective, Jung felt this opened up the possibility of the theory being taken seriously and hence creating a link between the primordial archetypal experiences and the modern mind set.[4] The theory of the collective unconscious was to be an interpretation of the abiding experience of archetypes appropriate for the modern age. "If we cannot deny the archetypes or otherwise neutralize them, we are con-fronted, at every new stage in the differentiation of consciousness to which civilization attains, with the task of finding a new *interpretation* appropri-ate to this stage, in order to connect the life of the past that still exists in us with the life of the present, which threatens to slip away from it." (Vol. 9–A, p. 157)

Thus, Jung wanted to create a theoretical framework that would be instrumental in archetypal phenomena becoming integrated into our modern world. He wanted some way to demonstrate how these numinous and often spiritually inspiring mythological images are really part of our experience, whether we acknowledge them or not. Jung wanted to accomplish the most essential task with which any systematic and disci-plined attempt to understand the irrational and emotionally charged archetypes would have to deal: a valid demonstration of the essential reality of the phenomena. In order to accomplish this goal, Jung felt he needed a theoretical framework that did not directly conflict with scientific knowledge and could even partially stake a claim to the authority of science itself. This is an implicit acknowledgment on Jung's part that science has to be taken seriously in any statement concerning those things which can be said to really exist in the world of our experience. Thus, Jung framed his theory within the context of scientific realism, accepting the view that the entities with which science deals for the most part really succeed in describing the world rather than being merely helpful fictions or conventions.

But even the most sympathetic appreciation of Jung's concern with the question of scientific compatability will have to acknowledge that the kinds of experiences that Jung included within the theory of the collective unconscious are among those aspects of life which could well be con-sidered as the least likely items for successful scientific scrutiny. In fact the archetypes in their numinous, symbolic, and even, at times, ineffable aspects seem often to point beyond words altogether toward a seemingly irreducible mystery. These phenomena include some of the most profound and moving experiences of life for which poetic description would seem frequently more appropriate than the value neutral dissecting analysis of the scientific method. It would seem that science and archetypes occupy different and seemingly incompatible domains of epistemological territory.

One way of dealing with this issue is to acknowledge it fully and attempt to understand the divergence in these ways of experiencing by means of broad general categories. For example, we could designate the way the world is seen from the imaginative, intuitive point of view as conditioned by the various archetypal images as the mythos. The contrasting category, the logos, would be a rationally discursive perspective on the world such as is ideally represented in the scientific attitude. We could also say that the logos offers us a theoretical account of the world, a cognitive understanding of it, whereas the mythos discloses the world in its presence and immediacy, thereby offering a sense of spiritual connection and the dimension of meaning. The table below gives an idea of the sort of differences of perspective that we are referring to by these terms.

Logos	*Mythos*
science	mysticism
rational knowledge	intuitive knowledge
reason	imagination
literal truth	metaphorical truth
philosophy	mythology
expression through conscious activity	expression through manifestations of the unconscious

These somewhat arbitrary categories, although not employed as terms by Jung himself, offer us a convenient means to appreciate the import of the theory of the collective unconscious and Jung's unique contribution to understanding the phenomena it describes. For Jung, in articulating a theoretical framework in terms of which the archetypal images could be understood and appreciated, was trying to create a logos of the mythos and thereby bring about a bridging of the two. In regard to this aim, it is important to bear in mind that the categories we have here labeled logos and mythos would not have designated for Jung two separate domains of reality, a natural versus a supernatural domain, for example. In terms of his ideal of a unified world picture, the *unus mundus,* what we are calling here "logos" and "mythos" were to be perceived as equally valid though different perspectives on the same one world. What was needed according to Jung's viewpoint was both an appreciation of the mythos perspective in a regrettably demythologized and desouled world as well as accountability to the rationally critical functions represented by the logos point of view. Any framework adequate to do justice to the reality of archetypes must then maintain this dual perspective. It would have to be open to the mythos perspective with its numinous, symbolic mysteries as well as able to withstand scientific critique.

To fully appreciate the significance of Jung's ideas about what we are calling here the "mythos-logos," it is helpful to see how his perspective relates to other contrasting views. In this way the significance of the parity of emphasis Jung gives to the two poles of experience can be more fully appreciated by seeing it in relation to outlooks that advocate the hegemony of one of the poles over the other. In advocating a kind of equiprimordiality of logos and mythos, Jung's outlook can be contrasted both with a perspective which devalues the mythos in relation to the logos as well as a view which takes Jung's appreciation of the mythos to the extreme that science itself is reduced to a subset of myth.

The ideas of Ernst Cassirer can serve as representative of the first contrasting position. So far as Cassirer is concerned, the existence of a mythological level of human nature is not in dispute. It is rather the contention that the mythos gives a deeper, truer, or even helpful additional view on reality that he apparently disclaims. Cassirer sees mythological conceptualizing as belonging to an earlier stage of human development in which mythos and logos were not sharply differentiated but conflated together:

> At first the world of language, like that of myth in which it seems as it were embedded, preserves a complete equivalence of word and thing, of "signifer" and "signified." It grows away from this equivalence as its independent spiritual form, the characteristic force of the logos, comes to the fore.[5]

Beginning in the West with the early Greek philosophers and accelerated by the development of science, the process of separation of logos and mythos is hailed by Cassirer as a progressive development that has the characteristic of a long and arduous struggle for emancipation from the rationally detrimental effects of mythological influence. "Indeed, the history of philosophy as a scientific discipline may be regarded as a single continuous struggle to effect a separation and liberation from myth."[6] Moreover, Cassirer believes that culture is continually threatened with the reversal of this progress of differentiation of logos and mythos. Modern humanity is threatened by a return of the pernicious influence of mythological thinking:

> The world of human culture may be described in the words of this Babylonian legend. It could not arise until the darkness of myth was fought and overcome. But the mythical monsters were not entirely destroyed. They were used for the creation of a new universe, and they still survive in this universe. The powers of myth were checked and subdued by superior forces. As long as these forces, intellectual, ethical,

and artistic, are in full strength, myth is tamed and subdued. But once they begin to lose their strength chaos is come again. Mythical thought then starts to rise anew and to pervade the whole of man's cultural and social life.[7]

We cannot hope to "rationalize" myth by an arbitrary transformation and re-interpretation of the old legends of the deeds of gods or heroes. All this remains vain and futile. In order to overcome the power of myth we must find and develop the new positive power of "self-knowledge." We must learn to see the whole of human nature in an ethical rather than in a mythical light.[8]

In contrast to Cassirer's view,[9] Jung did not believe that the influence of the mythos either could be completely subjugated by the logos or that the effort should be made to subjugate it. For rather than stripping away any claims to validity or truth made on behalf of experience from the standpoint of the mythos and seeing the mythos as merely a superstitious or animistic perversion of objective reality, Jung tries to affirm the value of both perspectives as ways of seeing the world.

One of the consequences of Jung's position is the claim that the logos and mythos cannot really be totally separated from each other. For example, he emphasized that when we think we have spelled out something with absolute precision and eliminated all traces of unconscious influence, this is never entirely the case:

> One may tend to dismiss such differences as redundant or expendable nuances of meaning that have little relevance to everyday needs. But the fact that they exist shows that even the most matter-of-fact contents of consciousness have a penumbra of uncertainty around them. Even the most carefully defined philosophical or mathematical concept, which we are sure does not contain more than we have put into it, is nevertheless more than we assume. It is a psychic event and as such partly unknowable.[10]

The two modes then interpenetrate each other with the logos never completely free of the mythos and the mythos likewise subject to rational influence and interpretation. Thus, the effort to deny one for the sake of affirming the other must necessarily be a futile endeavor. It is clear, moreover, that it is because Jung thinks that the mythological motifs are an innate and thus indispensable part of human nature that he believes that the mythos perspective cannot be radically overcome or discarded.

This point is similar to one that could be made with respect to metaphor. For Jung's view presupposes a position on metaphor which assumes that language cannot be purged of metaphor without catastrophic loss of referential function. Metaphor will be seen as permeating all languages and cannot be eliminated in favor of completely literal discourse. Moreover, myths can themselves be seen as extended metaphors so that the archetypes could then be understood as an innate set of basic metaphors in terms of which humans can see the world. Just as language cannot be freed from metaphor, so also human nature cannot be purified of archetypal perspective and mythological influence. As an innate aspect of human nature, the mythos will always be present either in overt or disguised form.

Having an access to the mythos, moreover, is essential from the standpoint of providing human existence with a sense of meaning and purpose. According to Jung we need symbols that are capable of mediating the experience of the archetypes. If we think of religion in terms of our scheme of mythos and logos, this particular point becomes clear. We might think that religion would belong to the mythos side, and this is indeed the source of the archetypal images from which religious revelation springs. However, once in consciousness, the archetypal images are interpreted and integrated into consciously elaborated theological and dogmatic frameworks. In the course of time, the original symbols, which were vehicles for channeling the mythos, may become "dead" symbols where they cease to mediate the archetypal images and become mere signs. They cease to help us to apprehend or experience the mythos and become merely additional aspects of our conscious experience. Thus, when religion becomes logos, completely rationalized with all of its mysteries literalized, it does not function any longer as mediator of the mythos, and we begin to see less and less meaning and point in the whole enterprise.

If religion is denied totally, however, this does not mean that we have discarded the mythos, that the mythos vanishes without trace. For in that case some other system of belief may begin to take over the function of mediating the mythos. One may, for example, come to be an adherent of some political ideology such as communism, which is replete with such myths as the eventual withering away of the state in the coming of the golden age.

> There is in the psyche some superior power, and if it is not consciously a god, it is the "belly" at least, in St. Paul's words. I therefore consider it wiser to acknowledge the idea of God consciously; for, if we do not, something else is made God, usually something quite inappropriate and stupid such as only an "enlightened" intellect could hatch forth. (Vol. 7, p. 71)

According to Jung's view, if we acknowledge the function of a mythic dimension to human existence, then we have a better chance of modifying it with rational considerations. Moreover, once the mythos is acknowledged there is then less chance of confusing it with the logos. This is closely analogous to consciously acknowledging that a particular way of speaking is a metaphor and thereby avoiding the risk of taking one's models of the world for the world itself; it is to avoid the problem of confusing the map with the territory. This acknowledgment of the mythos also has the major additional advantage of enabling one to see the limitations of a particular mythos perspective. Once a particular viewpoint is understood to be a model or extended metaphor, we are then alerted to the built-in limitations of looking at reality too exclusively in terms of this conception. This creates the possibility of a critique from the logos perspective, that is, the possibility of a rational critique.

The net result of not attempting to eliminate the tension between mythos and logos by devaluing one in favor of the other is to maintain a dual perspective on the world. Both are seen as necessary and important modes of cognizing with nonoverlapping functions. The potential imaginative sterility and nihilism of a logos alienated from the mythos is overcome. On the other hand, the mythos is not left completely free of rational critique. Although the logos cannot replace the mythos, it can prevent the mythos from overstepping its own legitimate bounds by insisting on literality, facts, and empirical grounds whenever appropriate. In this way the mythos is then made partially accountable to the logos.

Jung's perspective on the mythos-logos, in contrast to a view such as Cassirer represents, has the net result of advocating the value of the mythos in relation to the logos. However, Jung's outlook also needs to be contrasted with the ideas of someone like James Hillman.[11] For Hillman has taken up the cause of the mythos and attempted to understand all experience in terms of it. Rather than aiming for a logos of the mythos as did Jung, Hillman wants to articulate a mythos of the logos. For rather than attempting to develop a scientific approach to the archetypes, he advocates that we see science from the viewpoint of archetypes:

> In fact, the categories of logic and number, of science and theology, could themselves be reduced (i.e., led back) to more basic metaphors of myth. No concepts, no matter how general and abstract, could embrace the range of these archetypal metaphors.[12]

> By psychologizing scientific problems, methods, and hypotheses we can find their archetypal fantasies.[13]

Since he sees all psychology as depth psychology,[14] it is not surprising that Hillman does not recognize psychology as properly a science:

> In order to move toward a nonagnostic psychology we must first see through psychology's dominant belief in itself as a science. Clearly, from the ideas we have been shaping, archetypal psychology does not imagine itself or the psyche as belonging to science, even social or behavioral science.[15]

Hillman's program is thus best described as a relativizing of the logos by seeing it as a limited part of the mythos.

In contrasting Hillman and Jung's views on the mythos and logos, the fundamental differences hinge on the question of how broadly to apply the archetypal theory. Jung, in contrast to Hillman, wants to keep the archetypal theory grounded in the scientific attitude rather than using the theory as a sort of ideological device to critique all experience including science itself. The advantage that Jung's position offers is the prospect of creating bridges between the tradition of scientific knowledge and archetypal experience. By trying to approach the archetypes in a scientific spirit, Jung opens himself up to the results of critical and rational inquiry, that is, he makes his theory accountable to the logos point of view. This accountability offers the possibility of making archetypal experience an integral aspect of the modern world. For the logos accountability offers the prospect of a mythos appreciation which can be taken seriously without the necessity of having to subscribe to a philosophical viewpoint that argues for epistemological priority of the archetypal theory. Thus, in Jung's position, the logos perspective can maintain its autonomy and hence its critical function in relation to the mythos rather than being reductively "swallowed" and depotentiated by an all-inclusive mythos emphasis.

This contrast with other views has been undertaken in order to develop Jung's position on the mythos and logos as a key to understanding how his theory of archetypes can be seen in a scientific perspective. However, our discussion of the relevance of compatibility with a scientific point of view, of bridging the logos and mythos which Jung's emphasis on mythos and logos seems to entail, is still lacking an important aspect. Before the relevance of the question of scientific compatibility can be definitely established, we have to show how the extrascientific aspects of Jung's writings about archetypes can be reconciled with the intention to have the theory perceived within a scientific context.

For in addition to the tendency to accommodate his ideas about archetypes to a scientific perspective, there is also the tendency to want to go outside of a scientific viewpoint or beyond science such as we see in *Answer to Job* and the writings on synchronicity. And how are we to discriminate those aspects of Jung's writings which seem to be outside the scope of science, or to be even potential embarrassments to a scientific outlook, without grossly distorting the actual intent of Jung's work on the collective unconscious as a whole?

In this regard it is important to bear in mind that Jung was involved with archetypal experience on both a mythos as well as a logos level. Thus, an essay such as *Answer to Job* was not intended as a scientific work, nor was it perceived as such by Jung.[16] Rather it was an attempt to wrestle with the mythos of the God archetype and interpret it for the modern era. *Job* is then at the object-level of the mythos rather than the meta-level. From the standpoint of his therapeutic commitment, Jung had to be involved at the object-level of myth because it is from involvement with the mythos that he believed that the patient's healing sprang. Thus, it is not surprising that Jung has a stake in an articulation of both the mythos as well as the logos of archetypes, although his style of exposition easily leads to confusion when he rapidly switches from a mythos to a logos discourse and back again.

Concerning synchronicity there is an attempt to develop a notion complementary to science. For synchronicity is supposed to deal with acausal events. It also calls into question the reality of space and time in discussion of events that are supposed to involve a relativizing of space and time as ordinarily understood. At this point it seems that Jung was attempting to grapple with phenomena that he could not conceive as fitting into a scientific scheme of understanding. This tendency to want to go beyond science and talk in terms of a broader framework of which science would be one part also can be seen manifested in Jung's discussion of psychical phenomena such as ESP and spirit manifestations and hints, open to various interpretations, concerning the subsistence of archetypal entities independent of human minds.[17]

In spite of Jung's self-description as an empiricist, the sorts of ideas mentioned above clearly indicate a speculative bent to Jung's thinking which, particularly in the later part of his life, led him in an unmistakenly philosophical direction. The value of these thought-provoking and insightful contributions are not negated if we insist on a separate treatment of these apart from what can be defended as a legitimately scientific dimension to Jung's work. They remain valuable contributions in their own right. But often when Jung is dealing directly with the mythos, as in *Job*, they confuse the reader as to what Jung is aiming for, and as to the basis upon which the ideas rest. The astrological "experiments" discussed in the essay on synchronicity are an infamous case in point as they leave the reader to wonder what sort of experimental proof Jung seems to be after and whether such things are even possible for so-called acausal events. But even though there are these many strains of Jung's thought—a philosophical emphasis, a mythos emphasis, as well as a scientific emphasis—this is not to say that everything Jung said has to be evaluated from the critical standpoint of any one particular point of view. For it is the thesis of this work to show that in spite of the confusion that Jung creates by working over his material from these methodologically divergent perspectives, a legitimately scientific perspective can nonetheless be reconstructed from his thought.[18]

It may seem somewhat paradoxical to defend Jung's ideas from the point of view of orthodox and traditional ways of trying to understand the world when in fact Jung's "science," such as it is, does not fit neatly into the ideal of what science should be, if this ideal is taken from the natural sciences as a model. However, we have to be wary of falling into the trap of trying to make psychology scientific by modeling it on an already outmoded concept of science, as it could be argued the behaviorists have done in their emulation of classical Newtonian physics. Jung's scientific method is descriptive and phenomenological and it is part of the pioneering element in his thought to attempt to legitimate alternative ways of scientific investigation in the human sciences in the face of the prohibitive difficulties of employing experimental methods with regard to archetypal phenomena. Therefore the endeavor to argue for a consideration of a genuine scientific aspect of Jung's work should not be understood as an effort to contort Jung's imaginative and symbolic ideas onto a procrustean bed of outdated scientific orthodoxy. Jung's science already encorporates a brave new vision of what it means to be scientific which owes a great deal to the inspiration of relativity and quantum physics.

But if it is acknowledged that Jung's understanding of what it means to be scientific already embodies a nonrestrictive notion of science and is compatible with a non-Newtonian physics, this still does not complete the argument for the importance of a reconstruction from the scientific perspective which deliberately brackets out the speculative element of Jung's thought. For when we acknowledge that Jung's ideas are out on the growing fringe of science, this still does not effectively counter those who see Jung's aim as being primarily to transcend the spectrum of scientific thought altogether. For a critic might argue that in reconstructing Jung's idea of archetypes from the standpoint of a scientific outlook, we are in effect cutting out of the theory the progressive aspects of it where Jung was beginning to grope toward a new vision of reality transcending the limiting scope of scientific method. Why not, for example, assimilate Jung's theory of the archetypes to such speculative theses as David Bohm's implicit and explicit orders[19] or Rupert Sheldrake's theory of morphic resonance[20] by way of acknowledging that this was the sort of thing that Jung was trying to say all along? Like Jung in his speculative mode, Bohm and Sheldrake seem to be attempting to talk about what lies beyond the scope of time and space as we ordinarily understand them. Both Bohm and Sheldrake seem to be groping toward the formulation of a truly transempirical notion of reality such that what happens outside of time and space as ordinarily understood is the initiating impetus for the phenomena that we observe in the space-time world. Thus, Bohm and Sheldrake could be seen as working toward what amounts to a spiritualist account of reality, if we mean that to describe realities grounded in realms beyond space and time.

But it just will not do to turn Jung's archetypes into such a spiritualist view. For the archetypal theory is preeminently a psychological theory talking about those phenomena which fall within the range of human experience. It is a theory about what transpires within the space-time world, as the mythos that Jung is endeavoring to make sense of is very much within the world.[21] Jung did indeed hold to beliefs in ultimate spiritual realities, what we could call the "Mythos," which stand as it were beyond the symbols and images of the mythos. In addition to the God archetype, Jung also believed, for example, that there was a transcendent deity. But Jung is ever careful to note that his theory or archetypes is not intended to account for the ultimately spiritual, only for that which informs human consciousness and experience.

Jung, like many of us, including I am sure Bohm and Sheldrake, was anxious to see the eventual emergence of a unifying theory which can knit together into a coherent world-view the spiritualist world outlook with the more obvious and observable elements of reality with which science deals. But it seems to be a surer way to progress along the pathway to such a goal to take a theoretically conservative course starting from what can be relatively agreed on as known and gradually expanding the horizon of that to include more of the previously unknown rather than to assume the irrelevance of scientific knowledge in favor of ungrounded and sweeping speculative views.

The case of psychic phenomena, a consideration of which was the main impetus behind Jung's speculative forays beyond the scope of science, serves to illustrate this point. Precognition, clairvoyance, psychokinesis, out-of-body experience, and related events, if they are truly what they seem to be, violate several assumptions of the common sense world of which science is in some ways a sophisticated extension. Precognition, for example, seems to indicate backward causation in time where a future event causes a present premonition. Out-of-body consciousness, experienced by those under deep anesthesia and in other unconscious states, seems to violate the ordinary assumptions we make about the dependence of consciousness on certain brain states. In these events are indeed what they appear to be, this might well indicate that the world is not completely and adequately described by the working assumptions with which science deals, and that perhaps there is in fact a spiritual background to the everyday world with these psychic events being only, as it were, little windows from our ordinary experience into a vastly different reality.

But the theory that would explain these events, if it is going to be the unifying theory which we seek, must also account for the mundane and garden variety phenomena with which science already deals as special and limiting cases of some wider picture of reality. It would not help to have a theory that accounted for psychic events, but which failed to explain the ordinary and the everyday. Before a new visionary theoretical synthesis can be achieved, it has to be preceded by attempts to integrate the anomalous events into the already existing framework of knowledge. Only when such an effort has completely run its course can the anomalies, in their persistent perversity with respect to standard ways of understanding, eventually necessitate a rethinking of basic assumptions.[22]

Thus, even if the archetypes did eventually prove to be the sort of entities the full understanding of which necessitated alterations in some of our basic assumptions about the world, this change would have to be one grounded in an exhaustive effort to fit archetypal phenomena into a traditional scientific perspective.[23]

But before we can even begin to think in terms of such a grand metaphysical unification of the spiritual and the scientific, the preliminary task remains of exploring and demonstrating the reality of archetypes in our everyday experience. Just as J. B. Rhine's pioneering work at Duke University has changed the study of psychic phenomena from collecting interesting antedotes to a respected scientific field studying real features of the world, so analogously we need to show how a scientifically credible archetypal theory is possible so that the reality of archetypes can be decisively demonstrated. This demonstration opens the door to the prospect of illustrating the relevance of the theory to other branches of knowledge. With a firm grounding in the logos aspect, the mythos of the archetypal theory can come into its own. The reality and inescapability of a mythic dimension of human existence will then have been made evident.

With the naturalistic reconstructive approach we are taking in this study, we hope then to create the possibility for a critical assessment of the archetypal theory. One that can strike a middle path between those critics out to discredit Jung and dismiss him and those enthusiasts who uncritically espouse Jung's views and who seldom venture to go beyond Jung's own formulations.

Jung's Mental Constructs 1

Psyche

Preliminary Remarks

BEFORE the prospect of a rapprochement of Jung's theory of archetypes with the scientific world picture can be fully explored, it is essential to rationally reconstruct the theory so that it can be made clear exactly what assumptions, claims, and implications are involved in it. In this regard, it will be helpful to see Jung's views on this matter within the context of his psychology as a whole. However, within the scope of this study, we cannot attempt to trace the relationship between all of Jung's views and the archetypes. A principal omission in this regard is Jung's theory of individuation where he attempts to examine the role which the archetypes play in the development of personality.

But if we cannot consider all of Jung's ideas that are related to the archetypal theory, it is essential to gain an understanding of his mental constructs. Thus, as a preliminary to discussing the archetypal theory itself, we will examine these concepts. Our approach in this regard will be to begin with the mental constructs of the widest application. We will consider first, then, the most general of the Jungian mentalistic terms, the psyche.

Psyche-Body Relation

We find that an attempt to gain a clear idea of just what Jung means by the psyche runs into immediate difficulties. For Jung's psyche is both a primitive as well as a central term in his psychology. The psyche, its contents, structure, and dynamics is that about which Jung's psychology is primarily concerned. It is not surprising, then, that when Jung addresses himself to the specific task of characterizing the psychic as distinct from the nonpsychic, his characterization fails to satisfy us as a definition, leading instead to a discussion of the relationship of the psyche to other basic Jungian concepts.

We should not expect a definition of the psyche from Jung in any case since, according to his view, the psyche mediates all experience so that there is a sense in which it can be said that we cannot get outside of the psyche in order to examine what it might be in itself: "... there is no standpoint above or outside psychology that would enable us to form an ultimate judgment of what the psyche is." *(Man and His Symbols,* p. 47)

But if we are not to find a precise definition of the psyche in Jung's writings, we still need to determine the relation between Jung's idea of the psyche and traditional concepts in the philosophy of mind. For if Jung avoids explicit concern with philosophical issues, there is nonetheless an implicit theory of mind at work in his writings an understanding of which will help us to grasp the unifying theoretical element present in Jung's discussions of the psyche. Thus, before attempting to discuss Jung's characterization of the psyche in the subsequent section where we will see how Jung operationally distinguishes the psychic from the nonpsychic and places the psyche in perspective within his psychology as a whole, we will examine the use of the term psyche in contexts that highlight Jung's position on the question of reductionism and the mind-body relation. By such a strategy we attempt to gain a theoretical overview of Jung's psychological constructs which can serve as a guide to Jung's discussion of the constructs themselves.

At a first approximation, then, we will consider the psyche as roughly equivalent to mind[1] and discuss the problem of the intended relation between psyche and body in Jung's writings from the perspective of reductionism. Reductionism seems to be a promising approach to Jung's outlook on the mind-body as Jung likes to consider the psyche in terms of a system of energy relations, using "libido" to designate the psychic energy.[2] This energetic viewpoint seems to suggest either a reductionist position in which the psyche, understood as physical energy, is seen as reducible to physicochemical terms or else a vitalist position in which a special type of mind energy is postulated. Thus, a materialist identity thesis in this case of reductionism or a substantial dualism in the case of vitalism seem to be possible mind-body positions that suggest themselves as alternative views to which Jung might be thought to subscribe.[3]

The possibility that Jung might be taking a reductive position is suggested by the fact that the purpose of the energetic standpoint is to enable the psychologist to understand phenomena in such terms as entropy, conservation of energy, and equilization of differences in an analogous way to the manner in which physical phenomena can be understood. Thus, Jung believes that the concept of libido "accomplishes for psychology the same advance that the concept of energy introduced into physics." (Vol. 4, p. 112)

In the absence of any methods of exact measurement of the energy, quantitative estimations can be reached through appeal to the system of psychological values, as the value intensity of psychological phenomena will be held to be a quantitative estimate of the amount of psychic energy involved. (Vol. 8, p. 9)

However, Jung makes clear that the analogy between physical energy and psychic energy cannot be taken in too literal a sense:

> ... in spite of the nonmeasurability of psychic processes, the perceptible changes effected by the psyche cannot possibly be understood except as a phenomenon of energy. This places the psychologist in a situation which is highly repugnant to the physicist: the psychologist also talks of energy although he has nothing measurable to manipulate, besides which the concept of energy is a strictly defined mathematical quantity which cannot be applied as such to anything psychic.... If psychology nevertheless insists on employing its own concept of energy for the purpose of expressing the activity... of the psyche, it is not of course being used as a mathematical formula, but only as its analogy. (Vol. 8, p. 233)

Jung's energetic standpoint is then obviously not an attempt to bring about a reduction of psychology to psychophysics. Jung insists on the autonomous position of psychology in relation to other sciences:

> Since, unfortunately, we cannot prove scientifically that a relation of equivalence exists between physical and psychic energy, we have no alternative except either to drop the energetic viewpoint altogether, or else to postulate a special psychic energy—which would be entirely possible as a hypothetical operation. Psychology as much as physics may avail itself of the right to build its own concepts, ... (Vol. 8, pp. 15-16)

But this characterization of libido as a "special psychic energy" would seem to imply a vitalist position. This suspicion seems confirmed when we read: "From a broader standpoint libido can be understood as vital energy in general, or as Bergson's *élan vital,*" (Vol. 4, p. 248) and "... we would probably do best to regard the psychic process simply as a life-process. In this way we enlarge the narrower concept of psychic energy to a broader one of life-energy, which includes 'psychic energy' as a specific part." (Vol. 8, p. 17)

However, Jung makes clear that "this broader standpoint" is a hypothetical and problematic one.[4] In order to maintain its functional autonomy, psychology must not conflate its concept of psychic energy with a possible biological concept of vital energy:

> I have therefore suggested that, in view of the psychological use we intend to make of it, we call our hypothetical life-energy "libido." To this extent I have differentiated it from a concept of universal energy, so maintaining the right of biology and psychology to form their own concepts. (Vol. 8, p. 17)

There is also an explicit disclaimer of the concept of vitalism: "We shall not be disturbed if we are met with the cry of vitalism. We are as far removed from any belief in a specific life-force as from any other metaphysical assertion." (Vol. 4, p. 125)

We can see, then, that in regard to the question of reductionism, Jung wants to avoid commitment to either reductionism or vitalism. Jung's stand on this issue can then best be characterized as de facto antireductionist. Rather than attempting to defend the a priori nonreduction of psychological phenomena to physics or chemistry, Jung holds to a de facto antireductionism. This nonreduction as a matter of fact is supportable by the available empirical evidence and is strictly speaking neutral with respect to the issue of reduction in principle.

With regard to reductionism, it would seem clear that Jung wants to hold operationally to a nonreductionist view while leaving open the possibility that psyche and body might be shown to be different features of an ontologically homogeneous organismic totality. This approach of acknowledging a duality from an operational point of view while adhering to a theoretical unity can also be shown to be characteristic of Jung's position on the mind-body relation as a whole where there is discernible a dualistic as well as a monistic emphasis.

However, our discussion of the reductionism issue, while serving as a preview to Jung's treatment of the problem of mind-body relation, still leaves many questions unanswered. For if we are to show that the key to understanding Jung's view on this matter is gaining an insight into the tension between the monistic and dualistic emphases of his thought, it still remains to be made clear how dualism and monism can be reconciled within one intelligible theoretical framework. Moreover, the monistic pole of Jung's thought must be further explored; since from the previous discussion of reductionism, it is still unclear how Jung is to be defended from a claim of adhering to a substantial dualism, that is, how the dual phenomenological perspective which Jung insists on does not amount in the final analysis to substantial dualism.

In order to gain a satisfactory answer to these questions about Jung's theory of mind, we must approach the problem of the mind-body relation in Jung's thought from the perspective of Jung's phenomenological strategy. For, as we have seen in the case of reductionism, Jung wants to take into account in his psychology both aspects of the mind-body relation, that is, the relationship of the physical body to the mind as well as the phenomenologically distinctive characteristics of mental activity. Moreover, the sense of taking into account at work here is that of not explaining away one of the two aspects by exclusive appeal to the other:

> We must be able to appeal to an explanatory principle founded on reality, and yet it is no longer possible for the modern psychologist to take his stand exclusively on the physical aspect of reality once he has given the spiritual aspect its due. Nor will he be able to put weight on the latter alone, for he cannot ignore the relative validity of the physical aspect. (Vol. 8, p. 352)

Jung's aim in regard to his statements about the mind-body is not, however, to formulate a philosophical position that will reconcile material-ism and idealism. Rather Jung is attempting to formulate an operational outlook that will be broad and flexible enough to encompass the full range of psychological phenomena without arbitrarily excluding data on the grounds of narrow theoretical considerations. Jung's favorite way of expressing his standpoint on the mind-body relation is thus to emphasize the necessity of an essentially phenomenological orientation. For, from Jung's perspective, if we concentrate our attention on the psychic images themselves rather than seeking to investigate their ultimate ontological referents, we arrive at an operational point of view in terms of which the problematic of mind-body as it is ordinarily understood should not arise. "If I shift my concept of reality on to the plane of the psyche—where alone it is valid—this puts an end to the conflict between mind and matter, spirit and nature, as contradictory explanatory principles." (Vol. 8, p. 353)

Taking Jung's writings into account as a whole, however, it becomes evident that the appeal to a phenomenological perspective does not eliminate the necessity for articulating a position on the mind-body relation that has definite theoretical implications. That is to say, Jung is unable to strictly adhere to his phenomenological program and does in fact make statements which disclose a distinctive theoretical outlook on the mind-body relation. Moreover, an understanding of this theoretical viewpoint is essential in order to gain a comprehension of Jung's notion of the psyche as a whole. For in order to be able to follow Jung's reasoning throughout the discussion of the psyche from many different perspectives, it is essential to be able to see these perspectives as for the most part different theoretical emphases of a single viewpoint.

Taking a look at a representative sample of those passages in which Jung takes a theoretical stand on the mind-body relation, then, we discover that Jung wants to adhere both to an interactionist view as well as a panpsychist double aspect account.[5] In the following passages from Jung's works, we find these views clearly expressed:

Matter therefore would contain the seed of spirit and spirit the seed of matter.... The "psychization" of matter puts the absolute immateriality of spirit in question, since this would then have to be accorded a kind of substantiality. (Vol. 9-A, p. 109) [Panpsychism-double aspect account]

...all reality would be grounded on an as yet unknown substrate possessing material and at the same time psychic qualities. (Vol. 10, p. 411) [Double aspect account]

The materialistic premise is that the physical process causally deter-mines the psychic process. The spiritualistic premise is the reverse of this. I think of this relationship in the physical sense as a reciprocal one, in which now one side and now the other acts as a cause. One could also say that under certain conditions the physical process reflects itself in the psychic, just as the psychic does in the physical. (*Letters*, Vol. 1, p. 366, letter to Markus Fierz dated 7 May 1945) [Interactionism]

That even the psychic world, which is so extraordinarily different from the physical world, does not have its roots outside the one cosmos is evident from the undeniable fact that causal connections exist between the psyche and the body which point to their underlying unitary nature. (Vol. 14, p. 538) [Double aspect account-interactionism]

Since psyche and matter are contained in one and the same world, and moreover are in continuous contact with one another and ultimately rest on irrepresentable, transcendental factors, it is not only possible but fairly probable, even, that psyche and matter are two different aspects of one and the same thing. (Vol. 8, 215) [Double aspect account]

Mind and body are presumably a pair of opposites and, as such, the expression of a single entity whose essential nature is not knowable either from its outward, material manifestation or from inner, direct perception.... This living being appears outwardly as the material body, but inwardly as a series of images of the vital activities taking place within it. They are two sides of the same coin, and we cannot rid ourselves of the doubt that perhaps this whole separation of mind and body may finally prove to be merely a device of reason for the purpose of conscious discrimination—an intellectually necessary separation of one and the same fact into two aspects, to which we then illegitimately attribute an independent existence. (Vol. 8, p. 326) [Double aspect account]

From a consideration of the above quotations, the solution to the puzzle of how the dualistic and monistic emphases in Jung's mind-body outlook are to be reconciled presents itself. For it is clear that Jung does not consider the two referents involved in the interactionistic view as ontologically distinct substances or as corresponding to fundamentally different orders of nature. The interaction involved can then be understood as intrasystematic interaction involving two phenomenologically distinct aspects of one and the same ontological system. Rather than understanding the phenomenological duality of mental and physical within a Cartesian-like framework of separate substances, then, Jung sees this duality as a manifestation of an underlying unity.

Except for some notable exceptions to be considered below, the conception of Jung's theory of mind with its emphasis on a duality of phenomenological perspectives conceived within a monistic theoretical framework serves us as the theoretical guide we are seeking in order to gain an appreciation of the essential unity of Jung's view of the psyche. Thus, even when Jung talks about the possibility of "psychoid" processes operating outside the psyche or discusses his theory of synchronicity, it is clear how what Jung says on these topics can be easily accommodated in principle within his interactionist and panpsychist double aspect view.[6]

... the "psychoid" and essentially transcendental nature of the archetype as an "arranger" of psychic forms inside and outside the psyche. (*Letters*, Vol. 2, p. 22, letter to Dr. H. dated 30 August 1951)

... the archetypes are not found exclusively in the psychic sphere, but can occur just as much in circumstances that are not psychic (equivalence of an outward physical process with a psychic one). (Vol. 8, p. 515)

In so far as both modalities, archetype and synchronicity, belong primarily to the realm of the psychic, we are justified in concluding that they are psychic phenomena. In so far, however, as synchronistic events include not only psychic but also physical forms of manifestation, the conclusion is justified that both modalities transcend the realm of the psychic and somehow also belong to the physical realm. (*Letters*, Vol. 2, p. 447, letter to Karl Schmid dated 11 June 1958)

That there is no essential theoretical discontinuity between these later developments of Jung's idea of the psyche and Jung's theory of mind as just outlined is due, then, to the fact that Jung's theory of mind with its panpsychist double aspect perspective already emphasizes an essential continuity between mind and matter. Thus, the "'psychization' of matter," that is, the possibility that psychic attributes might occur in contexts outside the psyche itself is already compatible with the theoretical framework evidenced by Jung's earliest writings about the mind-body relation.

But while it may be possible to identify an underlying theoretical unity in the many different passages where Jung discusses his views of the psyche and the psyche-body relation, this is not to say that there are not some passages that cannot be satisfactorily reconciled with the Jungian theory of mind we have outlined above. These previously mentioned exceptions concern Jung's ideas on synchronicity and ESP, out-of-body experiences, and survival of bodily death.

With regard to synchronicity, although we can understand how Jung's reflections on this matter are a natural development of his theoretical model of the psyche, Jung appears to reach some provisional conclusions in discussions of synchronicity that are inconsistent with his views as a whole. For even though due to Jung's habit of discussing points of view in a hypothetical way, the reader must beware of concluding from a few isolated passages that Jung actually adheres to a controversial position; it nevertheless seems to be the case that Jung seriously considered a parallelistic model of mind-body relation as a consequence of his thoughts on synchronicity:

I must again stress the possibility that the relation between body and soul may yet be understood as a synchronistic one. Should this conjecture ever be proved, my present view that synchronicity is a relatively rare phenomenon would have to be corrected. (Vol. 8, p. 500, note 70)

... we must ask ourselves whether the relation of soul and body can be considered from this angle, that is to say whether the co-ordination of psychic and physical processes in a living organism can be understood as a synchronistic phenomenon rather than as a causal relation. (Vol. 8, p. 505)

Jung apparently felt that the parallelistic model of mind-body relation might be necessary to account for ESP phenomena which Jung understood as synchronistic events. In general synchronicity with its emphasis on the meaningful but noncausal connection between psychic and physical events tended to undermind the concept of the psyche as necessarily dependent on the brain or on a material substrate. Thus we find Jung making such statements as the following:

> We must completely give up the idea of the psyche's being somehow connected with the brain, and remember instead the "meaningful" or "intelligent" behaviour of the lower organisms, which are without a brain. Here we find ourselves much closer to the formal factor [synchronicity] which, as I have said, has nothing to do with brain activity. (Vol. 8, p. 505)

Similar conclusions are reached in speculations about life after death and out-of-body experiences:

> We may establish with reasonable certainty [at death] that an individual consciousness as it relates to ourselves has come to an end. But whether this means that the continuity of the psychic process is also interrupted remains doubtful, since the psyche's attachment to the brain can be affirmed with far less certitude today than it could fifty years ago. Psychology must first digest certain parapsychological facts, which it has hardly begun to do as yet. (Vol. 8, p. 412)

> These experiences [out-of-body experiences] seem to show that in swoon states, where by all human standards there is every guarantee that conscious activity and sense perception are suspended, consciousness, reproducible ideas, acts of judgment, and perceptions can still continue to exist.... If we are correct in this assumption, then we must ask ourselves whether there is some other nervous substrate in us, apart from the cerebrum, that can think and perceive, or whether the psychic processes that go on in us during loss of consciousness are synchronistic phenomena, i.e., events which have no causal connection with organic processes. (Vol. 8, p. 509)

In light of the ontologically monistic theory of mind we have claimed for him, it seems hard to understand how Jung could arrive at such conclusions which seem strongly implicated with a substantial dualism. However, it is not difficult to retrace the steps of Jung's reasoning on these points. Jung starts from the data of ESP and synchronistic phenomena. Accepting the descriptions of ESP phenomena as genuine events, Jung tries to understand them in the context of his theory of synchronicity by seeing the ESP phenomena as instances of synchronicity. Jung then reasons that a psychic relativity of space and time has been demonstrated in these cases since events seem to take place independently of our conventional understanding of the limitations of space and time. For example, Jung cites evidence that telepathy is not significantly effected by changes in distances between participating subjects. (Vol. 8, p. 433) Moreover, the phenomenon of precognition seems to indicate the existence of a situation in which our ordinary sense of time has been suspended.

With the hypothesis of the psychic relativity of space and time, the significance of considering ESP phenomena as instances of synchronicity becomes clear. For if a causal explanation of these events is ruled out, as it is in the theory of synchronicity, then a theoretically radical explanation, such as psychic relativity of space and time, seems to be required:

> The "absolute knowledge" which is characteristic of synchronistic phenomena, a knowledge not mediated by the sense organs, supports the hypothesis of a self-subsistent meaning, or even expresses its existence. Such a form of existence can only be transcendental, since, as the knowledge of future or spatially distant events shows, it is contained in a psychically relative space and time, that is to say in an irrepresentable space-time continuum. (Vol. 8, p. 506)

Jung concludes that since under some circumstances the psyche can apparently operate outside of our conventional conception of space and time, there is then the distinct possibility of a condition in which the psyche is not bound by space and time at all:

> The fact that extra-sensory perception is real proves that time and space are psychically relative. That means that they can be more or less annihilated. If that is the case, an extreme also is possible where time and space don't exist at all. If a thing is capable of non-existence then we must assume that it is also capable of absolute existence. (*Letters*, Vol. 1, p. 421, letter to Laurence J. Bendit dated 20 April 1946)

Jung is easy prey for the critic here since the assimilation of ESP to Jung's theory of synchronicity is questionable at best. Moreover, the theory of synchronicity itself is open to major criticism independently of the issue of its connection with ESP (see page 150, notes 18 and 19). Lastly, the dubious move from the psychic relativity of space and time to the condition of "absolute existence" outside space and time needs at least to be argued for in a more convincing way than the merest hints which Jung gives.

However, if Jung in his pioneering efforts to come to an understanding of the complete range of psychic manifestations did on occasion reach provisional conclusions which prove on careful analysis to have an anomalous relationship to his psychology as a whole, this is not a legitimate basis for the conclusion that Jung had no coherent and consistent theory of mind. For in order to understand the relationship between what we might call Jung's "standard theory of mind" (interactionism and panpsychist double aspect theory) and the passages which cannot be satisfactorily reconciled with this position, the sort of distinction we must bear in mind is that between a well-worked-out and empirically grounded concept, the notion of the psyche as embodied and closely tied to the functioning of the brain, versus tentative, provisional efforts to see how this outlook could be expanded, or perhaps revised in order to take into account the full range of extraordinary psychological phenomena.[7]

For the purpose of reconstructing Jung's views, then, we will set aside the statements quoted above where Jung speculates about a psyche which functions relatively independently of a brain and of quasi-psychic functions which operate synchronistically in physical nature. Thus, we will reconstruct Jung's theory of archetypes from the perspective of what we have called his standard theory of mind.

Characterization of the Psyche

Keeping these theoretical considerations about the mind-body relation in mind, we can now proceed to a discussion of Jung's characterization of the psyche. This characterization is to serve us as the basis for an operational understanding of the psyche so that we can see the relationship of the psyche to the other Jungian mental constructs. Although from Jung's point of view we cannot strictly delimit the psyche: "...no one knows what 'psyche' is, and one knows just as little how far into nature 'psyche' extends," (Vol. 8, p. 409) it is nonetheless possible to describe the phenomenological difference between the psychic and nonpsychic and thus arrive at a sort of operational definition.

Jung says then that: "What I would call the psyche proper extends to all functions which can be brought under the influence of a will." (Vol. 8, p. 183) Moreover, by will is understood a form of disposable energy. (Vol. 8, pp. 182-183) The sort of working model that emerges from this characterization, then, is a separation of the psyche and the truly psychological from the instincts and the only physiological in terms of the possibility of modification or flexibility in the otherwise rigid dynamisms of physiological compulsion.

An example of what is meant by the nonpsychic in terms of animal life is perhaps instructive. For in consideration of the insect world, there seem to be no exceptions to the rigid physiological determinism of behavior. An insect is essentially a physiological automaton. However, as we consider more complex forms of organisms with more centralized nervous systems, the hypothesis of the existence of at least a rudimentary form of consciousness becomes more probable. With the higher mammals, the existence of psychological processes becomes evident. Thus, Jung explicitly affirms the existence of psychic processes in dogs and domestic animals. (Vol. 8, pp. 173 and 189) For Jung, then, the psyche is not restricted to humankind but only finds its greatest development there as the outcome of a continuous developmental sequence of gradual phylogenetic

phylogenetic emergence.

In specifying the relationship between the instincts and the psyche, then, the instincts are conceived to be ectopsychic in origin. Jung summarizes his argument on this point in the following way:

> If we started with the hypothesis that the psyche is absolutely identical with the state of being alive, then we should have to accept the existence of a psychic function even in unicellular organisms....
>
> But if we look upon the appearance of the psyche as a relatively recent event in evolutionary history, and assume that the psychic function is a phenomenon accompanying a nervous system which in some way or other has become centralized, then it would be difficult to believe that the instincts were originally psychic in nature. And since the connection of the psyche with the brain is a more probable conjecture than the psychic nature of life in general, I regard the characteristic *compulsiveness* of instinct as an ectopsychic factor. (Vol. 8, p. 115)

In stating that instincts are ectopsychic, Jung does not of course wish to deny a psychological aspect to instinctual phenomena; and thus he wishes to make clear that the instincts can be considered from two points of view: as they appear in consciousness, their psychic impact, as it were, and as physiological stimuli:

> Instinct as an ectopsychic factor would play the role of a stimulus merely, while instinct as a psychic phenomenon would be an assimilation of this stimulus to a pre-existent psychic pattern. A name is needed for this process. I should term it *psychization*. Thus, what we call instinct offhand would be a datum already psychized, but of ectopsychic origin. (Vol. 8, p. 115)

A further clarification of Jung's model of the psyche comes into play when this ambiguous interface region between the psychological and the physiological is explicitly considered. For the psychological phenomena associated with the disposable energy of the will are, according to Jung's model, merely the end of a continuum with the physiological at one end and the psychic at the other. However, in the middle of this continuum, Jung identifies psychoid functions that are quasi-psychic yet not merely physiological. Instincts are examples of these psychoid phenomena which, though not psychic in the full sense of Jung's designation, yet have psychological aspects. Jung states, then, that the term "psychoid" is "...meant to distinguish a category of events from merely vitalistic phenomena on the one hand and from specifically psychic processes on the other." (Vol. 8, p. 177)

Since in order to be influenced by the disposable energy of the will a function or process must be capable of becoming conscious, the characteristic quality of those functions that are psychoid is their incapability of reaching full consciousness. The sense in which Jung sees the instincts as not capable of full consciousness is made clear in the following way:

> We speak of "instinctive actions," meaning by that a mode of behaviour of which neither the motive nor the aim is fully conscious and which is prompted only by obscure inner necessity.... Thus instinctive action is characterized by an *unconsciousness* of the psychological motive behind it, in contrast to the strictly conscious processes which are distinguished by the conscious continuity of their motives. (Vol. 8, p. 130)

However, the delineation of the psyche in terms of functions that can become fully conscious and hence capable of being influenced by the disposable energy of the will is not completed by distinguishing between the psyche and the instincts. For Jung makes the point that there is another type of function that limits the will and that cannot be described as instinctual in the physiological sense. This function is called "spiritual" and is mediated by those structures Jung calls the "archetypes." This spiritual function is like instinct a psychoid function incapable of full consciousness.[8]

A full discussion of what Jung means by the spiritual will be given in chapter 2. Here it will suffice to state that for Jung the compulsiveness associated with the nonpsychic realm is due not only to dynamisms of physiological origin, the instincts; but, in addition to this "lower" limit, the psyche has an "upper" limit where the psychic functions gradually fall under the influence of spiritual determinants. "Just as, in its lower reaches, the psyche loses itself in the organic-material substrate, so in its upper reaches it resolves itself into a 'spiritual' form about which we know as little as we do about the functional basis of instinct." (Vol. 8, p. 183)

But from a phylogenetic point of view, the question now arises why the spiritual function is said to be "higher" than the instinctual psychoid function, since the psyche appears to have developed out of the psychoid processes considered as a whole and thus to be "higher" than it in the sense of having developed later. The solution to this enigma seems to be that although the archetypal psychoid processes are probably present, at least in rudimentary form, throughout the animal kingdom, it is only with the development of the more advanced forms of consciousness that there is a clear separation between instinctual and spiritual psychoid functions.[9] Moreover, it seems to be just this separation that brings about the phenomenon of consciousness so that "... psychic processes seem to be balances of energy flowing between spirit and instinct, ... " (Vol. 8, p. 207)

In this separation of spiritual and instinctual functions, the instinctual energies seem to be channeled by the spiritual forms so that in a sense the spiritual function is that which allows the energies of humankind to be employed in other than instinctual activities. This is the sense in which the spiritual function is higher than the instinctual. From the standpoint of phylogeny, however, the designation "higher" is misleading since both types of psychoid processes are unconscious in relation to the later developing consciousness associated with the psyche. "Spirit and instinct are by nature autonomous and both limit in equal measure the applied field of the will." (Vol. 8, p. 183)[10]

Unconscious

Now it would seem that an understanding of the delineation of the psyche in terms of the will leads to the conclusion that the psyche is to be conceived as equivalent to consciousness or awareness in opposition to the psychoid functions, the distinguishing feature of which is their incapability of full consciousness and hence relative autonomy from the will. (Vol. 8, pp. 183-184) However, it is only when we consider the attribution of an unconscious dimension to the psyche that a full characterization of what Jung intends by his psyche construct can be completed.

In order to resolve this apparent paradox of the existence of an unconscious psyche, then, it is necessary to focus on the meaning Jung gives to the notion of the unconscious. He says that: "Since we perceive effects whose origin cannot be found in consciousness, we are compelled to allow hypothetical contents to the sphere of the non-conscious, which means presupposing that the origin of those effects lies in the unconscious precisely because it is not conscious." (Vol. 4, p. 140) Thus, " ... everything in the personality that is not contained in the conscious should be found in the unconscious." (Vol. 3, p. 204)

The unconscious understood in this negative way as the nonconscious is relatively unproblematic. Whatever is not immediately present in awareness is said to be unconscious. Memories, for example, can be said to be unconscious contents that can be brought into consciousness at will. Other unconscious contents such as repressed experiences or subliminal perceptions may also be brought into awareness, although a special effort or technique is needed. Since the latter are not as easily recoverable to awareness as the former, they are said to belong to a "deeper level" of the unconscious. The analogy of depth then amounts operationally to a function of energy. Contents with a certain critical energy stay in consciousness and lacking it become unconscious. When contents which are ordinarily unconscious become charged with energy, they intrude themselves into conscious awareness and produce a so-called lowering of consciousness with a consequent disruption of conscious intentionalities.

The boundary or dividing point between conscious and unconscious is thus an energy threshold. However, this idea that conscious and unconscious are qualitatively separate should not be understood to mean that a sort of energy membrane sharply divides conscious from unconscious contents. For it is rather the case that every psychic content is to some degree unconscious and that consequently the psyche is both conscious and unconscious at once:

> Consequently there is a consciousness in which unconsciousness predominates, as well as a consciousness in which self-consciousness predominates. This paradox becomes immediately intelligible when we realize that there is no conscious content which can with absolute certainty be said to be totally conscious,... (Vol. 8, pp. 187-188)

> We must, however, accustom ourselves to the thought that conscious and unconscious have no clear demarcations, the one beginning where the other leaves off. It is rather the case that the psyche is a conscious-unconscious whole. (Vol. 8, p. 200)

It becomes clear then how the characterization of the psyche in terms of the will allows for an unconscious dimension to the psyche. For it is only the possibility of an influence by the will that is necessary to characterize the psychic as distinct from the psychoid.

Moreover, rather than being identical with consciousness, the psyche is even better conceived as being for the most part unconscious, with the conscious part being of comparatively narrow scope. For in addition to those items of immediate awareness, there are other contents on the fringes of consciousness or just below the threshold of awareness. Jung catalogues these unconscious contents in the following way: "...lost memories, painful ideas that are repressed (i.e., forgotten on purpose), subliminal perceptions, by which are meant sense-perceptions that were not strong enough to reach consciousness, and finally, contents that are not yet ripe for consciousness"; (Vol. 7, p. 66) and, in other words, "...everything forgotten or repressed or otherwise subliminal that has been acquired by the individual consciously or unconsciously." (Vol. 17, p. 116)

Often these unconscious contents group together to form subliminal functional units which then become sort of "splinter psyches" or "fragmentary personalities." (Vol. 8, p. 97) These focal points of unconscious psychic activity are designated as the complexes. They are groups of often highly emotionally charged feelings, thoughts, and images that are associated together so that, for instance, an environmental stimulus which activates the complex results in the entirety of the associated psychic contents coming into play and affecting consciousness. This often leads to a response which is out of proportion to the initiating stimulus. For Jung the ego itself is also a complex, "the complex of consciousness." (Vol. 14, p. 357) "...the complex of the ego may well be set parallel with and compared to the secondary autonomous complex." (Vol. 2, p. 601)

Collective Unconscious

With the description of these unconscious components to the psyche, then, the concept of the psyche according to Jung's characterization of it in in terms of the will is complete. However, Jung goes on to describe the psychoid region of the unconscious that is designated as a collective unconscious in contrast to the region of the unconscious in relatively close association to consciousness which he calls the "personal unconscious."

> As to the no man's land which I have called the "personal unconscious," it is fairly easy to prove that its contents correspond exactly to our definition of the psychic. But—as we define "psychic"—is there a psychic unconscious that is not a "fringe of consciousness" and not personal? (Vol. 8, p. 200)

The above quotation should make it clear that although according to Jung's specification of what the psyche means in the strict sense it should be applied only to consciousness and the personal unconscious, Jung frequently uses the term to include the collective, impersonal portions of the unconscious as well. Thus, Jung often speaks of a collective psyche or of an impersonal, objective psyche. Further discussion on this point of how the collective unconscious can be said to be psychic on the one hand and not to fit into the definition of the psyche on the other must wait until further in the exposition (see pages 36-37). The crucial distinction involves discriminating between the psychic contents as they appear in consciousness and their postulated but unobserved determinants which are said to be psychoid rather than psychic. However, for our purpose here, it is sufficient to point out that there is for Jung an impersonal and collective aspect to the unconscious in contrast to the personal unconscious described above.

This collective unconscious is said, moreover, to constitute a deeper stratum of the unconscious than the personal. Whereas for the personal unconscious the "depth" of a content represents a corresponding lack of energy and hence a greater degree of nonassociation to the central focus of awareness, the collective unconscious is "deeper" in the additional sense of being the foundation of the "upper" layers. Consciousness and the personal unconscious then represent the individual and personal heterogeneity which develops through maturation from a common and universal homogeneity: "Individual consciousness is only the flower and the fruit of a season, sprung from the perennial rhizome beneath the earth;..." (Vol. 5, p. xxiv)

Jung thus uses the term "collective" to mean the opposite of personal or individual: "I have chosen the term 'collective' because this part of the unconscious is not individual but universal; in contrast to the personal psyche, it has contents and modes of behaviour that are more or less the same everywhere and in all individuals." (Vol. 9-A, pp. 3-4)

Jung argues that since the body may be said to have certain universal features that form a common basis for the emergence of individual differences, it would then be reasonable to expect that the psyche, which is intimately related to the body, would also have common and universal features:

> ...just as the human body shows a common anatomy over and above all racial differences, so, too, the human psyche possesses a common substratum transcending all differences in culture and consciousness. (Vol. 13, p. 11)

> For just as there is an objective human body and not merely a subjective and personal one, so also there is an objective psyche with its specific structures and activities... (Vol. 3, p. 267)

The idea of a collective unconscious thus understood as the common, universal element of the psyche would seem relatively unproblematic or perhaps even superfluous as a concept since no one would wish to deny that the psyche has foundations in the structure of the brain that are common to all people. However, the real import of Jung's theory of a collective unconscious is brought into clarity when Jung states that the contents of the collective unconscious are in fact psychic contents which come into awareness but which are not the direct consequences of the individual's own personal experiences: "...in addition to memories from a long-distant conscious past, completely new thoughts and creative ideas can also present themselves from the unconscious—thoughts and ideas that have never been conscious before." (*Man and His Symbols*, p. 25) The collective unconscious is then not only the structural element common to the psyches of all humans; it is also the active source of original psychic contents.

Additional features of Jung's concept of the collective unconscious come to light when we learn that

> ...ego-consciousness seems to be dependent on two factors: firstly, on the conditions of the collective, i.e., the social, consciousness; and secondly, on the archetypes, or dominants, of the collective unconscious. The latter fall phenomenologically into two categories: instinctual and archetypal. (Vol. 8, pp. 217-218)

Thus, both instincts as well as archetypes characterize the collective unconscious. Moreover, there is in addition a concept of collective consciousness that is to be distinguished from the collective unconscious. Jung states that by collective consciousness he has something similar in mind to Freud's idea of the superego. (Vol. 9-A, p. 3, note 2) Like the superego, the collective consciousness is partially conscious and partially unconscious. It consists of "generally accepted truths," (Vol. 8, p. 218) that is, of beliefs, values and ideals that are supposedly held in common by members of a community, and that serve as a sort of common ideological basis or cultural ideal for the community. The recent phenomenon of the so-called counterculture would then represent a process of development or change in the collective consciousness of our time.

The collective consciousness has its ultimate source in the collective unconscious. For through the influence of the collective unconscious on individuals, new ideals, ethical and religious systems, and basic scientific discoveries come into awareness for the first time. However, the symbolic quality of these images from the unconscious is eventually lost as the images and ideas are subjected to the interpretive powers of generations in order to assimilate them to the existing system of culture. Through this process the manifestation of the collective unconscious in one pioneer individual is gradually transformed into the cultural heritage and collective consciousness of the community. The result is then often the sort of transition that the religious insight of an individual undergoes in the change from the teachings of the individual in his lifetime to the formation of a doctrine of established belief by his later followers. It is the difference between an original religious experience and the dogma of an established church. Thus, Jung states that "... we can hardly avoid the conclusion that between collective consciousness and the collective unconscious there is an almost unbridgeable gulf over which the subject finds himself suspended." (Vol. 8, p. 218)

Jung makes the point that through the process of socialization and in attempting to adapt to the demands of society we tend to identify ourselves with the consequent roles that we must play in order to fit smoothly into the social order. This part of the personality Jung calls the "persona." The word means mask and like a mask the persona is the person that we pretend to be in order to have a well-defined niche in the community.

> When we analyse the persona we strip off the mask, and discover that what seemed to be individual is at bottom collective; in other words, that the persona was only a mask of the collective psyche. Fundamentally the persona is nothing real: it is a compromise between individual and society as to what a man should appear to be. (Vol. 7, p. 158)

By "collective psyche" in this context it is clear that the collective consciousness is meant. However, there are other passages in which the term "collective psyche" means collective unconscious. For example:

> It is therefore absolutely essential to make the sharpest possible demarcation between the personal and the impersonal attributes of the psyche. This is not to deny the sometimes very formidable existence of the contents of the collective unconscious, but only to stress that, as contents of the collective psyche, they are opposed to and different from the individual psyche. (Vol. 7, p. 94)

"Collective psyche" is then an ambiguous term leaving still to be specified the amount of unconsciousness that is implied. This formulation is sometimes preferable when speaking of the consciousness of a group, particularly when there is a strong group identity. For since the collective consciousness is grounded in the collective unconscious, there are then correspondences between the institutions of culture and the related archetypes. The effectiveness of the community leader, for example, is often a function of his capacity to fulfill the expectations brought about by the projection of the archetype of the hero or Old Wise Man upon him, and the guiding ideals of the community remain cohesive factors for the life of community only as long as they remain living symbols capable of constellating the appropriate archetypal configurations. The ambiguous collective psyche is then sometimes the best description of the Zeitgeist of a people, as it acknowledges the close relationship between the foundations of culture in the collective unconscious and the embodiments of those foundations in the accepted standards of collective life.

Moreover, Jung's use of the ambiguous collective psyche becomes easier to appreciate when it is made clear that for him the relationship of the personal psyche to the collective unconscious is closely analogous to the relationship of the individual to society. "Now, all that I have said here about the influence of society upon the individual is identically true of the influence of the collective unconscious upon the individual psyche." (Vol. 7, p. 154) Therefore, the psychology of a community is not basically different from the psychology of an individual: "...the psyche of a people is only a somewhat more complex structure than the psyche of an individual." (Vol. 10, p. 86)

Collective consciousness and the collective unconscious may thus both be subsumed under collective psyche due to the close relationship of the individual to the collective aspect in each case. The individual has then both an inner and an outer relationship to the collective as he must contend with society without and the collective unconscious within.

In so far as the similarities rather than the differences between collective consciousness and collective unconscious are emphasized as in collective psyche, questions then arise concerning the existence of distinct kinds of group psyches. That is, to what extent is the idea of a collective unconscious meant to be truly transcultural and to what extent is there intended to be a different collective unconscious for each distinct human community?

Evidence can be found in Jung's work to support either of the two possible positions suggested above. For example, we find: "The collective unconscious is simply the psychic expression of the identity of brain structure irrespective of all racial differences." (Vol. 13, p. 11) Also:

> When I first came across such contents [archetypal images] I wondered very much whether they might not be due to heredity, and I thought they might be explained by racial inheritance. In order to settle that question I went to the United States and studied the dreams of pure-blooded Negroes, and I was able to satisfy myself that these images have nothing to do with so-called blood or racial inheritance,... (Vol. 18, p. 37)

But there are also statements such as the following:

> No doubt, on an earlier and deeper level of psychic development, where it is still impossible to distinguish between an Aryan, Semitic, Hamitic, or Mongolian mentality, all human races have a common collective psyche. But with the beginning of racial differentiation essential differences are developed in the collective psyche as well. (Vol. 7, p. 152, note 8)

> Inasmuch as there are differentiations corresponding to race, tribe, and even family, there is also a collective psyche limited to race, tribe, and family over and above the "universal" collective psyche. (Vol. 7, pp. 147-148)

Part of the difficulty of understanding Jung on this point is due to the problematic interaction of form and content—to the difference between a common universal structure and its concrete embodiment in ways which are characteristic of individual cultures. Moreover, the word "collective psyche" tends to obscure these differences which arise from the fact that the collective unconscious is an abstraction derived from the phenomena of concrete cultures in which the archetypes exist as actual symbols and images.

However, in light of the totality of Jung's writings, it is not necessary to reconcile the two views quoted above, as it is clear that the view that there might be racial, ethnic, and geographic differences in the collective unconscious was one which had been clearly abandoned by Jung in his later writings after about 1929.[11]

But although Jung specifically rejects the idea of differences in the collective unconscious based on racial inheritance, this is not to say that Jung does not argue for the existence of distinct differences in the psychology of different ethnic, racial, and geographic groups. Rather than being the result of racial, ethnic, or geographic differences in the collective unconscious itself, however, the differences in the collective psyche which Jung defends in his later writings (i.e., after about 1929) are due to cultural influences. For different groups assimilate the archetypes into distinct cultural forms, and the phenomenological form of the archetypal images are then a direct result of cultural influence (see pages 57-58). Moreover, one archetype may be emphasized in one culture but not in another. Due to the ambiguity of collective psyche, then, Jung can discuss significant differences in the collective psyches of different groups due to cultural determinants while still maintaining the essential uniformity of the collective unconscious itself.[12]

In addition to the question of racial, ethnic, and geographic differences in the collective unconscious, the use of the latter term raises another question which must be considered at this point. For it is tempting to understand collective unconscious in such a way that a sort of group mind is postulated to exist as a superindividual entity. Moreover, from the limited perspective of the individual ego, the collective unconscious is experienced as something outside of and alien to one's personality so that, phenomenologically, it seems as if the collective unconscious exists as an entity in its own right independently of the individual.

At times Jung writes in such a way as to suggest that he believes that what phenomenologically seems to exist in this regard is actually the case:

> In our ordinary mind we are in the worlds of time and space and within the separate individual psyche. In the state of the archetype we are in the collective psyche, in a world-system whose space-time categories are relatively or absolutely abolished. (*Letters*, Vol. 2, p. 399, letter to Stephen Abrams dated 21 October 1957)

> Accordingly the capacity to nullify space and time must somehow inhere in the psyche, or, to put it another way, the psyche does not exist wholly in time and space. It is very probable that only what we call consciousness is contained in space and time, and that the rest of the psyche, the unconscious, exists in a state of relative spacelessness and timelessness. For the psyche this means a relative eternality and a relative nonseparation from other psyches, or a oneness with them. (*Letters*, Vol. 1, p. 256, letter to Pastor Fritz Pfäfflin dated 10 January 1939)

> Hence there is only one collective unconscious, which is everywhere identical with itself, from which everything psychic takes shape before it is personalized, modified, assimilated, etc. by external influences. (*Letters*, Vol. 1, p. 408, letter to Pastor Max Frischknecht dated 8 February 1946)

We have already seen how the phenomena of parapsychology and Jung's theory of synchronicity based in part on these phenomena lead Jung to conclusions that are difficult to reconcile with his psychology as a whole. In this instance, Jung seems to want to postulate a collective psyche that is independent of space and time, and which thus exists relatively independently of individual psyches.

However, it would be unfair to Jung to state that he unequivocally asserted such an idea, although he seems to be groping towards the formulation of such a view in his later writings. In any case, in line with our program of naturalistic reconstruction, the idea of the collective unconscious as a superindividual entity, that is, an entity that exists over and above the psyches of individuals, will not be assumed in the following.[13]

Theory of Archetypes: Part 1   2

Introduction

Preliminary Remarks

OUR discussion of the notion of a collective unconscious serves as an introduction to the concept of the archetype. For in addition to the instincts, the collective unconscious is said to contain archetypes. It is the notion of archetypes that gives Jung's collective unconscious its real substance, and it is the resolution of questions concerning the archetypes upon which the real point of a concept of a collective unconscious depends. Many such questions inhabit the fringes of consciousness while reading about the archetypes: What really is an archetype? What sort of ontological status is it supposed to have? What is the relationship between the archetypes and the instincts? Where do the archetypes come from? What is the difference between the archetype in itself and the archetype as it appears in consciousness? What are the chief archetypes? What causes their appearance in consciousness?

These many questions about the archetypes reflect the many aspects and perspectives from which the idea can be considered. In order to gain an insight into the unifying elements of these different perspectives on the archetype, our exposition will proceed with a conceptual overview followed by a detailed discussion of the different aspects of the concept.

Characterization of the Archetype

It will be remembered from the above discussion of the collective unconscious that the contents of this portion of the psyche were said to be objective and impersonal in the sense that the collective unconscious is the supposed source of original contents that appear in consciousness but which seem not to have been conscious before. For example, an individual has a dream, vision, or fantasy composed of alien images to which he has no personal associations. Moreover, parallels to the phenomenon's basic themes can then be found in materials drawn from comparative symbology which are unknown to the person previous to his experience of the archetypal event.

The following dream illustrates these characteristic archetypal qualities:

In my dream I am at an amusement park with my wife and another couple. The first amusement we decide to see is a sort of "haunted house." To enter we descend a flight of stairs into a cool, damp cellar consisting of an empty main room. Looking into one room I see nothing. At this point a ghostlike figure appears. I recognize the "ghost" as a child dressed in a costume and am friendly to it. The "ghost" then leaves. In the next room, I see a table. Upon the table is a small, incomplete childlike body. A large knife is hovering in the air over the table and proceeds to dismember the body. Blood gushes out, spurting into the air in great streams. I think that this "show" is a little too much for an amusement for the general public, although I personally am not affected by the gore. The "body" then begins to carry on a normal conversation with me while the blood continues to spurt and gush over the table top. The show is then over and the body disappears.[1]

In this particular case, it is the archetypal motif of ritual dismemberment which is the most outstanding feature of the dream. The dreamer had no idea as to what this image might mean and was unfamiliar with the frequent occurrence of this theme in the literature of alchemy.[2]

What Jung means by an archetype, then, is a disposition in the collective unconscious to produce such an image in consciousness as the one above. Jung distinguishes between the actual image, which he calls the "archetypal image," and the archetype per se, which, as a disposition of the unconscious, is unobservable in principle.[3] However, the term "archetype" is frequently used indiscriminately for both the archetypal manifestation and the archetypal disposition. The archetypal image is then a concrete instantiation of the hypothetical, unobservable archetype per se.

Archetypal contents that emerge into awareness assume a form which is a reflection of the individual consciousness. This fact that archetypes appear in a personal form seems to be an instance of the tendency to structure awareness of unfamiliar phenomena so that they resemble familiar forms of experience.

The unconscious supplies as it were the archetypal form, which in itself is empty and irrepresentable. Consciousness immediately fills it with related or similar representational material so that it can be perceived. For this reason archetypal ideas are locally, temporally, and individually conditioned. (Vol. 13, p. 346)

In the case of the dismemberment dream, this assimilation of the archetypal motif into an individual context is illustrated when the uncanny and alien ritual of dismemberment, concerning which the dreamer had no knowledge, was represented in the familiar setting of an amusement park.

Ontological Status of the Archetype

The archetype can be said to have the ontological status of a hypothetical construct. Like the electron, the archetype can be detected only through the effects which it produces, and, as with the electron, this unobservability is not held to make the archetype any less real than directly perceivable objects like chairs and doorknobs. Unlike the electron, however, the archetypes are unobservable in principle. Since the unconscious can only be known indirectly through its effect on consciousness, there is no possibility of a direct perception of these unconscious contents. Thus, the archetypes per se are only possibilities to form observable phenomena with the determinate form in which they appear being the result of the interaction between this disposition in the collective unconscious and the informing consciousness.

In basing the ontology of the archetypes on a position of scientific realism, Jung wants to carefully distinguish his unobservable theoretical entities from metaphysical concepts such as Plato's forms. The difference is that the archetypes are empirically derived and grounded. They are the product of Jung's therapeutic work in which he found it increasingly difficult to fit all of the phenomenological material into an explanatory framework which included only a personal unconscious. There exists, then, the possibility of falsification to the extent that the archetypal theory fails to provide adequate explanation for the observed phenomena. The relationship between experience and the postulated concepts of metaphysics, on the other hand, is too vague to allow for the possibility of disconfirmation in principle.

Relationship of Archetypes and Instincts

Since the archetypes are not the product of an individual's personal experience, they must then be the result of inheritance. Rather than inherited experiences or inherited images, however, the archetypes are transmitted as the disposition to form images and ideas. There are close parallels here with the instincts, which rather than being inherited behaviors are instead inherited dispositions to produce certain behaviors when activated by the appropriate environmental releasing stimuli. With this similarity to the instincts in mind, Jung often refers to the archetypes as patterns of behavior:

> ...they prove to be typical attitudes, modes of action—thought-processes and impulses which must be regarded as constituting the instinctive behaviour typical of the human species. The term I chose for this, namely "archetype," therefore coincides with the biological concept of the "pattern of behaviour." (Vol. 3, p. 261)

Just as the body develops evolutionarily conditioned modes of responding to external and internal stimuli, Jung hypothesizes the development of analogous phylogenetic patterns for the psyche. The archetypes are then somewhat like psychic instincts. Moreover, since the body is not functionally a separate entity from the mind, these "mental instincts" are parallel psychic counterparts to the inherited modes of bodily response. " ... there is good reason for supposing that the archetypes are the unconscious images of the instincts themselves, ... " (Vol. 9-A, p. 44)

The fact that archetypes can be understood as patterns of behavior emphasizes, then, their biological aspect and their continuity with naturalistically understood processes. With a widening of the traditional use of "patterns of behaviour," this allows for the possibility of archetypes in animals. "There is nothing to prevent us from assuming that certain archetypes exist even in animals, that they are grounded in the peculiarities of the living organism itself ... " (Vol. 7, p. 69)

Archetypes as A Priori Conditioning Factors

However, the archetypes can also be seen from the cognitive point of view as inherent categories of apprehension. (Vol. 6, p. 376) This perspective underlines their role as the structuring elements of the psyche and focuses on those aspects of the archetypes which seem least directly connected with instincts as ordinarily understood. It may seem difficult, then, to grasp how the archetypes can be at once both patterns of behavior and "a priori conditioning factors." However, man's characteristic pattern of behavior is to develop consciousness that can then act at variance with or in relative independence of the instincts understood as drives of the body. And, since for Jung, the mind and body are not really separate entities but merely different aspects, his shift from the archetypes as patterns of behavior to talk of archetypes as categories of the psyche can be seen as a plausible move rather than as a logical leap. "As *a priori* conditioning factors they represent a special, psychological instance of the biological 'pattern of behaviour,' ... " (Vol. 11, p. 149, note 2)

Now in characterizing the archetypes as a priori conditioning factors, what Jung has in mind is similar to the idea of categories worked out by Kant.[4] Moreover, it sometimes appears as if Jung is attempting to broaden Kant's concept so that in addition to necessary forms of cognition, the archetypes will also be categories of the imagination. Specifically the archetypes are held to be forms of thought, perception, and imagination. (Vol. 9-A, p. 44) However, the comparison of the archetypes to the Kantian categories is only of limited usefulness. For the archetypes can be said to be necessary only in the biological sense of being part of our inheritance that will then necessarily influence us. They are not necessary in the sense that they could not have been other than they are. The archetypes are products of evolution and are thus subject to whatever contingent environmental forces made them an enduring part of the genotype. A hominoid on a different planet could then conceivably develop different archetypes.[5]

Moreover, Kant's categories were the necessary formal aspects to which any experience must conform, whereas Jung's archetypes are the forms of only certain types of experience. Thus, the archetypes are more properly described as primordial images than as categories in Kant's sense. For the archetypes as "thought-forms," (Vol. 7, p. 66) that is dispositions to form certain typical images and thoughts, come into consciousness only under unusual circumstances, rather than being the structuring aspect of experience in general. This is then what Jung has in mind when he states: "Only, in the case of our 'forms,' we are not dealing with categories of reason but with categories of the *imagination*." (Vol. 11, p. 518)

From the point of view of similarity with Kant, the archetypes can be seen to be universal, inborn, and formal elements of the psyche. (Vol. 9-A, p. 44) Moreover, the individual and personal aspects of the psyche are held to develop from a universal substratum in the collective unconscious. From this perspective the ego is itself an archetype in the sense that it is prefigured as an a priori possibility in the collective unconscious of the individual before it emerges by a process of differentiation. All of the complexes, in fact, although they are predominantly manifestations of the personal unconscious, have a "nuclear element" which is composed of an archetype in addition to experientially derived elements. (Vol. 8, p. 11)

> ... every complex, has or is a (fragmentary) personality. At any rate, that is how it looks from the purely observational standpoint. But when we go into the matter more deeply, we find that they are really archetypal formations. (Vol. 5, p. 255)

What this archetypal basis of complexes amounts to is that a complex which can be traced to events in the individual's personal history is often "magically" complicated because the personal situation has been assimilated to the archetypal one. For example, problems originating from the relationship with the parents are frequently the result of the fact that the individual has since childhood seen the parents as gods. The father is perceived as God the Father and the mother in terms of the Archetype of the Great Mother or Earth Mother. The troubled individual then cannot successfully distinguish between the parents as individuals and the archetypal projections in terms of which he or she has habitually perceived them.

For every typical human situation there is a corresponding archetype so that the experience of the individual in such a situation invariably falls under the influence of an archetypal pattern. In this respect the description of the archetypes as "patterns of instinctual behaviour" seems amply justified.

However, the archetypal notion runs the risk of being overgeneralized into triviality if the idea of the archetypes as formal a priori conditioning factors is taken as a guide for explaining all human behavior. For example, the archetypes can be seen as the phylogenetic forms to which ontogeny supplies the content. But, although this understanding of the archetypes is hypothetically plausible, it is misleading from an operational point of view. For although in principle all aspects of the personality are founded on the common structure of the collective unconscious out of which individuality emerges like an island out of the ocean, the archetypes cannot be exclusively appealed to in order to form a comprehensive theory of behavior. This would be an incomplete and one-sided perspective ignoring the vitally important ontogenetic factors influencing individual development. In the case of the complexes, for example, Jung identifies them with the personal unconscious. The archetypal nucleus is called upon as an explanatory principle only when the psychological situation seems incomprehensible from an exclusively personal point of view. That there is a common and universal structure to the psyche is then a true statement, but not always an informative one for all distinct aspects of behavior.

Further Implications of Kantian Influence

On the basis of the discussion so far, it could be fairly concluded that, on the whole, it is more accurate to understand the archetypes as patterns of behavior than to think of them in terms of Kant's theory of knowledge. This conclusion, however, would be unwarranted as the full extent of Kant's influence on Jung's idea of the archetypes has yet to be described.

Jung's insistence on the label of empiricism to characterize his work, for example, is a consequence of his methodological ideal of staying within the bounds of possible experience. Moreover, in terms of Jung's thought, the concept of the psyche describes these bounds. There is no possibility of getting outside the psyche to determine how the psyche interprets the world for all experience is most immediately and inescapably psychic experience. The psyche is the mediator of all experience, both from within and without. If a thinker comes up with a metaphysical scheme which he thinks grasps the essential nature of reality, Jung then alerts us to the need for a psychological critique. The claims of universal validity which the system-maker has put forth transcend possible experience and are justified only on the basis of intuition. It is just at this point that Jung's theory of archetypes assumes a deflationary role by explaining the appeal of the metaphysical system on the basis of its conformity to the fundamental aspects of the thinker himself rather than to conformity of the system with the ultimate nature of reality:

> When a speculative philosopher believes he has comprehended the world once and for all in his system, he is deceiving himself; he has merely comprehended himself and then naïvely projected that view upon the world. (Vol. 3, p. 185)

Archetypes and Scientific Theories

To complicate matters at this point is the fact that basic scientific insights are held to be founded on archetypes. For example, Robert Mayer's idea of the conservation of energy, (Vol. 7, p. 67) the concept of the atom, (Vol. 9-A, p. 57) and Kekulé's discovery of the structure of the benzene ring (*Man and His Symbols*, pp. 25-26) are all understood as illustrating the effect of archetypes.

> ...we speak of "atoms" today because we have heard, directly or indirectly, of the atomic theory of Democritus. But where did Democritus, or whoever first spoke of minimal constitutive elements, hear of atoms? This notion had its origin in archetypal ideas, that is, in primordial images which were never reflections of physical events but are spontaneous products of the psychic factor. (Vol. 9-A, p. 57)

This archetypal basis of scientific theory is supported when it is shown that the ideas have been present in the history of civilization for many centuries. In Kekulé's case the solution to his theoretical dilemma came during a state of relaxation when, dozing before his fireplace, he seemed to see snakelike atoms dancing in the fire. When one of the snakes formed a ring by grasping its own tail, the idea of the benzene ring was conceived in a flash of insight.[6] This image of a snake (or dragon) biting its own tail is called the "uroboros" and dates from at least as early as the third century B.C. (*Man and His Symbols*, p. 26)

Naturally the role of the unconscious must always be seen in proper relation to the activity of consciousness in these cases. Had Kekulé not already spent great amounts of time and energy consciously thinking about the problem of the structure of benzene, the situation of an insightful archetypal constellation could not have occurred. Moreover, there was a great deal of effort necessary after the fireplace episode before the structure of benzene was finally worked out. Notwithstanding the well-documented and critical role of the unconscious, then, it should not be thought that scientific theories exist preformed in the collective unconscious.

We might well imitate Kant at this point and ask how this apparent conformity between symbols from the collective unconscious and scientific theories is possible. Moreover, it needs to be made clear why scientific ideas derived from the archetypes are held to be genuine discoveries and advances, whereas similarly derived metaphysical ideas are restricted to a sphere of only subjective validity. In the case of science, then, the archetypal constellation sometimes proves to be instrumental in bringing about a progressive theoretical advance for science when the image from the unconscious is assimilated in terms of the already existing body of knowledge. Many other ideas from the same source are never put to scientific use because they do not happen to be compatible with the progress of science.

Thus, with scientific theories archetypes are sometimes an important influence within the context of discovery. Regardless of the origin of a scientific hypothesis, however, in order for it to become acceptable to the scientific community, it must be validated in terms of criteria of scientific methodology. These criteria of acceptability involve relating the theoretical terms of the hypothesis to observation statements in such a way as to constitute an empirically derived decision procedure which will indicate what observational states of affairs will count for or against the hypothesis. With metaphysical theories based on archetypal experience, on the other hand, the relationship between the theory and observations is not specified in such a way as to form the basis for an objective decision procedure which could be used to adjudicate conflicting metaphysical claims.

Moreover, the archetypal images are always the partial result of the individual traits of the embodying consciousness, with aspects of personal history and cultural background being always associated with their appearance. Thus, the personal factor cannot be eliminated in order to arrive at an objectively valid metaphysical statement. In addition to the inevitable contamination of the personal factor, the archetypes can be said to be unavoidably anthropomorphic. As the product of human evolution, they mirror humankind and are humankind. Although the archetypes represent humankind's relationship to the world, it is only from the historically conditioned human standpoint reflecting how the universe affects human beings.

There is for Jung, nonetheless, a possibility of evaluating the pragmatic value of the metaphysical ideas considered from the standpoint of their ability to further and enhance human existence. Thus, very similar to Nietzsche, Jung would judge metaphysical ideas on the basis of their life-affirming quality while maintaining that the final truth of the ideas in terms of which of them mirror best the ultimate structure of reality could not be decided.

In Jung's view we must be careful to distinguish subjective, psychological truth from objective truth about the external world; that is, the function of the mythos must be distinguished from that of the logos. Thus, although it is an error to think of the archetypes in an objective way in the sense that they represent literally true statements about objective states of affairs, yet the archetypes have a psychological validity and are psychologically true in the sense that it is possible to interpret them in a subjectively meaningful way. The validity of the archetypes in terms of applicability to the human situation must then be acknowledged even in the absence of the possibility of a scientific validation of statements based on them. For example, the existence of a God cannot be either proved or disapproved scientifically, yet the existence of an internal God-image or its equivalent must be acknowledged as a psychologically real and effective event:

> The gods cannot and must not die. I said just now that there seems to be something, a kind of superior power, in the human psyche, and that if this is not the idea of God, then it is the "belly." I wanted to express the fact that one or other basic instinct, or complex of ideas, will invariably concentrate upon itself the greatest sum of psychic energy and thus force the ego into its service. (Vol. 7, p. 72)

The Symbolic Nature of the Archetypes

The way in which Jung characterizes the distinctive psychological validity of the archetypes is by emphasizing the symbolic nature of the archetypal images. The archetypes are said to be "symbolic formulas." (Vol. 6, p. 377)

The symbol for Jung is to be sharply distinguished from the reference function of signs. Signs are representations of known things. The trademark of a company, for example, simply represents the company itself. Symbols, on the other hand, cannot be said to be logically equivalent to their referents. The symbol points beyond itself to an unknown:

> Thus a word or an image is symbolic when it implies something more than its obvious and immediate meaning. It has a wider "unconscious" aspect that is never precisely defined or fully explained.... As the mind explores the symbol, it is led to ideas that lie beyond the grasp of reason. (*Man and His Symbols*, p. 4)

Symbols function as interconnecting links between the conscious and the collective unconscious, as they bring into consciousness in representable form the otherwise unknowable archetypes. The symbols mediate the experience of the archetypes and because of the unavoidable personal characteristics due to embodiment in an individual consciousness are products of both the collective unconscious and consciousness.

There is then in the symbol a synthesis of known and unknown and of real and unreal:

> If it were only real, it would not be a symbol, for it would then be a real phenomenon and hence unsymbolic.... And if it were altogether unreal, it would be mere empty imagining, which, being related to nothing real, would not be a symbol either. (Vol. 6, p. 111)

> The symbol ... unites the antithesis between real and unreal, because on the one hand it is a psychic reality (on account of its efficacy), while on the other it corresponds to no physical reality. (Vol. 6, pp. 128-129)

To a large extent, then, what we add to the picture of the archetype by calling the archetypal images "symbols" is an emphasis on the living intensity of the archetypes as they are experienced. The archetypal images are not abstract intellectual concepts, but symbols which are not transparent to reason and the intellect. Moreover, these symbols have a certain aura of fascination. They appeal not only to the intellect as puzzles for the understanding but to the emotions as well. "They are as much feelings as thoughts;..." (Vol. 7, p. 66) This characteristic quality of the symbol to evoke emotion is termed its "numinosity," the numen being the specific energy of the archetypes.

With the description of the numinosity of the archetypes, the close relationship between archetypal images and religious motifs becomes evident. For Jung accepts Rudolf Otto's characterization of religious experience as a "careful and scrupulous observation of...the *numinosum*,..." (Vol. 11, p. 7) "We might say, then, that the term 'religion' designates the attitude peculiar to a consciousness which has been changed by experience of the *numinosum*." (Vol. 11, p. 8)

Although originating through individual experiences of the collective unconscious, religion is, strictly speaking, a phenomenon of collective consciousness. And since not all experiences of the archetypes result in their being assimilated in terms of a religious frame of reference, another wider designation is needed to characterize the effect of the numinous quality of archetypes. Thus, the archetypes are said to be "spiritual" factors.

In a sense spiritual and archetypal are almost equivalent and interchangeable terms. For when we have understood the transpersonal nature of the archetypes,[7] their numinosity and their ability to generate images which serve as the foundations of culture, we have then made the meaning of the spiritual more definite. What keeps us from asserting this equivalence of meaning, however, is the instinctual perspective. For the archetypes are said to be "patterns of instinctual behaviour." (Vol. 9-A, p. 44) And it is the instinctual aspect of humankind that seems to stand in sharpest contrast to what we wish to designate as spiritual.

However, Jung points to Christian prejudice as the origin of the apparent antithesis between spirit and nature:

> ...very remarkable opposition of spirit and nature. Even though spirit is regarded as essentially alive and enlivening, one cannot really feel nature as unspiritual and dead. We must therefore be dealing here with the (Christian) postulate of a spirit whose life is so vastly superior to the life of nature that in comparison with it the latter is no better than death. (Vol. 9-A, p. 210)

A more in-depth perspective, then, reveals the paradoxical relation between spirit and instinct. For they seem to be similar processes of psychic energy that are distinguished by the application of this energy into diametrically contrasting modes.

Moreover, it is in the description of the relation between the spiritual and instinctual that Jung's psychological viewpoint is in sharpest contrast to that of Freud. For Jung does not conceive all psychic energy as being instinctual energy as does Freud. He uses the term for psychic energy, libido, in a way that does not imply its equivalence with instinctual energy. There is then for Jung no need of a concept of sublimation in which instinctual energy must be siphoned off for cultural purposes. Any diversion of the flow of libido from its natural instinctual channels in Jung's view leads only to neurotic maladjustment. However, there is more psychic energy available for the human being than is utilized by the natural instinctual processes. This excess psychic energy can be used for other than instinctual purposes, and we might say that this excess energy represents a degree of freedom for humankind to pursue cultural activities for their own sake. The symbolic images from the collective unconscious then serve as "transformers" of energy in the sense that the archetypes represent inherent patterns for this energy flow. (Vol. 5, p. 232)

Since the spiritual uses of psychic energy are the result of the influence of the archetypes that are themselves the product of evolution, it becomes evident that the development of the spirit in humankind is our characteristic pattern of behavior.

> In reality of course the world-spurning passion of the "spirit" is just as natural as the marriage-flight of insects. (Vol. 5, p. 396)

> The spiritual appears in the psyche also as an instinct, indeed as a real passion, a "consuming fire," ... It is not derived from any other instinct, ... but is a principle *sui generis*, a specific and necessary form of instinctual power. (Vol. 8, p. 58)

Archetypes and Instincts

In order to fully understand the meaning of the term "spiritual," a further clarification of the archetype-instinct relation is necessary. For we need to grasp how the spiritual is to be of the same type of stuff as the instincts and yet seemingly different from and even opposed to them.

A look at animals other than human beings helps to gain an insight into what Jung has in mind in this regard. For in the examples of patterns of behavior in animals, we see clearly the unity which in humankind becomes a tension of opposites between spirit and instinct.

A key word "pattern" is then the link that enables us to connect the behavior of animals with the archetypes and instincts in humankind. For the instinctual behavior of animals is not to be understood as just a blind impulsion to action. Rather, for each instinctual act there is present a total pattern that includes a sort of image of the instinctual situation:

> There are, in fact, no amorphous instincts, as every instinct bears in itself the pattern of its situation. Always it fulfils an image, and the image has fixed qualities. The instinct of the leaf-cutting ant fulfils the image of ant, tree, leaf, cutting, transport, and the little ant-garden of fungi. If any one of these conditions is lacking, the instinct does not function, because it cannot exist without its total pattern, without its image. Such an image is

an *a priori* type. It is inborn in the ant prior to any activity, for there can be no activity at all unless an instinct of corresponding pattern initiates and makes it possible. (Vol. 8, p. 201)

The instinctual acts of animals then seem to be unified by a pattern that includes a sort of intuitive recognition of the goal of the instinctual acts as well as the physiological mechanisms which supply the necessary energy.

Of course, in the case of animals, our use of "image" must be metaphorical; but it is Jung's point that this regulating principle of the instinct, the factor which especially in the insects makes the operation of instinctual behavior amazingly precise and selective rather than haphazard, can be recognized.

The organizing factor of the instinct together with its specific energy make up a unified pattern of behavior for animals. In humans, on the other hand, the representations of this formal factor of instinct can come into awareness as actual images. Thus, whereas in animals the archetypes and the instincts exist in a fused, undifferentiated state; in humankind, with the formation of consciousness, they become separable and distinct.

In the human realm, then, the archetypes become the forms that regulate the instincts. Moreover, the archetypal images are said to represent the meaning of the instincts and to be "the unconscious images of the instincts themselves." (Vol. 9-A, p. 44) The archetypes thus act as guiding factors for the release of instinctual energy in appropriate ways characteristic of humankind as a species.

But what are these human instincts? Jung recognizes five types of instinctual factors for people: "hunger, sexuality, activity, reflection, and creativity." (Vol. 8, p. 118) He conceded that any attempt to enumerate the human instincts is at least a matter of controversy. The principal reason for this confusion as to what constitutes an instinct in a person is the complication of the psychological factor. For the criterion of what to count as psychic is the ability of the functioning of the will to modify the otherwise automatic and compulsive instincts. It would seem evident, then, that the reason we cannot decide on what to count as purely instinctual in a person is due to the fact that instincts are always in part influenced by the psyche. Thus, Jung says that the instincts per se are ectopsychic and serve the function only of a stimulus, whereas the determining factor for human behavior is always the result of an interaction between the ectopsychic instinct and the psychic situation of the moment. (Vol. 8, p. 115)

This mutual interaction between psyche and instinct in human beings has the result of making the instinctual element ambiguous. For, on the one hand, all psychic processes seem to be founded on an instinctual base; whereas, on the other hand, psychic processes also influence the working of the instincts. "...the instincts are a condition of psychic activity, while at the same time psychic processes seem to condition the instincts." (Vol. 11, p. 330)

Thus, the twofold nature of instinct becomes more evident in human behavior where for each instinctual action we have to take into account both the aspect of "dynamism and compulsion" as well as that of "specific meaning and intention." (Vol. 10, p. 287) For each instinctual action, then, we can pose the question as to its meaning.

Moreover, it is just the archetypal images that are the psychic factors which provide the meaning for the instincts. They are thus the necessary forms of instinctual behavior for humankind, and it is by an understanding of the process of "psychization," the assimilation of the physiological stimulus to a preexistent psychic pattern that the sense of saying that something represents the meaning of an instinct for humankind is made clear. (Vol. 8, p. 115)

On the other hand, in the animals that have only a rudimentary psyche, there is nevertheless present a unified pattern of behavior as the instinctual acts are the ways in which the animal realizes its inherent nature, its possibilities of becoming what it can be. The appropriate fulfillment of the instinctual nature of an animal is then its way of realizing its meaning. If we say that the archetypes in humankind are the images of the instincts and represent their meaning, we are thus emphasizing this continuity with the lower animals. Humans also have their characteristic patterns of behavior, and the archetypes act as the patterning factors for these human instincts. Will the fulfillment of the instincts in human beings then also lead to an unfoldment of their inherent human nature? The answer to this question must of course deal with the factor of the psyche. What is only dimly prefigured in animals becomes in humans with the growth of consciousness their particularly human way of being. For a human being to realize its nature then implies the development of consciousness. This development is like an instinct in the sense that it comes into being conditioned by the archetypal patterns. However, its nature is to exist as a factor that can operate as a will and hence control and regulate the "other" instincts. The nature of consciousness contains then the possibility of being able to act against nature:

> It is recognized that man living in the state of nature is in no sense merely "natural" like an animal, but sees, believes, fears, worships things whose meaning is not at all discoverable from the conditions of his natural environment. Their underlying meaning leads us in fact far away from all that is natural, obvious, and easily intelligible, and quite often contrasts most sharply with the natural instincts. We have only to think of all those gruesome rites and customs against which every natural feeling rises in revolt, or of all those beliefs and ideas which stand in insuperable contradiction to the evidence of the facts. All this drives us to the assumption that the spiritual principle (whatever that may be) asserts itself against the merely natural conditions with incredible strength. One can say that this too is "natural," and that both have their origin in one and the same "nature." I do not in the least doubt this origin, but must point out that this "natural" something consists of a conflict between two

principles, to which you can give this or that name according to taste, and that this opposition is the expression, and perhaps also the basis, of the tension we call psychic energy. (Vol. 8, p. 52)

That the archetypes seem to enter the human picture on two levels—as patterns of instinctual behavior and as spiritual factors—is due to the fact that one of the innate human patterns, the tendency to develop consciousness, can act against the other lower drives and become a channel of psychic energy in its own right independently of the instincts. Therefore the archetypes seem to have two paradoxically opposite qualities: "...the archetype is partly a spiritual factor, and partly like a hidden meaning immanent in the instincts,..." (Vol. 8, p. 222) Only in human beings, then, is there this potential split between the natural tendencies and the realization of the species-most potentiality of being. This split, which is strictly analogous to that between the conscious and unconscious, is a state of necessary tension since the development of awareness and the giving in to the unconsciousness of instinctual motivations tend to work against each other and to a large extent are mutually exclusive activities. However, Jung's psychological viewpoint as a whole can be understood as the attempt to show how this necessary tension between conscious and unconscious and between spirit and instinct need not necessarily be a conflict. For the integrated personality is one that learns to live with a balance between these forces of tension rather than excluding one for the sake of the other.

But if we can reconcile ourselves to the mysterious truth that the spirit is the life of the body seen from within, and the body the outward manifestation of the life of the spirit—the two being really one—then we can understand why the striving to transcend the present level of consciousness through acceptance of the unconscious must give the body its due, and why recognition of the body cannot tolerate a philosophy that denies it in the name of the spirit. (Vol. 10, p. 94)

Theory of Archetypes: Part 2   3

The Origin of the Archetypes

Archetype and Myth

THE next aspect of the archetypal theory which we must take up for discussion is the question of the origin of the archetypes. Where do the archetypes come from? One way of approaching this problem is to consider the relationship between archetypes and mythological motifs. For myths and fairytales are one of the most characteristic ways in which the archetypes manifest themselves, and the mythological motifs (mythologems) are paradigm archetypal images. If we can discover how myths originate, perhaps this will then shed light on the question of the origin of the archetypes.[1]

In designating mythological motifs as typical archetypal images, the previous discussion in chapter 2 may be recalled where we discussed the characteristic symbolic nature of the archetypal images and their religious or spiritual significance. The mythological feature of archetypal manifestation can be seen as consistent with this previous discussion in that the myth (in contrast to the mythologem) is a cultural product and a phenomenon of the collective consciousness. The myth, then, is the end product of a conscious elaboration of an original unconscious content that often involves the efforts of many generations of storytellers. Thus, the numinous quality of the mythologem, the immediate impact of the living intensity of the unconscious revelation, is lessened in the process of assimilation of the mythologem to mythic expression.

When Jung states that the religious expression of the archetypes is more numinous than that of myths: "The so-called religious statement is still numinous, a quality which the myth has already lost to a great extent," (Vol. 11, p. 301) it would seem that a distinction between mythic and religious expression of archetypes in terms of numinosity was intended. But the religious expression of the archetypes can also suffer the same fate as myths and cease to become "living" symbols. Moreover, there are examples from primitive cultures where the mythological and religious coincide: "A tribe's mythology is its living religion, ..." (Vol. 9-A, p. 154) Attempting to distinguish between mythic and religious expressions of archetypes in terms of numinosity also raises the awkward question of the point at which a religious expression of the archetypes would cease to be religious and become mythological.

However, a comparison of passages of Jung's work employing the two terms reveals that Jung is not particularly concerned with establishing strict criteria of usage which would keep them distinct. For example:

> ...esoteric teaching. This last is a typical means of expression for the transmission of collective contents originally derived from the unconscious.
> Another well-known expression of the archetypes is myth and fairytale. (Vol. 9-A, p. 5)

> ...myths of a religious nature can be interpreted as a sort of mental therapy for the sufferings and anxieties of mankind in general ... (*Man and His Symbols*, p. 68)

> I was driven to ask myself in all seriousness: "What is the myth you are living?" ... So, in the most natural way, I took it upon myself to get to know "my" myth, and I regarded this as the task of tasks, for—so I told myself— how could I, when treating my patients, make due allowance for the personal factor, for my personal equation, which is yet so necessary for a knowledge of the other person, if I was unconscious of it? I simply had to know what unconscious or preconscious myth was forming me, from what rhizome I sprang. (Vol. 5, pp. xxiv–xxv)

In speaking about his personal myth as in the above, it is evident that myths are often used as vehicles of the most symbolic and numinous manifestations of the unconscious. Thus, Jung's use of the term "myth" deviates somewhat from the ordinary usage. Sometimes he means myth to refer to the symbolic archetypal images themselves, the mythologems, and at other times he uses myth in the conventional way to indicate the cultural product as an aspect of the collective consciousness. When this dual sense of myth is taken into account, it would seem clear that Jung means that the original symbolic expression of archetypes may be either mythic or religious (spiritual) in form.[2]

In attributing a positive function to myths even in the case of modern humans, it is evident that Jung does not see myths as a sort of primitive inferior science, or simply as a crude form of prescientific explanation. This is because of the symbolic nature of myths. For if we understand that mythological statements are not really about the external physical world but are actually psychological statements, then we are less apt to criticize the myths for their variance with current scientific knowledge. Thus, myths have a psychological validity and accurately depict the nature of the human situation.

The inability of primitives and other unsophisticated individuals to adequately distinguish the subjective and objective frequently leads, then, to the phenomenon of projection in which an unconscious content is perceived as belonging to an object and as being a property of the object. Through the agency of projection, natural phenomena take on qualities stemming from the collective unconscious so that "... the whole of mythology could be taken as a sort of projection of the collective unconscious." (Vol. 8, p. 152)

In spite of this confusion about inner and outer observed in mythological thinking, Jung asserts that mythology should not be understood as an attempt to formulate a type of scientific explanation in which the mythos is made to serve as a substitute for the logos:

> There can be no doubt that science and philosophy have grown from this matrix, but that primitives think up such things merely from a need for explanation, as a sort of physical or astronomical theory, seems to me highly improbable. (Vol. 8, p. 153)

It would seem rather that the anthropomorphism seen in mythology, the projection of human qualities onto natural phenomena, is an attempt to grasp the meaning of nature in human terms. It is, then, the symbolic meaning of natural phenomena that captures the interest of the mythmakers. If we look at alchemy, for example, only as a sort of protochemistry, this cannot explain how the interest in it continued in spite of the failure to produce the desired objective results over periods of hundreds of years.[3] The alchemist is, of course, taken in to an extent by his own projections; but Jung points out that the hubris of assuming that our scientific world-view is thus superior to one founded on mythological projections is not justified, since if the unsophisticated mind anthropomorphizes the world, we have in the present era "mechanicomorphized"[4] it with the result that the symbolic quality of our existence is impoverished. We must then avoid the mistake of trying to see mythology wholly as an attempt at explanation in objective terms when its explanations are symbolic in nature.

Origin of Myths in the Psyche

Once we fully grasp the symbolic function of myth, it is clear that the expression of the archetypal psyche by means of mythic images cannot be a straightforward mirroring of natural events. Yet in some way mythological images seem to arise as the psyche's primordial response to physical phenomena. It is clear, however, that the relationship between the physical process and images of mythological motifs is not understood by Jung as being one of simple representation. When he says then that the archetypal image is not to be understood as an allegory of the physical process, he means that the objective content of representation is experienced symbolically and hence takes on psychic aspects due to projection:

> It is not the world as we know it that speaks out of his unconscious, but the unknown world of the psyche, of which we know that it mirrors our empirical world only in part, and that, for the other part, it moulds this empirical world in accordance with its own psychic assumptions. The archetype does not proceed from physical facts, but describes how the psyche experiences the physical fact, and in so doing the psyche often behaves so autocratically that it denies tangible reality or makes statements that fly in the face of it. (Vol. 9-A, p. 154)

Thus, original archetypal (mythological) images are postulated as being the resultant of an interaction between a physical event and the primitive psyche, with the physical process being interpreted in terms of a psychic fantasy content. Moreover, it is the subjective part, the fantasies that arise concomitant with the physical process, that are the formative elements for the mythological motif:

> What we can safely say about mythical images is that the physical process imprinted itself on the psyche in this fantastic, distorted form and was preserved there, so that the unconscious still reproduces similar images today. (Vol. 8, p. 153)

> It is not storms, not thunder and lightning, not rain and cloud that remain as images in the psyche, but the fantasies caused by the affects they arouse. (Vol. 8, pp. 154-155)

Still to be explained, however, is the process of psychic imprinting through which an original mythological image becomes an enduring aspect of the collective unconscious that can then produce images of similar form even to the present day. When we read Jung on this point, there seems to be an evident appeal to a theory involving inheritance of acquired characteristics. For although Jung is careful to make clear that it is the disposition to form images rather than the images themselves that are inherited, yet this inherited disposition is held to be a sort of condensation of the repeated experiences resulting from typical human situations:

> These archetypes, whose innermost nature is inaccessible to experience, are the precipitate of the psychic functioning of the whole ancestral line; the accumulated experiences of organic life in general, a million times repeated, and condensed into types. In these archetypes, therefore, all experiences are represented which have happened on this planet since primeval times. (Vol. 6, p. 400)

The repetition of these typical human experiences leaves a sort of function trace in the psyche which then can act to produce analogous mythological images in succeeding generations. Thus, the archetypes are described as "mnemic deposits":

> From the scientific, causal standpoint the primordial image can be conceived as a mnemic deposit, an imprint or *engram* (Semon), which

has arisen through the condensation of countless processes of a similar kind. In this respect it is a precipitate and, therefore, a typical basic form, of certain ever-recurring psychic experiences. (Vol. 6, pp. 443–444)

This reference to the influence of Richard Semon seems to clarify what Jung had in mind as a mechanism by which archetypes might be inherited. For the exposition of Semon's theory in his book *The Mneme* reveals a sort of theory of racial memory that tries to integrate the factors of memory, habit, and inheritance under one theoretical principle and which appeals explicitly to the idea of the inheritance of acquired characteristics.[5] For example:

> ... the engraphic effects of stimulation are not restricted to the irritable substance of the individual, but that the offspring of that individual may manifest corresponding *engraphic modifications.*[6]

However, Jung's mention of Semon and use of his terminology does not constitute a complete endorsement of his theory. In particular, Jung is sensitive to the chicken and egg dilemma in relation to the question of the origin of the archetypes. For the archetypes can not only be seen as the product of past experiences but also as themselves conditioners of experience. Instead of seeking an explanation of where the archetypes come from by saying that they are the result of the influence of physical processes on the psyche, then, there is the alternative of conceiving the archetypes as part of the inherent nature of the psyche itself:

> The fact that the sun or the moon or the meteorological processes appear, at the very least, in allegorized form points to an independent collaboration of the psyche, which in that case cannot be merely a product or stereotype of environmental conditions. From whence would it draw the capacity to adopt a standpoint outside sense perception? ... In view of such questions Semon's naturalistic and causalistic engram theory no longer suffices. We are forced to assume that the given structure of the brain does not owe its peculiar nature merely to the influence of surrounding conditions, but also and just as much to the peculiar and autonomous quality of living matter, i.e., to a law inherent in life itself. (Vol. 6, p. 444)

Later View on Origin of Archetypes

Jung in the course of his work abandoned Semon's theory of engrams and talk of mnemic deposits disappears from his later writings. Archetypes were then simply said to be part of the inherited brain structure, thus leaving the mechanism of hereditary transmission unspecified. "Archetypes are systems of readiness for action, and at the same time images and emotions. They are inherited with the brain-structure—indeed, they are its psychic aspect." (Vol. 10, p. 31)

With Jung's retreat from the position that archetypes are "deposits of the constantly repeated experiences of humanity," (Vol. 7, p. 69) we see that the correlations he had previously drawn relating physical phenomena to the formation of mythological images must also be reconsidered.[7] With the abandonment of the engram theory, Jung is no longer certain he can reconstruct the process by which the objective physical event and the interpretive psyche interact to form myths. He seems, on the whole, in his later work (as exemplified in the quotations immediately below) to have come to the conclusion that mythological motifs are not amenable to a straightforward naturalistic explanation, as if they were caused by physical events.

Thus, the question of how archetypes (mythologems) originate is now seen by Jung as no longer a legitimate question since it implies the need for a special explanation of how the archetypes came to be in the psyche, whereas Jung now sees the archetypes as developing along with the psyche as part of its inherent pattern of functioning:

> Empirically considered, however, the archetype did not ever come into existence as a phenomenon of organic life, but entered into the picture with life itself. (Vol. 11, p. 149, note 2)

> These images are "primordial" images in so far as they are peculiar to whole species, and if they ever "originated" their origin must have coincided at least with the beginning of the species. They are the "human quality" of the human being, the specifically human form his activities take. This specific form is hereditary and is already present in the germ-plasm. (Vol. 9–A, p. 78)

The hope expressed earlier, then, that Jung's ideas on the way in which myths originate would prove to be the clue to solving the riddle of the origin of the archetypes proves to be unjustified, and we are left without a definitive answer to the question of how the archetypes originate. Jung is naturally quite happy to abandon questions of ultimate origin to the sphere of metaphysics: "Whether this psychic structure and its elements, the archetypes, ever 'originated' at all is a metaphysical question and therefore unanswerable"; (Vol. 9–A, p. 101) and "... it is impossible to say where the archetype comes from, because there is no Archimedean point outside the *a priori* conditions it represents." (Vol. 9–A, p. 69, note 27)

It is evident that, by saying in effect that the question of the origin of the archetypes is not a useful one to ask, Jung is attempting to avoid the stigma of the doctrine of inheritance of acquired characteristics with which he had become implicated during his flirtation with Semon's engram theory. For from the Lamarckian point of view, it makes sense to ask how the archetypes come to be in the psyche and to postulate possible environmental causative conditions. With his withdrawal from implicit support of the Lamarckian position, Jung sees no point in raising the question.

However, asking about the origin of archetypes need not imply a Lamarckian answer. One might legitimately wish to know whether archetypes have a natural, biological origin or nonnatural origin as the result of the intervention of spiritual agencies.

> The question is nothing less than this: Does the psychic in general—the soul or spirit or the unconscious—originate in *us,* or is the psyche, in the early stages of conscious evolution, actually outside us in the form of arbitrary powers with intentions of their own, and does it gradually take its place within us in the course of psychic development?...
>
> This whole idea strikes us as dangerously paradoxical, but, at bottom, it is not altogether inconceivable. (Vol. 10, pp. 69–70)

In line with our program of naturalistic reconstruction, we will set aside the possibility of a spiritual origin of archetypes that Jung's philosophical neutrality on this allows. Disregarding the possibility of a nonnatural origin of archetypes, then, a natural origin of archetypes would seem to call for the archetypes coming into being through the same evolutionary processes as shape the rest of the organism.[8]

Archetypal Image and Archetype Per Se

Function of the Distinction

Another difficult challenge for understanding in the archetypal theory is the significance of the distinction Jung draws between the archetype per se and the archetypal image. The archetype per se was said to be not truly part of the psyche at all but rather psychoid and to be incapable of consciousness. As a consequence, it in principle cannot be directly observed. The essential question in this regard would seem to be how such claims as the above can be justified from the empirical point of view.

But that nothing is principle would count as a direct observation of an archetype is a result of the total conceptual framework of the archetypal theory, which as a whole is grounded empirically. With regard to its empirical basis, then, the archetypal theory is not significantly different from other scientific theories. Moreover, if, from the phenomenological point of view, the suggestion is made to do away with the hypothetical construct of the archetype per se and instead speak only of archetypal images, the reply is that this move would mean that a theory of archetypes, as it is conceived in this study, is no longer possible.[9] For there must be postulated an underlying common collective aspect to the psyches of individuals that will make the archetypal manifestations more than personalistic and idiosyncratic products. What counts as evidentially conclusive for the presence of archetypes is just the appearance of contents that prove to constitute universal themes or motifs which can be recognized in contexts that transcend the individual's personal sphere of reference. Unless the archetypes are to be reduced to the merely personal, then, there must be postulated an archetype per se that will be the transpersonal organizing principle for the personally and culturally determined archetypal manifestation.

Individuation of the Archetypes

However, in emphasizing the necessity of maintaining the archetype per se as a necessary hypothetical construct in terms of which the phenomenology of the archetypal images can be understood, it should not then be thought that the archetypes can be easily individuated, so that, for example, an unproblematic list of the archetypes could be agreed on. For Jung emphasizes that the phenomenological material does not justify definitive conclusions about the nature of the archetype per se:[10]

> When one carefully considers this accumulation of data, it begins to seem probable that an archetype in its quiescent, unprojected state has no exactly determinable form but is in itself an indefinite structure which can assume definite forms only in projection. (Vol. 9-A, p. 70)

Thus, the number of archetypes and the point of differentiation between one archetype and another is indeterminate:

> Empirically speaking, we are dealing all the time with "types," definite forms that can be named and distinguished. But as soon as you divest these types of the phenomenology presented by the case material, and try to examine them in relation to other archetypal forms, they branch out into such far-reaching ramifications in the history of symbols that one comes to the conclusion that the basic psychic elements are infinitely varied and ever changing, so as utterly to defy our powers of imagination. (Vol. 9-A, p. 70)

> Although he [the investigator] is forced, for epistemological reasons, to postulate an indefinite number of distinct and separate archetypes, yet he is constantly overcome by doubt as to how far they are really distinguishable from one another. They overlap to such a degree and have such a capacity for combination that all attempts to isolate them conceptually must appear hopeless. (Vol. 11, p. 288)

Ira Progoff suggests that the use of the word archetype as a noun is misleading. " . . . in the final analysis it is incorrect to speak of *archetypes* as nouns, if we are implying by that that each has a specific and individual existence."[11]

Archetype Per Se as Hypothetical Construct

In considering the problem of the nature of the archetype per se, Kant's influence on Jung's views must again be acknowledged. For Jung accepts the Kantian distinction between the thing-in-itself and that which appears. In these terms, then, the archetype per se is held to be inaccessible on analogy with Kant's noumenon, whereas the archetypal image is that which appears in the phenomenal realm:[12]

... the archetype *per se*, its psychoid essence, cannot be comprehended, that it possesses a transcendence which it shares with the unknown substance of the psyche in general. (Vol. 10, p. 453)

When I say "atom" I am talking of the model made of it; when I say "archetype" I am talking of ideas corresponding to it, but never of the thing-in-itself, which in both cases is a transcendental mystery....
   One must therefore assume that the effective archetypal ideas, including our model of the archetype, rest on something actual even though unknowable, just as the model of the atom rests on certain unknowable qualities of matter. (*Letters*, Vol. 2, p. 54, letter to H. Haberlandt dated 23 April 1952)

However, it is unnecessary to follow Jung's Kantian way of construing the archetype per se. For rather than implicating the archetypal theory with a problematic phenomena/noumena distinction, we can interpret the archetype per se as an unobservable, hypothetical construct. Thus, although Jung holds that the archetype per se is an ultimate mystery, the archetypal theory only requires that it be the unobservable and mostly unknown structuring principle responsible for the archetypal image.

Phenomenological Characteristics of the Archetypal Images

In any case, our efforts to discover the nature of the archetype directly are frustrated since the archetypal image always reflects the personal history of the consciousness in which it is embodied. Thus, when we attempt to abstract the archetype itself from its personal and cultural matrix, the result is that the distinctiveness of the archetype vanishes, and we can no longer say what it would be like in itself. But if the archetype is then essentially an "irrepresentable form," the question becomes how we are to distinguish collective archetypal manifestations from merely personal contents of consciousness. It would seem that there must be definite phenomenological differences between the archetypal images and other contents if we are to be justified in speaking of the existence of a collective unconscious containing archetypes. For in the absence of any common features that the individual archetypes manifest in every person, we must have general criteria for recognizing what constitutes an archetypal content.

As previously mentioned in the example of an archetypal dream (page 36), archetypal images characteristically have an alien, impersonal character so that they do not appear to be contents that were once conscious and then were forgotten or repressed. But this does not mean that the contents attributed to the collective unconscious contain images that the dreamer cannot recognize at all. Rather it seems that the strange and alien contents amount to fantastic rearrangements of items of experience already known to the dreamer. If one dreams of God, for example, the image may be conveyed as that of the figure of Superman. The archetypal images are for the most part, then, something familiar appearing in an unfamiliar context. Thus, mythological motifs may appear in dreams but with modern substitutes for the principal characters:

> We have only to disregard the dependence of dream language on environment and substitute "eagle" for "aeroplane," "dragon" for "automobile" or "train," "snake-bite" for "injection," and so forth, in order to arrive at the more universal and more fundamental language of mythology. (Vol. 11, p. 289)

It would be perhaps advantageous to distinguish the objective from the subjective aspects of the phenomenology of archetypes. Subjectively the archetypal appearance is characterized by its symbolic qualities. It has an aura of numinosity and seems to point beyond itself to an unknown. From the third person point of view, however, the symbolic nature of the archetypes is less evident as we have to do only with a content of consciousness whose origin is unknown, so that what may appear objectively to be a symbol may upon closer examination prove to be a sign with a simple representational explanation.

In order to verify the presence of an archetype, then, both the views of introspection and extraspection are necessary.[13] The symbolic nature of the person's experience and his for the most part absence of personal association to the material is taken into account along with the presence of the same theme or motif in material drawn from the history of symbols. The ability of these historical parallels to provide an explanation of the meaning of the otherwise unexplicable content is then the crucial factor justifying the employment of the archetypal hypothesis. When such a procedure provides the most plausible explanation for the presence of contents of consciousness, we can say that an archetype is present.

Rather than taking one particular image or dream in isolation, however, the determination of which contents are said to be archetypal is best arrived at with an examination of a series of dreams or other similar experiences. In this way the margin of error involved in any introspective evaluation is lessened. Then we are also able to see how the alleged archetype functions is more than one context. From the objective point of view, it is not so much how the supposed archetype appears as what it does and how it functions that is crucial for deciding about the presence of archetypes. This is especially so since the archetypes often appear as images that are themselves ordinary, although the role they play in the dream as a whole is archetypal. For example, the images of actual persons known to the dreamer may function as archetypal images.[14]

Although there is thus no definite objective criteria by which one can identify archetypal images out of the context of the function they play in particular manifestations, Jung does gives us an idea of the objective features that, as a matter of fact, are associated with the appearance of many archetypes:

An infallible sign of collective images seems to be the appearance of the "cosmic" element, i.e., the images in the dream or fantasy are connected with cosmic qualities, such as temporal and spatial infinity, enormous speed and extension of movement, "astrological" associations, telluric, lunar, and solar analogies, changes in the proportions of the body, etc. The obvious occurrence of mythological and religious motifs in a dream also points to the activity of the collective unconscious. The collective element is very often announced by peculiar symptoms, as for example by dreams where the dreamer is flying through space like a comet, or feels that he is the earth, or the sun, or a star; or else is of immense size, or dwarfishly small; or that he is dead, is in a strange place, is a stranger to himself, confused, mad, etc. (Vol 7, p. 160)

On the whole, the fantastic nature of the archetypal imagery often bears an alarming similarity to or even identity with the symptoms of schizophrenia. But schizophrenics, although they have gained an access to the collective unconscious, has been, figuratively speaking, swallowed up by it so that they have lost the ability to function as an ego and relate in a practical way to the objective world. In a sense they are unable to wake from their symbolic fantasies, so that these are more symptoms of psychic breakdown than they are numinous symbols that can be meaningfully integrated into the total pattern of their life.

The difference between archetypes and the dissociated products of schizophrenia is that the former are entities endowed with personality and charged with meaning, whereas the latter are only fragments with vestiges of meaning—in reality, they are products of disintegration. (Vol. 8, p. 122)

The phenomenology of the archetypal manifestation is often of immediate therapeutic relevance as the contents of the unconscious take on dark and menacing aspects when the point of view that they represent is not being acknowledged by the conscious mind.

The guise in which these figures appear depends on the attitude of the conscious mind: if it is negative towards the unconscious, the animals will be frightening; if positive, they appear as the "helpful animals" of fairytale and legend. (Vol. 5, p. 181)

Collective Compensation of Archetypal Images

If the form in which the archetypes appear is thus influenced by the attitude of the conscious mind, it would seem that the manifestation of the archetypes are not random and due to chance, but that their appearance is conditioned by certain necessary circumstances in the individual. Moreover, an understanding of these conditions should shed light on the nature of the relationship between the collective and personal aspects of the psyche. For by calling the collective unconscious the impersonal and objective portion of the psyche, the integral part this aspect of the unconscious plays in the life of the individual is not given adequate consideration. In this regard we find, then, that the archetypes behave in an analogous fashion to other contents of the unconscious in the sense that their appearance functions in a compensatory fashion to consciousness. That is, the unconscious supplies contents that compensate the conscious attitude by representing features of the person's total situation which are overlooked, repressed, or undervalued by the conscious personality. The appearance of the archetype thus usually indicates the need for a collective compensation. What this means is that the true nature of the person's situation corresponds to a universal and typical human pattern, so that what it is that is missing from the person's conscious attitude is an understanding of the broader human perspective that an appreciation of the basic patterns of human existence would give.

> The archetypal structure of the unconscious corresponds to the average run of events. The changes that may befall a man are not infinitely variable; they are variations of certain typical occurrences which are limited in number. When therefore a distressing situation arises, the corresponding archetype will be constellated in the unconscious. (Vol. 5, p. 294)

One instructive example to make clearer the meaning of collective compensation can be drawn from Jung's work on the UFO phenomenon. After extensive research lasting a decade, Jung concluded that the UFO phenomenon represented a sort of modern myth in which the archetype of the Self, an archetype expressing "order, deliverance, salvation, and wholeness," (Vol. 10, p. 328) was being projected into the heavens. Although unable to reach a definite conclusion about the physical reality of the reported objects, Jung makes a convincing case for the activation of the Self archetype as a compensation for the ominous world situation following World War II in which nuclear annihilation seemed possible at any moment.

> We have here a golden opportunity of seeing how a legend is formed, and how in a difficult and dark time for humanity a miraculous tale grows up of an attempted intervention by extra-terrestrial "heavenly" powers... (Vol. 10, pp. 322-323)

The archetype of the Self then functions to direct attention within to the possibility of the realization of an inner center of order and personal unity. With the world threatened with destruction, the Self can provide an inward source of meaning and unity.

Archetypal manifestations are thus the compensatory response of the unconscious to typical human situations, with the response being a representation of an inherent pattern of human functioning. In this way the archetype supplies the insight of a universal perspective to what are universally experienced problems.[15] This enables individuals to grasp the meaning of their situation in its more than personal aspect. If an actual person appears in archetypal guise in dreams, for example, we can see that the activation of some universal human pattern is complicating the personal relationship. A woman known to the dreamer may then represent the anima archetype and hence be a vehicle of symbolic projection.[16]

The Archetypes as Autonomous Factors

In our investigation of the conditions under which the archetypes come into consciousness, we have emphasized the similarity of behavior of archetypes to other contents of consciousness in that their appearance is the result of the overall compensatory influence of the unconscious. In this regard it must also be pointed out that the archetypes behave in a similar fashion to the complexes of the personal unconscious, that is, they are autonomous factors. Thus, although archetypes as a rule arise in response to the needs of the individual, the end result of their activation may be that the archetype subjugates or even possesses the person.

The archetypes are then not only objects of consciousness but also subjects that can be described as having intentionalities which may oppose that of the ego personality:

> They are spontaneous phenomena which are not subject to our will, and we are therefore justified in ascribing to them a certain autonomy. They are to be regarded not only as objects but as subjects with laws of their own. From the point of view of consciousness, we can, of course, describe them as objects, and even explain them up to a point, in the same measure as we can describe and explain a living human being. But then we have to disregard their autonomy. If that is considered, we are compelled to treat them as subjects; in other words, we have to admit that they possess spontaneity and purposiveness, or a kind of consciousness or free will. We observe their behaviour and consider their statements. This dual standpoint, which we are forced to adopt towards every relatively independent organism, naturally has a dual result. On the one hand it tells me what I do to the object, and on the other hand what it does (possibly to me). (Vol. 11, p. 362)

In describing the archetypes as autonomous factors, Jung wants to hold to the distinction between the complexes as contents of the personal unconscious and the archetypes of a collective unconscious. For the word "complex" is used primarily to refer to the autonomous contents of personal origin, to those contents that develop ontogenetically. The archetype, on the other hand, is inherited and thus seems impersonal in the sense that it cannot be explained in terms of the person's own life history. Naturally, this clear separation between the personal and collective aspects of the unconscious is, in reality, always more or less an interrelation. For the complexes appear to have a nucleus which contains an archetypal component and the archetypes are always manifested in images made up out of combinations drawn from the individual's store of experience. Nevertheless, it is still possible to discriminate between those contents of consciousness that owe their origin primarily to the individual and his or her experience from those that are impersonal and that point beyond the individual.

The archetype behaves like a complex, then, in that it is a locus of thoughts, feelings, and images that function in a unified way as a sort of personality. Rather than indicating that the archetypes are actually entities outside humankind, however, the personification that the archetypal images manifest are typical of autonomous contents which exist in the unconscious without being integrated with the conscious personality. The less acknowledgment and understanding an unconscious element is accorded, then, the more it tends to function independently of the conscious personality and even assume the characteristics of a personality itself. And since the archetypes are symbolic, numinous factors that do not originate from one's personal experience, the ability to integrate them into one's personality has definite limitations. They are, in fact, wider than the individual; they have a universal, collective meaning that the individual can only participate in but cannot hope to completely assimilate. There is often the real danger that the archetypes will even assimilate the ego personality. "It is perfectly possible, psychologically, for the unconscious or an archetype to take complete possession of a man and to determine his fate down to the smallest detail." (Vol. 11, p. 409) Plausible examples of this phenomenon are to be seen in the lives of Christ and Hitler.

The archetypes have a dual nature, being potentialities for both evil as well as good. Thus, what to one person proves to be a healing experience giving meaning to life, may prove to another less stable consciousness to be a source of evil, disorientation, or madness.

Characterization of the Chief Archetypes

Among the most common archetypes that show a distinct personality are the shadow archetype and the anima and animus. The shadow is a representation of the personal unconscious as a whole and usually embodies the compensating values to those held by the conscious personality. Thus, the shadow often represents one's dark side, those aspects of oneself that exist, but which one does not acknowledge or with which one does not identify. In dreams it usually appears as a figure of the same sex as the dreamer.

The anima archetype appears in men and is his primordial image of woman. It represents the man's biological expectation of women, but also is a symbol of a man's feminine possibilities, his contrasexual tendencies.

The experiences of one's mother and other actual women are a third contributing factor to the form of the archetype. The anima often appears in dreams as a strange or unknown woman. The animus archetype, the analogous image of the masculine that occurs in women, may appear as a series of strange men.[17]

The personification of the above archetypes is often of such a distinct character that dialogues of significant therapeutic value can be carried on between the ego and the shadow or anima/animus in the conscious state. This form of communication with the unconscious was enthusiastically recommended by Jung. (Vol. 7, p. 201)

In addition to the archetypes mentioned above, there are many other archetypes that appear in personified form notably the Old Wise Man, the Great Mother, the Earth Mother, the Divine Child and the archetype of the Self. Any attempt to give an exhaustive list of the archetypes, however, would be a largely futile exercise since the archetypes tend to combine with each other and interchange qualities making it difficult to decide where one archetype stops and another begins. For example, qualities of the shadow archetype may be prominent in an archetypal image of the anima or animus.

One archetype may also appear in various distinct forms, thus raising the question whether four or five distinct archetypes should be said to be present or merely four or five forms of a single type. There would seem, then, to be no definitive decision procedure for determining the exact boundaries of an individual archetype. For what is to count as a typical situation and thus indicate the presence of an archetype cannot be decided a priori, so that for instance we cannot determine on the basis of general considerations that there must be so many archetypes. And from the phenomenological point of view, the appearance of distinct types of archetypal images does not permit us to conclude anything definite about how many archetypes per se there may be. Therefore, it would seem evident that a complete cataloging of the archetypes in such a way as to determine their exact number could not be accomplished except in an arbitrary manner.

In addition to the personified forms mentioned above, there are many archetypes that do not appear in personal form. For example, the archetype of the Self may be manifested as a stone, diamond, flower, or as a four-sided figure. Animals, plants, and natural objects such as the wind, a lake, or a mountain may also figure into archetypal images. There is in fact no determinate condition regulating what form an archetype must assume. This is not to say, however, that there are not definite conditions an image must satisfy in order to count as archetypal. But these conditions depend more on the function of the image in the overall context of the manifestation than they do on the specific form.

With regard to the question of personification, a paradoxical situation seems to exist since Jung says that all autonomous contents of the unconscious are personified. "All autonomous psychic factors have the character of personality,..." (Vol. 10, p. 42) On the other hand, the archetypes, which presumably are all more or less capable of autonomous function in the unconscious, do not all appear in the form of persons. It would seem clear, then, that personification is being used in a general sense to mean ascription of traits of personality to an entity rather than implying that what is personified must appear as a distinct personality or in the form of a person.

Archetypes and Synchronicity

In our discussion of the phenomenology of the archetypes, dreams have been emphasized as a characteristic state of consciousness in which the archetypes come into awareness. Fantasies and visions are other altered states of consciousness in which archetypes frequently appear. But in addition to these modes of manifesting themselves, Jung states that the archetypes may also affect nonpsychic physical processes. This effect of the archetypes is described by Jung's theory of synchronicity. In synchronistic events, then, there is a meaningful correspondence between a physical event and a psychic content with the possibility of a causal connection between the two having been ruled out. These events are the often recorded meaningful coincidences that seem to defy understanding in terms of either causality or chance.

An example Jung describes from this therapeutic work serves to illustrate these ideas:

> A young woman I was treating had, at a critical moment, a dream in which she was given a golden scarab. While she was telling me this dream I sat with my back to the closed window. Suddenly I heard a noise behind me, like a gentle tapping. I turned round and saw a flying insect knocking against the window-pane from outside. I opened the window and caught the creature in the air as it flew in. It was the nearest analogy to a golden scarab that one finds in our latitudes, a scarabaeid beetle, the common rose-chafer (*Cetonia aurata*), which contrary to its usual habits had evidently felt an urge to get into a dark room at this particular moment. (Vol. 8, p. 438)

There would seem to be no plausibility of attempting a causal explanation here, although chance seems a possible rational explanation. Other examples of synchronistic events, however, seem to eliminate the possibility of the meaningful coincidence being the result of the chance intersection of random events. A good illustration of synchronicity where chance is ruled out occurs in experiments attempting to verify the phenomenon of extrasensory perception, ESP. Jung referred to the card guessing techniques pioneered by J. B. Rhine at Duke University. (Vol. 8, p. 432) These tests are sometimes structured so that the subject tries to guess the sequence of a deck of cards before they are shuffled by a randomizing machine. As the subject is guessing the sequence of a future order of the cards, this of course also eliminates the possibility that the order of the cards can have a causal effect on the mental state of the subject.

In the ESP tests the meaningful coincidence is between a content of consciousness, the person's idea of what cards will appear, and the actual order of the cards. The archetypal theory comes into play, then, as Jung says that an archetype is manifesting itself synchronously in both a psychic content and a physical process. The term "synchronous" is used instead of simultaneous in the formulation of the synchronistic hypothesis to indicate that the meaningful coincidence between the psychic and physical events need not occur at exactly the same time. The physical event can be slightly before or after the psychic content.

In the ESP examples, it is the archetype of magical effect, the expectation that a miraculous event can occur, that seems to be at work.[18] Evidence for this is the fact that the results of the experiments are positively correlated with the emotional state of the subject, so that an enthusiastic, hopeful subject can score well above chance probability at the beginning of the experiments; and then his score will move toward the chance probability as the novelty of the experiments lessen, or if he becomes bored or depressed. (Vol. 8, p. 434)

The archetypal influence is clearly seen in the first example given. The woman patient was at a crisis point in her analysis due to a too narrow rationalistic view that did not leave her sufficiently open to the possibility of change which could result from taking seriously the irrationally produced contents of the unconscious. The meaningful coincidence was then the turning point in this regard and produced the needed change in attitude allowing the analysis to progress to a successful conclusion. The scarab motif, moreover, is a classic symbol of rebirth (Vol. 8, p. 439) so that it would seem that the patient's situation of impasse had constellated the archetype of rebirth and renewal.

Jung postulates that an archetypal ordering principle is at work in these instances of synchronicity bringing about a situation in which an outer event and a psychic content are expressions of the same meaning. The archetypes in these cases seem to be localized as much in matter and in the environment as they are in the psyches of individuals:

> The psychoid archetype has a tendency to behave as though it were not localized in one person but were active in the whole environment. (Vol. 10, pp. 451-452)

> ... the archetypes are not found exclusively in the psychic sphere, but can occur just as much in circumstances that are not psychic (equivalence of an outward physical process with a psychic one). (Vol. 8, p. 515)

The phenomena with Jung describes in his theory of synchronicity undoubtedly exist and his efforts to take account of these events in his overall theory of the psyche seems a worthwhile and needed endeavor. However, as we have previously noted, the theory of synchronicity leads Jung to make statements that cannot be unproblematically reconciled with his views as a whole when, as a consequence of reflections about synchronistic phenomena, he suggests that the psyche need not be considered necessarily dependent on the brain and that psychoid processes can operate at large in physical nature (see pages 20-23). From the standpoint of our naturalistic reconstruction of Jung's theory of archetypes, then, the requisite strategy would seem to call for a setting aside of synchronicity so as not to implicate an already complex and manifold theory with additional theoretical notions of unusual difficulty and debatable cogency. In any event the concept of the archetypes is not logically tied to the notion of synchronicity. Although synchronicity may well require something like an archetypal hypothesis to make it intelligible, the reverse is certainly not the case.[19]

Archetypes and Temporality

One final topic that must be taken up before our exposition of the archetypal theory is complete is the aspect of the changes in archetypes through time. Two distinct questions seems to be involved. In the first place, are there emergent archetypes, that is, do new archetypes come into being in response to the changing situation of human beings? Secondly, how can we account for the changes that archetypal images manifest through time as, for example, the changes that the God archetype undergoes when the Yahweh of the Old Testament is experienced as the Christian Trinity and Devil?

It seems evident that an answer to our first question must hinge on our idea of the origin of the archetypes. As will be remembered, it was concluded in this regard that the archetypes are inherited in a similar fashion to other biological structures. If we assume, then, that human evolution operates according to the same principles that are at work in other species where we can observe evidence for evolution working through many generations, we would expect that the chances of new archetypes coming into being through the evolutionary process would constitute a very low probability. For the evolutionary process works in an accumulative fashion in the sense that the origins of new structures occur, as a rule, as an addition to the pattern of the existing genotype. Highly evolved creatures, then, tend to be more complex organisms. Moreover, as a structure becomes highly evolved, there is less probability of major changes occurring in it, since the chance that single changes in the genotype will lead to an improvement in the overall structure compatible with the rest of the existing genotype is very small. We would not expect, then, the appearance of human beings with new basic structures for the body, a third eye or an extra limb. These occurrences would be monstrosities rather than improvements to be passed on to the next generation. Analogously, the origin of completely new archetypes through evolution would seem to be unlikely, especially in the light of the basic structuring function that the archetypes are held to play in the psyche. The archetypes are the phylogenetically old aspects of the psyche and hence those parts least liable to be changed to the overall benefit of the organism.[20]

However, there are in fact distinctive aspects of human evolution that must be taken into acount and that complicate the evolutionary script so far as development of psychic elements is concerned. The possibility has to be considered that there is a coevolutionary link operating between genes and culture in which culture itself acts as a selective pressure effecting the inheritance of genetic factors which in turn influence the development of cultural forms. The sociobiologist Edward O. Wilson has worked out a detailed theory of gene-culture coevolution.[21]

But even if Wilson's work is open to question, the distinctive nature of the cultural factor in its effect on human evolution has to be taken into account. For with the development of culture, humans are no longer subject to the unmediated effects of environment upon which the theory of natural selection is based. Moreover, a good argument can be made for the case that the distinctive quality of *Homo sapiens* as a separate species appears phylogenetically on an equal pace with the development of culture. Thus, culture has to be seen as one of the prime movers in the rapid evolutionary development from the prehuman species to *Homo sapiens*. As innate factors conditioning the development of the mythic and religious aspect of human nature, the archetypes must have undergone a rapid evolutionary development during the explosive emergence of *Homo sapiens*.

Thus, if we are to understand archetypes as a natural part of the developing human organism, this precludes the possibility that archetypes are eternal and unchanging like Platonic forms.[22] However, we must also be careful not to overestimate the rate of change in the genetic basis of archetypes. With the rapid and chaotic changes with which we are all too familiar in the latter half of the twentieth century, it is tempting to ascribe at least part of the reason for so much change and diversity to basic changes in human nature. But, in spite of all the new cultural forms, human nature itself seems to be relatively stable. For example, the rapidly changing technology of warfare seems to have taken place in a setting in which the aggressive and conflictual basis of human nature seems alarmingly essentially unchanged from centuries past. It is very likely therefore that a contemporary human is genetically very similar to what humankind was like ten thousand years ago.

And although it took only two million years for the rapid evolutionary development of the human brain and mind to result in the most advanced forms of *Homo sapiens* starting from *Homo habilis*,[23] this is still a vast time scale compared with the approximately five to six thousand years of the entirety of human civilization. Thus, even though the prospect of changes in the genetic basis of archetypes has to be allowed as a possibility in the very long run, practically speaking new archetypes are unlikely to emerge in the foreseeable future. This is not a surprising conclusion for what would a completely new typical human situation be like corresponding to which new archetypes could arise? It would seem that changes in the basic human situation—birth, marriage, initiation, work, friendship, recreation, death—can only be variations of situations that have existed contemporaneously with the emergence of humankind as a distinct species.

To account for the many changes in archetypal manifestation that can be readily observed in the history of civilization, we must then seek for another explanation rather than ascribing these variations to changes in the basic nature of the archetype itself, to fundamental changes in the archetypes per se. In this regard the crucial importance of cultural and individual development in shaping the archetypal image must not be underestimated, as the basic patterning influence of the archetype per se can take on a seemingly limitless variety of forms.

Changes in the archetypal images of particular archetypes then mirror and keep pace with cultural change. Rather than a dragon as the devouring monster, we have *Jaws* and *Aliens*. *E.T.* becomes the magically helpful animal; the familiar clash of archetypal good and evil is given a fresh twist as *Star Wars*, and the story of the Divine Child is presented as *Superman*. The UFO phenomenon is a particularly instructive example in this regard:

> It is characteristic of our time that the archetype, in contrast to its previous manifestations, should now take the form of an object, a technological construction, in order to avoid the odiousness of mythological personification. (Vol. 10, p. 328)

Thus, although we do not expect there to be new archetypes per se, there are always new symbols and new myths as the archetypal images undergo a gradual transformation under the influence of changing culture corresponding to the varied personal and cultural background of the individual experiencing the archetypes.[24]

Critiques of the Theory of Archetypes

4

Introductory Remarks

IN the preceding chapters we have reconstructed Jung's archetypal theory by way of illustrating how the concept of the collective unconscious can be understood naturalistically so that the archetypes can be be seen as part of the natural order rather than as being possibly occult or supernatural entities.[1] Before continuing with the line of reasoning designed to show how the theory of archetypes as reconstructed has a legitimate place within the domain of scientific investigation, we must in this chapter first consider various general criticisms of Jung's views of archetypes that attempt to undercut Jung's particular approach to the phenomena he describes irrespective of the scientific merit of the notion of the collective unconscious.

The ambiguity and openness to different possible interpretations characteristic of Jung's formulations gives the unsympathetic critic an abundance of possible avenues of attack. Jung is particularly vulnerable when passages are criticized out of their proper context or without regard to what is said in other writings. For it is frequently necessary to read Jung's explanation of a theoretical point in several different writings in order to gain a complete understanding of what he is saying in light of the overall development of his ideas. Jung, then, offers more than the usual difficulties for the reader,[2] and as a consequence, a significant amount of Jungian criticism is grounded in misunderstanding of Jung's basic ideas. We will be content here with two examples of this type of criticism. Rather than being instances of simple errors, they are more aptly described as " . . . a mixture of distortion and misunderstanding, which is obviously motivated by ill will."[3]

The first sample comes from the pen of Philip Rieff. In the passage below, this unfortunately influential critic slides from a discussion of the role of fantasy in mediating the experience of the archetypes to two subsequent passages on the same page where it is apparent that he is equating "illusion" and "archetype." Although Rieff may feel that the archetypes are illusions, it should not be supposed, as he implies, that this in any way approximates Jung's meaning of the term. It would seem that Rieff wants the reader to think that because archetypal images can be produced through a type of fantasy activity—Jung calls it "active imagination"—archetypes are then merely "forms of fantasy"[4] in the sense of being a system of illusions:

> What exactly is this "creative impulse" which Jung sets up as the highest activity of man? On first glance, one would think it is merely a new term for *art*; but actually Jung implies something much more general, public as well as private. What Jung means by fantasy is, in a word: *illusion....*
>
> More than ever before, then, both the high culture and the individual sense of well-being depended, for their very existence, on erotic illusions. If old illusions no longer functioned satisfactorily, then they must be replaced by "something new." Jung dedicated his life to the production of something new in the way of saving illusions....
>
> Jung despised the fundamental "unspirituality" implied by Freud's suspicious treatment of the dynamics of the unconscious. Just there, in the unconscious, are those superior illusions that would compensate mankind for the barren interdicts of Christianity and the almost equally barren interdicts of psychoanalysis.[5]

Our second sample of misconceived criticism comes from Edward Glover, whose book *Freud or Jung?* is the fortunately as yet unsurpassed nadir of anti-Jungian literature. The following statements reveal that he fails to appreciate even so basic an idea as the importance of the unconscious in Jung's psychology. Glover is apparently unaware of the distinction Jung draws between collective consciousness and the collective unconscious and thus deduces the absurdity that Jung is actually proposing a brand of conscious psychology:

> Now in so far as Jung is convinced of the overwhelming importance of the Collective Unconscious (and it must be remembered that although he appears to be sincerely convinced of this, he also adduces considerations which if correct would reduce its importance to the level of purely conscious forces and factors) he is clearly an ardent champion of the constitutional factor.... Indeed it is hard for any Freudian who takes the trouble to immerse his mind in Jungian psychology to avoid the horrid suspicion that Jung is nothing more or less than a pre-Freudian who having at first let himself be carried in the stream of Freudian thought has ever since striven to make his peace with conscious psychology.[6]

But, by thus dismissing from further discussion criticisms based on misunderstandings of what Jung's archetypal theory implies, we must not then also exclude certain systematically biased critiques. These criticisms are based not so much on a misunderstanding of what Jung says as on the failure to see how Jung's archetypes can be made comprehensible within the scope of a particular conceptual framework for understanding human experience.[7] Consequently these critiques recur as a type or species of criticism that adherents of a given intellectual persuasion typically raise against Jung in regard to the archetypes.

What is at stake, then, in the consideration of such systematic critiques is the intelligibility of the archetypal hypothesis from the perspective of a given image of humankind. Criticism from such a point of view could readily be understood as having begged the questions at issue. However, this consideration is not a sufficient reason to disregard the criticisms discussed below. For in addition to helping us understand the point of common types of criticism, we must consider whether the phenomena for which the archetypes purport to provide an explanatory framework could not be accounted for in less cumbersome ways. Perhaps from the perspective of these other images of humankind, archetypes can be shown to be no longer necessary. At any rate, a discussion of such criticism will better enable us to gain a critical viewpoint on Jung's image of humankind.[8]

Psychoanalytic Criticism

If we consider, then, the characteristic criticism of Freudians to the archetype concept, this is usually a claim to the effect that all unconscious contents can be accounted for in terms of an individual's personal history without the need for an hypothesis of a collective unconscious. According to this line of argument, the latter should then be eliminated in favor of a more parsimonious explanation couched in developmental terms. As a case in point, Glover argues as follows:

> ...but at the very least we must examine the embryonic stages of individual development to see whether they could not account satisfactorily for those mental contents that led Jung to develop his theory of the collective or racial unconscious.[9]
>
> ...*many Jungian archetypes are capable of adequate explanation in terms of purely individual thought but also that so long as we have not fully explored the early forms of individual thinking, the validity and universality of the collective archetype is under strong suspicion.*[10]

A second representative instance of Freudian systematic criticism is taken from Nandor Fodor's *Freud, Jung, and Occultism*. In the passage cited below, he gives examples of dreams that from the Jungian point of view would provide good paradigm cases of archetypal images. He concludes that these images can be adequately understood in terms of Freudian psychology without the need for a concept of a collective unconscious of archetypes:

> The chief point of interest, however, is whether the concept of the Old Wise Man and the archetype of transformation make any novel contribution to the interpretation of the dream. They do not. Unconscious

> guidance and sublimation cover the situation just as well. The spiritual element is a beautiful unconscious fantasy. The Jungian contribution is only verbal—but it is stimulating and appeals to the imagination.[11]

> Was then the Carpenter of his dream an archetype of the Self or just a personification of the integrating drive? It makes no difference whichever way you look at it.[12]

> [Archetype of the] Shadow or neurosis. It makes no difference. The meaning is the same.
> The Jungian approach yields nothing that the Freudian does not imply.[13]

In considering the force of this type of objection, it is important to note that what is at issue is not the existence of the phenomena for which the archetypal theory is to provide an explanatory framework so much as how these phenomena are to be interpreted. The British psychoanalyst Anthony Storr admits for example that: "It is not difficult to prove the existence of an inner world of highly irrational images;..."[14] and "The existence of the mythological substratum to human experience is recognized by analysts of entirely different theoretical orientations, though they would use another nomenclature."[15]

Although Fodor and Glover argue that Freud's psychology can account for the images alleged to be archetypal without need for any theoretical adjustment of basic Freudian theory, another school of psychoanalytical thought has developed a concept of "internal objects" to account for the type of phenomena at issue. This neo-Freudian school is composed of those influenced by the writings of Melanie Klein. According to the Kleinian view, then, the images that Jung would call archetypes are the result of a process of introjection in which items of experience in the child's immediate environment such as the mother's breast are internalized and become incorporated into the child's ego as internal objects.

In the passage cited below, we see an example of how this explanatory device of introjection of internal objects attempts to account for the allegedly archetypal images within the context of an essentially Freudian psychology that explains unconscious images in terms of individual development:

> In reality parents and child possess limited power of goodness and badness, wisdom and foolishness. The child's phantasy makes gods and demons and all those unearthly creatures of them which folklore and mythology, religious legends and artistic creation present to us in sublimated, and the imagination of the insane in more unsublimated, form. Moreover, the child places his self-created figures inside his own body and treats them as live entities alien to himself and beyond his control.[16]

The proper Jungian reply to this line of criticism will appeal to evidence that the images said to be archetypal have collective features that rule out an interpretation solely in terms of individual development. The reasoning in support of the collective nature of such features will consist of a demonstration of the correspondence of the images with symbols in the history of culture that are unknown to the individual previous to his imaginal experiences. Thus the spontaneous appearance of the same symbols in cultures widely separated in space and time will be seen as necessitating a concept of the collective unconscious.

The soundness of such reasoning is naturally open to question in various ways. In the case of the individual who experiences allegedly archetypal images, how is the absence of previous cultural influence established, for example? Moreover, would not a theory of cultural diffusion better account for the appearance of the same symbols in different cultures?

However, the sort of systematic attack on the archetypal theory with which we are concerned here is not so much interested in directly impugning the evidence for a collective unconscious as it is in trying to show how its own interpretive framework makes the allegedly archetypal phenomena intelligible without the need for a concept of a collective unconscious. We will then reserve an examination of the evidence given in support of the collective unconscious for a later chapter (pages 133-138). For it is our task in the present section to indicate the manner in which the Freudians and Kleinians see the Jungian interpretation of the phenomena at issue as not merely false or unsupportable by the evidence given, but as violating basic assumptions they appear to hold about the nature of humankind.

The sort of assumption on which the tension between the Jungian and Freudian images of humankind seems to turn involves the issue of description of human experience in terms of "spiritual" predicates. As will be recalled from previous discussion (pages 44-48), we were unable to grasp what Jung means by the spiritual until we had contrasted the spiritual and instinctual. The spiritual was said to be that which channels the energies of human beings into cultural activities for their own sake, thus representing a determination of human activity that can function autonomously of instinctual determination understood in a narrow, physiological sense. The emphasis of the Jungian image of humankind is then on the existence of a source of creative symbolic activity that may manifest itself in artistic, religious, and even scientific ways, but which is not to be understood merely as an outgrowth of sexuality.

By contrast, what might be characterized as a Freudian image of humankind seeks to explain all aspects of human activity in terms of the development of the individual's instinctuality. Thus, the attempt is made to give the so-called spiritual aspects of humans a reductive biological interpretation. Since it is difficult to see how creative symbolic activity relates directly to the biological needs of the individual, it is easy to believe from this perspective that the symbolic manifestations must be either infantile phenomena or delusions. Thus, Storr states:

> As will be perceived, I am putting forward suggestions as to possible myths which can be variously regarded either as paranoid delusions or as religious beliefs.... I think that Kleinians and Freudians would argue that religious beliefs are as unnecessary as delusions, provided a man has sufficiently rewarding interpersonal relationships.[17]

> Psychoanalysts consider that the inner world and its images are infantile phenomena, admittedly powerful determinants of a man's idea of the external world, and therefore of his behavior, but actually a hindrance in adaptation to reality. The mythological level of the psyche is, in this view, a misconstruction which ought to be outgrown or overcome if a person is to be properly orientated toward people in an adult way, and toward the external world as it actually is.[18]

This way of understanding as instinctual perversities that which from the Jungian perspective constitutes mankind's human-most potentialities for being seems to lead to an incomplete and nondescriptive image of the human situation. The suspicion that there has been an effort to explain away a vitally important aspect of experience through a biological reductionism is reinforced by the often emotionally worded attacks on Jung. If the archetypes were really only infantile phenomena or delusions, then one wonders if they would elict such emotional counterattacks. As a case in point Glover states that " ... he [Jung] proceeds to invest *human* ideas and images with an atmosphere politely described as mysticism, but which the less polite observer would call an atmosphere of religiosity."[19]

With such differing ways of looking at the human condition as that represented in the writing of Freud and Jung, we cannot attempt here to provide conclusive arguments in favor of Jung's views versus those of Freud. Such a task would carry us beyond the purpose of this study. In so far as what we say here about Jung and his theory of archetypes proves to be intelligible and to offer a genuine gain in understanding the human situation, this may perhaps count against a Freudian perspective, if a comparison with Freud's ideas fails to provide an equally satisfactory explanation. But beyond what we have said about the archetypes, no effort will be made to conclusively validate the importance of a spiritual dimension to experience. Such a question cannot be resolved only through argumentation, but must be settled as the course of time proves the relative merits of the Freudian or Jungian images of humankind.[20]

In any case, it seems evident that the claim that the archetypal theory must be rejected on grounds of parsimony cannot be upheld. For although it is readily admitted that Jung's archetypal theory is a more cumbersome theoretical device than Freudian explanation in terms of individual development, in contrast to Freud, Jung's idea of archetypes reflects the characteristic quality of the objects of experience it seeks to explain. To charge Jung with violation of parsimony is thus beside the point until another theory can provide a simpler explanation that at the same time is able to adequately characterize the phenomena.

Jung's view has an obvious advantage over Freud in that, in dispensing with the idea that dreams and other unconscious products are systematically distorted by the unconscious, Jung can have his theoretical explanations of the images in close agreement with the phenomenological content. The actual content of the images must then for Jung be taken seriously, not as mere disguises for sexuality.

A passage from Fodor serves to illustrate this point. He once had a dream involving a coal mine and under the influence of having read Jung attempted a Jungian type of explanation in terms of the archetype of transformation.[21] His interpretation along these lines proceeds in part:

> Coal preeminently stands for transformation—of vegetable life (and imprisoned sunshine) into stone. Moreover, coal is something valuable; it is called black diamond, not quite without reason, as both coal and diamond are made of carbon.... Treasure is undoubtedly referred to and, if it is in the mine or if it is to be mined, it has been mined from the unconscious.[22]

Then in an attempt to discount the importance of this interpretation he remarks: "It is interesting to note that, under the influence of Jung, I completely ignored the obvious uterine element in the coal mine..."[23] The interpretation of the coal mine as uterus does not have much phenomenological plausibility; that is, we fail to see on what grounds the interpretations of the coal mine as representing a uterus can be adequately defended. If a coal mine is a uterus, then any enclosed space could on the basis of this reasoning be a uterus and any elongated object a penis.

By comparison with the Freudian interpretation, the Kleinian theoretical model can take the phenomenology of the images successfully into account. However, its explanatory device of the introjection of internal objects lacks credibility and empirical foundation. The internal objects thesis seems to be, moreover, a sort of ad hoc addition to the Freudian theory, an attempt to save at any cost the perspective of explanation in terms of individual development.

Perhaps someday a theory will succeed in accounting for what Jung calls "archetypes" without the necessity of a concept of collective unconscious and yet without explaining away the phenomena. However, there is no good reason to believe that the Freudian or Kleinian approach is in fact such an account.[24]

Theological Criticism

The second type of systematic criticism we will discuss comes from the theological point of view. Rather than opposing the archetypal theory with an alternative psychological interpretation of events as was the case with the Freudian and Kleinian approaches, the theologians are concerned with the issue of psychologism. They object to Jung's theory of archetypes since, in their understanding, Jung's theory attempts an illegitimate psychological reduction of the transcendental concerns of religion. In regard to the psychological interpretation of religious assertions, Father Josef Goldbrunner thus remarks that: "In the language of science this thinking of Jung's must be called psychologism, the levelling down of supra-psychic realities to the level of purely psychic reality."[25] It is, then, not so much the theory of the archetypes to which the theologians object, as it is Jung's use of the theory to understand and explain religious experience in a psychological way that attempts to be metaphysically neutral with respect to such issues as the existence of God.

The Jewish theologian Martin Buber voices this type of criticism of Jung. He feels that Jung's psychological treatment of God in terms of a God archetype has the effect of making God into an entity that has reality only within the psyche. Thus, he accuses Jung of overstepping the legitimate scientific bounds of psychology and indulging in a type of psychologically based theology:

> In short, although the new psychology protests that it is "no world-view but a science," it no longer contents itself with the rôle of an interpreter of religion. It proclaims the new religion, the only one which can still be true, the religion of pure psychic immanence.[26]

> Jung does not exercise such a restraint when he explains that God cannot exist independent of men. For, once again, if this is a statement about an archetype called God, then the emphatic assurance that it is a psychic factor is certainly unnecessary (What else could it be?). But if it is a statement about some extra-psychical Being which corresponds to this psychic factor, namely the statement that no such Being exists, then we have here, instead of the indicated restraint, an illict overstepping of boundaries.[27]

The validity of Buber's criticism must be evaluated in the face of what Jung has to say about God. Jung distinguishes God-as-he-is-experienced, the psychic God-image or God archetype, from a possible God entity transcending possible psychic experience to which the God-image could correspond. In terms of his scientific methodological ideal of avoiding undecidable metaphysical claims, Jung's assertions about God are then to be restricted to psychological statements about the God-image:

> Psychologically, however, God is the name for a complex of ideas grouped round a powerful feeling; the feeling-tone is what really gives the complex its characteristic efficacy,... (Vol. 5, p. 85)

> The idea of God is an absolutely necessary psychological function of an irrational nature, which has nothing whatever to do with the question of God's existence. The human intellect can never answer this question, still less give any proof of God. Moreover such proof is superfluous, for the

idea of an all-powerful divine Being is present everywhere, unconsciously is not consciously, because it is an archetype. There is in the psyche some superior power, and if it is not consciously a god, it is the "belly" at least, in St. Paul's words.... Our intellect has long known that we can form no proper idea of God, much less picture to ourselves in what manner he really exists, if at all. The existence of God is once and for all an unanswerable question. (Vol. 7, p. 71)

What Jung says above about God seems relatively unproblematic. However, Jung frequently uses his God-image construct in ways that imply that it has the same meaning as the ordinary traditional religious usage of God:

"Absolute" means "cut off," "detached." To assert that God is absolute amounts to placing him outside all connection with mankind. Man cannot affect him, or he man. Such a God would be of no consequence at all.... this urge to regard God as "absolute" derives solely from the fear that God might become "psychological." This would naturally be dangerous. An absolute God, on the other hand, does not concern us in the least, whereas a "psychological" God would be *real.* (Vol. 7, p. 235, note 6)

Yet Jung is not agnostic and affirms his personal view that there is something to which the psychological God-image corresponds:

This is certainly not to say that what we call the unconscious is identical with God or is set up in his place. It is simply the medium from which religious experience seems to flow. (Vol. 10, p. 293)

We find numberless images of God, but we cannot produce the original. There is no doubt in my mind that there is an original behind our images, but it is inaccessible. (Vol. 18, p. 706)

All that I have learned has led me step by step to an unshakable conviction of the existence of God. I only believe in what I know. And that eliminates believing. Therefore I do not take His existence on belief—I *know* that He exists.[28]

From these different perspectives from which Jung talks about God, we can begin to understand why his views attract theological criticism. For Jung believes that he can restrict himself to the "facts" of religious experience and that without committing himself to any metaphysical assertions arrive at certain valid empirical statements about God-as-he-is-experienced. But since these assertions will be based on a cross-cultural comparison of religious symbology, they may come into conflict with the dogma of a specific religion where the archetypally based religious experiences have undergone a prolonged period of interpretation.

Thus, Jung says that the doctrine of the *privatio boni* and its implication: "*Omne bonum a Deo, omne malus ab homine*" is not supportable by existing archetypal evidence:

> ...I have felt compelled to contest the validity of the *privatio boni* so
> far as the empirical realm is concerned....
> Criticism can be applied only to psychic phenomena, i.e., to ideas and
> concepts, and not to metaphysical entities. These can only be confronted
> with other metaphysical entities. Hence my criticism is valid *only within
> the empirical realm*....It seems to me, however, that the existing
> empirical material, at least so far as I am acquainted with it, permits of no
> definite conclusion as to the archetypal background of the *privatio boni*.
> Subject to correction, I would say that clear-cut *moral* distinctions are
> the most recent acquisition of civilized man. (Vol. 11, pp. 305-306)

For the most part, however, Jung feels that his empirical formulations
leave the door open for at least theoretical compatability with metaphysical religious statements based on faith. Since these metaphysical statements, such as the assertion that a God exists who transcends the psyche,
are supported by faith rather than by experience, they cannot be either
empirically validated or disproved. For even the numinous experience of
the God archetype reveals only that a certain psychically conditioned
factor exists.

Thus, Jung's reply to theological criticism is that he is making empirical
statements about the God archetype rather than uttering metaphysical
truths. He is not talking theologically but scientifically:

> You evidently did not know that epistemologically I take my stand on
> Kant, which means that an assertion doesn't posit its object. So when I
> say "God" I am speaking exclusively of assertions that don't posit their
> object. About God himself I have asserted nothing, because according to
> my premise nothing whatever can be asserted about God himself. All
> such assertions refer to the psychology of the God-image. Their validity is
> therefore never metaphysical but only psychological. All my assertions,
> reflections, discoveries, etc. have not the remotest connection with
> theology but are, as I have said, only statements about psychological
> facts. (*Letters*, Vol. 1, p. 294, letter to Josef Goldbrunner dated 8 February
> 1941)

In spite of all Jung's protests of innocence, the theologians have
nonetheless good reasons to be upset with Jung's archetypal treatment of
religion. It is not that Jung has explained away religion by reducing it to
psychology—his psychological treatment maintains the authentic existence of numinous experience that transcends reference to the personal
ego to an indeterminable extent. Rather the difficulty is that the Jungian
image of humankind with its archetypal understanding of the spirit is in
real conflict with a traditional religious viewpoint based on faith. Thus,
although Jung is attempting to approach religious concerns from a strictly
empirical point of view and is not advocating that his views be interpreted
in a religious way, it is hard to avoid perceiving the manifest incompatibility

with a traditional religious viewpoint. For if one holds Jung's theory of archetypes to be true, then traditional religious understanding can only claim to be a relative and limited interpretation. In a letter Jung once admitted this point:

> If the Christian truth is not supreme and solely valid, then it believes it has lost its *raison d´être* and, if I may express my humble opinion, it *would* have lost it. It would instantly have to turn into a sort of philosophical syncretism. I think that this is a most serious point. (*Letters*, Vol. 1, pp. 269-270, letter to W. E. Hocking dated 5 May 1939)

Jung's claim, then, is that all experience that could count as supporting a religious understanding, since it must be a psychic experience, falls within the domain of his theory. The religious interpretation of this experience is thus always open to question and to possible psychological critique:

> ...I approach these problems in a way that has often been charged with "psychologism." If "psychology" were meant, I should indeed be flattered, for my aim as a psychologist is to dismiss without mercy the metaphysical claims of all esoteric teachings....Let the convinced Christian believe, by all means, for that is the duty he has taken upon himself; but whoever is not a Christian has forfeited the charisma of faith. (Perhaps he was cursed from birth with not being able to believe, but merely to know.)...One cannot grasp anything metaphysically, one only can do so psychologically. Therefore I strip things of their metaphysical wrappings in order to make them objects of psychology. (Vol. 13, p. 49)

> The fact that I am content with what can be experienced psychically, and reject the metaphysical, does not amount, as any intelligent person can see, to a gesture of scepticism or agnosticism aimed at faith and trust in higher powers, but means approximately the same as what Kant meant when he called the thing-in-itself a "merely negative borderline concept." Every statement about the transcendental is to be avoided because it is only a laughable presumption on the part of a human mind unconscious of its limitations. Therefore, when God or the Tao is named an impulse of the soul, or a psychic state, something has been said about the knowable only, but nothing about the unknowable, about which nothing can be determined. (Vol. 13, p. 54)

Such a position, although technically leaving open a loophole for religious faith, undermines the grounds for believing in the extrapsychological truth of such faith, that is, a truth that would be more than just valid relative to a particular psychological perspective. The choice of one religious interpretation of archetypal experience over another or over an atheistic interpretation must then be on the basis of which particular root metaphor one finds congenial to their individual psychology.

Moreover, there is some real question to what extent Jung is successful in maintaining his discourse about religious concerns on a solely empirical, psychological level. The appropriation of the emotionally loaded word God to mean the psychological God-image opens him up to the criticism that he is indulging in theological discourse. In his *Jung, Gods, and Modern Man*, Antonio Moreno complains then that "Jung, the philosopher-psychologist, interprets man's ideas of God within the framework of his own ideas of God."[29] Works such an *Answer to Job* leave the impression that what is being expressed is more a personal religious testament than an objective psychological discussion.

The claim that Jung's theory of archetypes constitutes a psychologistic treatment of religion is then justified in the sense that his theory offers a psychological framework for understanding with which a traditional religious perspective can be made compatible only by assuming the subservient role of an undecidable metaphysical interpretation based on the so-called archetypal facts.

The question remains, however, to what extent this "psychologism" is the basis for a valid criticism of the archetypal theory. For the fact that psychologism can be established does not necessarily mean that something is wrong with the theory. It would seem clear that psychologism is an objection only to a misuse or misapplication of the archetypal theory rather than to the theory itself. If, for example, the claim is made that the psychological perspective is the only valid way to understand a religious, philosophical, or aesthetical work or event, then there exists the manifest possibility of an illegitimate reductionism. Freud's psychologistic understanding of religion and art in terms of sublimation of sexuality seems an example of this pernicious "nothing but"[30] psychologistic application of a theory.

But surely there is a legitimate psychological element in religion, art, and philosophy that can be discussed without the implication that these disciplines are nothing but confused psychology. Jung's application of the archetypal theory beyond psychology to these other areas is for the most part sensitive to this problem. But, of course, examples can be found where Jung is guilty of failing to appreciate a work in its own terms because of his awareness of the psychological element. He seems to arbitrarily dismiss the philosophies of Georg Hegel and Martin Heidegger in this manner:

> ...Hegel, who in my very incompetent opinion is not even a proper philosopher but a misfired psychologist. His impossible language, which he shares with his blood-brother Heidegger, denotes that his philosophy is a highly rationalized and lavishly decorated confession of his unconscious. (*Letters*, Vol. 2, p. 501, letter to Joseph F. Rychlak dated 27 April 1959)

Moreover, it can be readily seen how it is Jung's Kantian strategy that brings him into direct conflict with the theologians. Jung will give a psychological treatment of the phenomena and leave the theologians and metaphysicians with the impossible task of talking about noumena. But we need not follow Jung on this point; the archetypal theory can be made intelligible without the need for a Kantian distinction between phenomena and noumena. In this way much of the theological criticism loses its force. For there is no longer the necessity for the misleading emphasis on the *merely* phenomenal nature of the God-image we experience.[31]

But with the abandonment of this Kantian distinction, the question about the independent subsistence of archetypes reappears. For instead of the archetypes being only psychic entities, the psyche could be considered as just one place in which they manifest themselves.[32] The alternative thus presents itself to interpret the archetypes as transcendent metaphysical entities.

Our argument against such an interpretation in terms of what we have called "a naturalistic reconstruction" can now be shown to have the advantage of helping to separate the scientific aims of a theory of archetypes from unnecessary metaphysical and theological complications. For Jung was perhaps misguided in believing that Kant's doctrines would preserve the scientific character of his theory and prevent metaphysical and theological discourse in its name. It is not clear that Kant succeeded in preventing the claims of science and religion from becoming competing systems of explanation, and, in any case, Jung in fact fails to strictly adhere to Kant and sometimes indulges in discourse that is of a metaphysical and theological nature. (*Answer to Job*) In light of these difficulties, then, our naturalistic reconstruction is intended to provide a way of showing how the theory can be construed so that its scientific import is not needlessly implicated with nonscientific discourse.

The Challenge of James Hillman's Archetypal Psychology 5

Preliminary Remarks

T HE systematic challenges to Jung's theory of archetypes that we have discussed in the previous chapter aimed to show how the phenomena which the theory of archetypes are supposed to describe can be accounted for by other simpler theories or else that the theory fundamentally misrepresents those phenomena. However, with the views of James Hillman, we have to consider an alternative interpretation of the theory of archetypes that takes the theory in a direction incompatible with the scientific attitude. Rather than attempting to refute the archetypal theory, it might well be said that Hillman loves it to death. For he applies it so universally that the theory becomes a kind of ideology in terms of which all phenomena have to be interpreted. Thus, rather than attempting to demonstrate how the archetypal theory can be construed so as to meet scientific criteria, Hillman would judge science by archetypal standards.

Although it might seem that Hillman's interpretation of the archetypal theory was simply another equally valid perspective with which to understand the archetypal phenomena so that we do not have to choose between Jung's original version and Hillman's alternative, the radical nature of Hillman's metapsychological views necessitates a detailed rebuttal. For to accept Hillman's ideas on the relationship between science and archetypes would mean that Jung's whole project of a reconciliation of a theory embracing archetypal phenomena with the scientific world-view is fundamentally mistaken. Thus, there are real incompatibilities between Hillman's and Jung's views of archetypes and these incompatibilities need to be addressed before the idea of a rapprochement of an archetypal theory with science can be accepted as a meaningful and viable enterprise.

Characterization of Hillman's Views on Archetypes

A major difference in Hillman's approach from Jung's original formulations is evident in his rejection of the distinction that Jung made between archetype per se and archetypal image. Hillman rejects this distinction because he wants to avoid the Kantian idealism he sees inherent in it in which the archetypal images would represent the phenomena and the archetypes per se the equivalent of the noumena in Kant's system.[1]

As we have previously discussed in chapter 3, the archetype per se, archetypal image distinction does not have to be construed in a way that implies acceptance of a Kantian idealism. However, the considerations that were brought forth there do not fully address the real import of Hillman's objection to the distinction. For Hillman wants to focus attention on the imaginal aspect of archetypes as opposed to *anything* to which the archetypal image might possibly be said to refer or stand for:

> In fact, the image has no referent beyond itself, neither proprioceptive, external, nor semantic: "images don't stand for anything" (Hillman, 1978a). They are the psyche itself in its imaginative visibility; as primary datum, image is irreducible.[2]

Another related part of Hillman's view is his rejection of Jung's distinction between the personal and the collective aspects of the unconscious. All psychic manifestations are thus to be interpreted archetypally no matter how personal they may seem:

> (Platonism never made a sharp separation between your or my personal soul and the soul in general, just as archetypal psychology cannot separate the personal and the collection unconscious, for within every complex, fantasy, and image of the personal psyche is an archetypal power.)[3]

If we consider the mythos/logos categories mentioned in the introduction, then Hillman's program in general is one of highlighting the mythos as a way of understanding the world to the denigration of the logos. If we take dreams as a representation of the mythos for purposes of illustration, it is as if Hillman wanted to say that the dream is real, but the external world to which the dream refers is relatively unreal. This position contrasts with Jung's attempt to legitimate the reality of the dream while respecting the reality of the external world, and is an inversion of a positivistic position that affirms the reality of the external world while denying any meaningful sense to dreams.[4] Hillman, in fact, actually speaks of dreams in this fashion:

> The dream is not compensation but initiation. It does not complete ego-consciousness, but voids it.[5]

We must reverse our usual procedure of translating the dream into ego-language and instead translate the ego into dream-language.[6]

The imaginal perspective assumes priority over the natural organic perspective.[7]

Hillman arrives at this radical and rather startling view by extending Jung's notion that archetypes underlie and structure all of our conceptions. "The archetypal position implies that all knowing may be examined in terms of these psychic premises. It suggests nothing less than an archetypal *epistēmē*, an archetypal theory of knowing."[8]

Rather our aim is to remember that all knowledge can be psychologized. And that by being psychologized, it also becomes a means of psychological reflection. Therefore all teaching is relevant to the soul as long as its literalism is psychologized. Every statement in every branch of learning in every university department is a statement made by the psyche through men and women and is a psychological statement.[9]

From Hillman's perspective, everything must be experienced as an image of the psyche in order to be experienced at all. Moreover, since these psychic images are conditioned by archetypes, the fantasy images must be in some sense ultimately real since everything is reducible to them, but they are just what they appear to be:

All consciousness depends upon fantasy images. All we know about the world, about the mind, the body, about anything whatsoever, *including the spirit* and the nature of the divine, comes through images and is organized by fantasies into one pattern or another.... Because these patterns are archetypal, we are always in one or another archetypal configuration, one or another fantasy, including the fantasy of soul and the fantasy of spirit.[10]

To hold that "we are not real" means that the reality of persons and every act of consciousness is a reflection of a fantasy-image: for these are the only actual existents that are not reducible to something other than their imagery; only they are as they literally appear; only fantasies are utterly, incontrovertibly real.[11]

In Hillman's view, what psychology ought to be involved in, its proper work, is the explication of the archetypal perspective in all of experience. This appreciation of the pervasiveness of the archetypal Hillman calls "psychologizing." But to see things mythically from the standpoint of archetypes will mean to see them metaphorically, since the mythologems are understood by Hillman to be metaphors. "Archetypes are semantically metaphors."[12] Thus, psychologizing will also mean "deliteralizing" so that nothing is taken as literally what it is except the archetypal images themselves. *"Through psychologizing I change the idea of any literal action at all—political, scientific, personal—into a metaphorical enactment.*"[13]

The net result of Hillman's position is that psychology itself gets deliteralized. For in seeing all psychology on the model of depth psychology,[14] the entirety of what Hillman would acknowledge as the proper domain of psychology falls outside of the objective, literal realm of science. Psychology and science become incompatible:

> So it would seem that an adequate psychology must be one that cannot take itself or any of its ideas literally.[15]

> Psychology is thus not a discipline of truth, as is science or philosophy or theology.[16]

> They [Freud and Jung] could not free themselves from psychological conceptualizing, and so they tended to conceive myths metapsychologically (whereas we are trying to imagine our metapsychology mythically).[17]

We might well call Hillman's position "imaginative realism." It is clear that such a view, if tenable, rules out the possibility of the kind of scientific realism that Jung is aiming for in his efforts at rapprochement with a scientific viewpoint in his archetypal theory.

Hillman's perspective at first sight seems to be a potentially reasonable one vis-à-vis Jung's original position. For as Ernst Cassirer can argue for the primacy of the logos and Jung for an equiprimordiality of logos and mythos, then Hillman's view as the third option, the primacy of the mythos seems open for exploration and development. If Hillman's position is a legitimate third point of view, then it would seem that the differences between Hillman and Jung could not be settled in a straightforward way. For as Jung and Hillman come from different starting assumptions about the relations between mythos and logos, this would seem to mean that they inevitably argue through each other. However, there are several serious drawbacks to Hillman's view of the primacy of the mythos, and, because of these difficulties, it is questionable to what extent Hillman's position constitutes a genuine alternative to Jung's outlook on mythos and logos. Moreover, notwithstanding any real inconsistencies that might be shown to plague Hillman's perspective, there are also some undesirable consequences attendant upon acceptance of his view that must be understood before we see his position as possibly supplanting Jung's outlook.

But before we can fully appreciate what is entailed by the Hillman line, we must endeavor to discover more of its underlying logic. In this regard it is clear that, in opting for the primacy of the mythos, Hillman is arguing from a kind of romantic appeal where the literal is dissolved into metaphor and truth into poetry. From Hillman's point of view, myth and reality seem to coincide. This is still acceptable as long as Hillman is intent on merely showing us the myth *in* every reality. But is Hillman arguing only that there is fantasy in everything or additionally that, in the final analysis, everything is just a fantasy, that everything reduces to fantasy?

In an analogous fashion, we might argue that there is metaphor in every statement. But then we could not conclude that every statement is a metaphor. Clearly we are not justified in concluding the latter from the former, unless we also want to assert that the difference between the two terms is a distinction without a difference.

But Hillman does not in fact seem to be straightforwardly arguing against the meaningfulness of a distinction between these terms. In the following example, he clearly acknowledges a legitimate role to the literal and hence the logos:

> We should hasten to qualify that psychologizing does not mean *only* psychologizing, or that statements may not have content, merit, and import in the area of their literal expression. Philosophical and scientific assertions are, of course, not only psychological statements. To reduce such assertions wholly to psychology commits the psychologistic fallacy, or "psychologism." This point is important.[18]

But if Hillman is not arguing that the literal is really metaphor and reality really just fantasy, that is, that the logos is merely another form of the mythos, then on what grounds can he advocate the primacy of the mythos? Moreover, what is the basis for the difference that Hillman draws between Jung's view and his own on this question? For the less radical aspect of Hillman's program, the emphasis on the mythos aspect in every logos expression, does not seem to differ significantly from Jung's original view since Jung would certainly agree that every aspect of reality is, to some extent, involved in metaphor, fantasy, and myth.

It is clear that the intent of Hillman's program of psychologizing is not so much to deny differences between logos and mythos altogether, but rather to weaken the distinction and level down the differences by emphasizing the common fantasy element in both mythos and logos. The argument will then be that, since fantasy is a common element in every human endeavor, the perspective that articulates and understands this dimension, that is, the mythos, has got to be more fundamental than that which is understood and articulated, the logos. Thus, Hillman argues that depth psychology (i.e., his archetypal psychology) is more primordial than a scientific psychology since both are manifestations of the soul, and depth psychology grasps this point whereas scientific psychology does not:

> But the psychological perspective is supreme and prior because the psyche is prior and must appear within every human undertaking. The psychological viewpoint does not encroach upon other fields, for it is there to begin with, even if most disciplines invent methods that pretend to keep it out.[19]

> Whether psychologists can stand for it or not, psychology inherently assumes superiority over other disciplines, because the psyche of which it is the advocate does indeed come before any of its compartmental activities, departmentalized into arts, sciences, or trades.[20]

Thus, there can be no outside of myth and fantasy—no way to break through to any truth unconditioned by the mythos. Hillman's claim for the primacy of the mythos amounts then to the assertion that the mythos perspective is more ultimate and more basic than any other. The logos may have its own legitimate functions, but these do not impinge on those of the mythos. The logos can then be safely ignored and we can talk as if certain aspects of reality were just mythos. Because of this the mythos is not accountable to the logos, that is, it is independent of logos judgment:

> In fact, the categories of logic and number, of science and theology, could themselves be reduced (i.e., led back) to more basic metaphors of myth. No concepts, no matter how general and abstract, could embrace the range of these archetypal metaphors.[21]

> Its fantasy of itself [an adequate psychology] must be one that allows psychologizing to continue as an open process of ideation. It may not be based upon axioms and laws, or even rely upon hypotheses. Instead it will have to consist of fictions.[22]

> Our premises present a world that escapes both the demands of logic for definition and the demands of empirical science for demonstration. Fictions take their place in the realm traditionally reserved for the soul, between the world of spirit (metaphysics and intellect) and the world of nature (science and sense perception). They furnish psychology with its own psychic premises, not borrowed from metaphysics and the sciences, which offer a mode of seeing through metaphysics and the sciences.[23]

Critique of Hillman's View

At least part of the credibility of Hillman's position rests on a situation where the mythos terms, myth and fantasy, are understood in one sense figuratively, and in another sense literally. We can best approach this point by considering the phrase: the myth of science. Science is a sort of myth too. From Hillman's point of view, science is another fantasy of the soul. But is science just a fantasy of the soul? Is the myth of science really the same kind of thing as say the myth of Icarus? Hillman's view seems to imply the latter. But when we say the myth of science, the word "myth" is being used in a metaphorical sense. Science involves a myth in the same way that every rational or irrational endeavor involves myth, that is, they all fall under the influence of one archetype or another. But this fact does not itself denigrate the difference between what we come to accept on the basis of science and what we perceive through mythic fantasy. In other words, just because of the universal scope of influence of archetypes, the real differences we want to acknowledge between science and myth remain largely unaffected. Within the context of the "myth" of science, we still have scientific knowing and mythic expression of timeless truths.

Moreover, the fact that the great scientific theories are based on theoretical models that involve extended metaphors does not really weaken the difference between science and myth. For the essence of science is the eventual accountability of these models to literal truth conditions determined by experimental outcomes.

In addition, Hillman's attempt to elevate the mythos to primacy by denigrating the importance of the logos fails just because of the inevitable interdependence of these two perspectives. For just as we cannot really ever get rid of or totally dispense with the mythos, we cannot literalize our speech totally, for example, so also is the logos dimension unexpungeable from experience. Hillman would have us focus all our awareness on the mythos perspective disregarding almost totally any logos aspect. In regard to dreams, for example, he wants us to focus on the images and disregard any thought about what the images might mean in respect to translating their significance for events in the everyday world. But this simply will not do because the mythos is itself meaningless unless it does relate at least indirectly to the logos perspective of things. Dreams are meaningless unless they have at least some indirect relation to our waking, nondream world. Metaphors, likewise, are meaningless without an implicit relation to the literal world. For we evaluate the mythos not entirely in terms of itself, but also in terms of how it helps us to appreciate and understand the logos. We judge metaphors, then, on how well they serve to illuminate the nonmetaphorical.

Although Hillman says that he wants to deliteralize psychology and understand his metapsychology mythically, it is unlikely that he can really stick with this and avoid inconsistency. He cannot say, for example, that his point of view is only a fantasy or an extended metaphor, and at the same time that his position is superior to Jung's and an improvement over his original perspective, as is clearly implied by his polemical rhetoric attacking Jung's views.

Moreover, Hillman's inconsistency in asserting that his psychology is not concerned with truth while also arguing for the superiority of his way of looking at things indicates the impossibility of getting around the logos. Although we can deny the logos and pretend we are not considering it, the logos perspective gets smuggled back into our outlook. Hillman is not content, then, to simply assert that his purported deliteralized psychology is simply another *style* of psychologizing. He means us to see it as the enlightened way to do psychology. All of our statements about the mythos thus are made inevitably from a logos-wise point of view. For we cannot go back to a primitive outlook where mythos and logos are merged together, and where myth has to be both meaning-giver as well as literal, historical explanation. When we disregard the logos, it comes back into our view unwittingly so that the effort to deliteralize everything only results in the undesirable situation where the mythos has to function illegitimately as the logos, and we run a real risk of construing the metaphorical as the literal and fantasy as concrete reality.

Hillman's move away from the logos towards a one-sided mythos point of view results in his having to acknowledge the situation where his psychology falls partly within the scope of religion. In fact, Hillman would have us recognize that, from his viewpoint, the archetypes are properly speaking Gods:

> By setting up a universe which tends to hold everything we do, see, and say in the sway of its cosmos, an archetype is best comparable with a God.[24]

> Archetypes are psychic structures, but *not only this*, for they are also Gods who cannot be encompassed by anyone's individual soul.[25]

> A re-vision of psychology means recognizing that psychology does not take place without religion, because there is always a God in what we are doing.[26]

> Here we are opening into "the religion of psychology" by suggesting that psychology is a variety of religious experience.[27]

Of course, as we might well imagine, the "Gods" of Hillman are not meant to be understood literally, for taking gods literally would involve us in the fantasy of theology.[28] However, when Hillman places a capital *G* in front of gods, this again indicates the difficulty of unwittingly slipping back into logos thinking, for Hillman's Gods are to be real but not literally real. The difference is easy to lose as is illustrated by these quotes:

> The imaginal has become real; for many, *the* real.[29]

> A study of man can never give a sufficient perspective, for man is fundamentally limited; he is a frail *brotos*, *thnetos*, a poor mortal thing, not fully real. Gods are real.[30]

Although Hillman speaks in the name of the mythos, the inescapability of the logos means that his approach really has the effect of functionally merging the two. This conflation of the mythos and logos is then one distinct disadvantage of taking the Hillman line.

But the credibility of Hillman's outlook is also considerably weakened by its ideological character that has a ready-made answer to any criticism. Any point of view from which we might criticize Hillman, from a scientific or theological perspective, for instance, can be "seen through" as just another manifestation of fantasy, as just more illustrations of the viewpoint itself. Hillman has claimed an epistemological stance more primordial than any nonpsychological point of view and thus not really subject to criticism from any other perspective. This is an unfortunate consequence of the Hillman program because it puts Hillman's ideas on the level of faith or belief rather than subjecting them to the possibility of rational critique from other viewpoints. Considering the innovative and pioneering nature of Jung's archetypal thesis on which Hillman's position is partly based, this is an undesirable outcome. Jungian psychology as a whole then loses credibility to the extent that it becomes identified with what Hillman is doing. For until the archetypal theory is able to meet its critics and eventually gain widespread acceptance in its present or some modified form, Hillman's radical use of the theory simply confuses the issues.

Thus, although aspects of Hillman's perspective on the archetypal theory may have something of value to offer as an alternative model in terms of which to understand archetypes, Hillman fundamentally fails to demonstrate that his overall outlook on the mythos and logos is superior to Jung's original position, and that Jung's attempt to achieve a reconciliation with science is misconceived. Because of the inconsistencies and undesirable consequences attendant upon Hillman's view, it cannot be accepted as an adequate alternative theory of archetypes.

Jung and the Scientific Attitude: Part 1

6

The Question of Scientific Status

Preliminary Remarks

WITH the completion of our discussion of various critiques of the theory of archetypes from the standpoint of general considerations and of the Hillman point of view, we can now proceed with our exploration of the question of the scientific status of the archetypal theory. Is Jung's notion of archetypes one that can be reconstructively construed as an idea which can be appropriately classified as belonging within the context of science?

In emphasizing the issue of the scientific status of the archetypal theory, we do not mean to imply that for any of Jung's ideas to be meaningful they must be shown to be genuinely scientific. Certainly such works as *Answer to Job* are meaningful and insightful though most probably not science. Jung was too complete an individual to have been only a scientist, and his writings often reflect his extrascientific views and interests. But the fact that Jung at times exceeds the accepted boundaries of scientific inquiry, as in *Job*, is all the more reason to assess the scientific nature of the archetypal theory. For the many facets of Jung's personality—philosopher, therapist, "speculating heretic" (Vol. 11, p. 307), scientist—invite the unsympathetic and shortsighted critic to dismiss Jung's views carte blanche as hopelessly unscientific or "mystic." In order to show why the archetypes merit serious scientific study and consideration, we must then address ourselves to the questions surrounding the alleged scientific status of the archetypal theory.

Outline of an Approach to the Question

Our approach to the question of the scientific nature of Jung's theory of archetypes will of necessity be a rather indirect one. Before proceeding to a discussion of the scientific merit of Jung's theory in terms of such issues as possibility of falsification, type and quality of explanations and predictions to be expected, and nature of evidence for the theory (these questions are taken up in chapter 8), we must in the present and subsequent chapter approach the question of scientific status from the point of view of attempting to show that Jung's theory of archetypes is not patiently unscientific. That is to say, we must show how the theory can meet various objections that constitute reasons on the basis of which the designation "scientific" would be an inappropriate description of it.

In terms of extant criticism, the most prevalent criticism of Jung's theory in this regard is the accusation that it is in some sense a mystical rather than a scientific approach to the phenomena. Although it can be rather easily shown that Jung's theory is not an overt and self-conscious attempt at mystical utterance, an examination of the context of issues out of which the question of mysticism arises serves as an introduction to the question of the manner in which the archetypal theory can meet criticism that it represents a paradigmatically unscientific approach. With the limited issue of the relation between mysticism and the archetypal theory clarified, then, more general questions concerning the issue of an unscientific approach can be brought into focus.

Our treatment of these more general questions will entail an examination of Jung's scientific attitude, that is, the way in which Jung understands the archetypal theory to be scientific in principle. In regard to this issue, two pivotal questions will prove to be the problem of the relation between a scientific discourse about archetypes and an extrascientific discourse, and the question of the manner in which the archetypal theory can satisfy acceptable criteria of rationality for a scientific theory, that is, whether or not the theory in the final analysis will prove to be sufficiently grounded in the logos. In addition to the treatment of these questions, our examination of whether Jung's theory of archetypes is implicated with a patently unscientific approach must also consider the issue of Jung's methodology (pages 119–124), the manner in which Jung understands his study of archetypes to employ a legitimate scientific method.[1]

As the examination of the question of mysticism leads us into discussion of more general issues, our approach will be to see in what way Jung understands his theory to be able to meet these challenges to its scientific nature. We will then attempt to determine to what extent Jung's scientific intentions are in fact carried through and whether or not they are adequate for the task of articulating the theory in such a way that it can be clearly shown to be a legitimate scientific enterprise.

The Charge of Mysticism

In attempting to gain perspective on the question of the scientific validity of the theory of archetypes, we must begin by considering the issue of mysticism. Clarification of this question is especially crucial for the scientific validity of the archetypal theory since Jung's views on archetypes are subject to be summarily dismissed from serious scientific consideration if it can be shown that the label of mysticism is appropriate in characterization of them. Judging from the extant literature about Jung, moreover, it would seem that Jung's views are frequently either identified or closely associated with a mystical framework of understanding. For example, in an article entitled "The Mystical and Scientific Aspects of the Psychoanalytic Theories of Freud, Adler, and Jung," Edward Burchard states:

> But it is only in Jung [in contrast to Freud and Adler] that we find a conscious and deliberate repudiation of rationality and empirical science and a lush proliferation of concepts which are indistinguishable in form and intention from those of Christian and Oriental religious mystics.[2]

In a similar vein Paul Friedman and Jacob Goldstein echo the theme of the employment of a paradigmatically unscientific approach:

> Jungian psychology, with its emphasis on the archaic and its tendency to passive preoccupation with symbolic content, stands in strong contrast to the rationalism and determinism characteristic of Western thought in general and of modern science in particular.[3]

Philip Rieff, although not employing the pejorative term "mysticism," criticizes the Jungian point of view from a similar standpoint by stating that Jung's ideas are validated from the perspective of revelation rather than scientific method:

> There is no arguing with revelation. Jung's was a personal language of faith, revelatory, and therefore beyond danger of being invalidated by argument or contrary experience. . . .
> Against the democracy of the scientific intellect, he represents the aristocracy of emotional profundity.[4]

> Because it offers no criteria of validity, other than the therapeutic experience of conviction, Jungian theory amounts at once to a private religion and an anti-science.[5]

Before the question of the scientific credibility of the archetypal theory can be critically discussed, there must be a clearing of the air concerning mysticism. For although it may well seem that "mysticism" signifies nothing other than "unscientific" when used to describe an allegedly scientific theory,[6] we still need to discover the reasons for this characterization of Jung's views. For an examination of the possible grounds for ascription of the label of mysticism will lead us beyond the narrower question of Jung's appeal to mystical frameworks of understanding to the more general issues of the rationality of the archetypal theory and the relation of scientific and extrascientific discourse about archetypes.

However, our discussion of these more general considerations must wait until we have indicated what relationship exists between Jung's idea of archetypes and mysticism. The possibility that Jung's archetypal theory is nothing more than a sort of appeal to mysticism must then be considered as the most extreme sort of criticism that it represents a paradigmatically unscientific approach.

Thus, in order to investigate the possibility that Jung's archetypal theory does in fact make an appeal to a mystical framework of understanding, we will need to explicate the relationship between Jung's views and mysticism. But, before we can address this task, it will be necessary to first gain an understanding of what is meant by mystical experience.

Mysticism Characterized

W. T. Stace in his *Mysticism and Philosophy* argues that genuinely mystical experience can be divided into two basic types. A so-called extroverted mystical experience is to be distinguished from an introverted one. In the extroverted experience, there is a "...unifying vision, expressed abstractly by the formula 'All is One.' The One is...perceived through...the multiplicity of objects."[7] Thus, the extroverted mystic perceives a oneness of all things that is distinguishable from the individual things themselves. The introverted mystic, on the other hand, experiences a oneness in a consciousness otherwise devoid of all ideational content. "The Unitary Consciousness, from which all the multiplicity of sensuous or conceptual or other empirical content has been excluded, so that there remains only a void and empty unity."[8]

In addition to the experience of oneness, Stace lists other characteristics shared by both types of mysticism: "Sense of objectivity or reality. Feeling of blessedness, joy, happiness, satisfaction, etc. Feeling that what is apprehended is holy, or sacred, or divine....Paradoxicality....Alleged by mystics to be ineffable,..."[9]

Is Jung a Mystic?

If we accept Stace's criteria of mystical experience as constituting a satisfactory guideline for determining what types of experience could be called mystical in a strict sense of the term, the question then presents itself: Is Jung a mystic from the standpoint of personal experience? Although we wish to focus on the crucial issue of whether Jung attempts to defend his archetypal theory from the point of view of a mystical framework of understanding, the issue of Jung's personal mystical experience is also relevant since the case for arguing that Jung's ideas appeal to a mystical justification would be strengthened if we could establish that he had first hand experience of mystical states of consciousness.[10] For in light of the usually intense nature of such experiences, we would have good reason to expect that such experience would have some influence on the development of Jung's overall viewpoint.

In regard to Jung's personal mystical experience, we discover, then, that although Jung in his autobiography reports several instances of paranormal psychic experiences, and in one case an out-of-body experience, plus visions, and instances of hearing voices or conversing with spirits,[11] there do not seem to have been any genuine cases of mystical experience. Moreover, in deciding about the nature of Jung's altered states of consciousness, it is important to note that the visions and voices that Jung describes do not qualify as genuine mystical states. Stace points out that visions and voices are not really mystical phenomena:

> Not only is this the opinion of most competent scholars, but it has also been the opinion which the great mystics themselves have generally held.[12]

> The main point is that the most typical as well as the most important type of mystical experiences is nonsensuous, whereas visions and voices have the character of sensuous imagery. The introvertive kind of mystical states are, according to all the accounts we have of them, entirely devoid of all imagery.[13]

On the basis of the negative evidence, then, we might feel justified in concluding that Jung had no genuine mystical experiences. For in view of the disclosure of the types of unusual experiences that Jung does reveal in his autobiography, it would be reasonable to expect a description of a mystical state had there been one to report.

But if we can conclude that from the standpoint of personal experience Jung is not a mystic, the question remains as to the extent of a possible appeal to a mystical framework of understanding in justifying his views on archetypes. That is, we need to understand the relation that exists between mysticism and Jung's archetypes in order to examine the possibility that Jung means his archetypal theory to be understood from an essentially mystical point of view in terms of which a scientific approach with its appeal to publicly observable data and empirical criteria of validation would not be applicable. Justification of the archetypal theory in terms of a mystical framework of understanding would involve, then, essentially an acceptance of mystical experience as an inexplicable and irreducible datum in terms of which other aspects of experience could be understood, but which would not itself be considered as a type or kind of more general experience; it would mean an abandonment of the logos for a one-sided mythos point of view.

As a first approach to understanding the relation between mysticism and Jung's ideas, it is important to note that, at least in regard to the introverted mystical state, Jung argues against its possibility. That is, in terms of the first characteristic, he says the experience of a oneness in a consciousness devoid of all thought, imagery, and sensation is impossible:

> "*As long as Sunyata*[14] *is cognized by a subject it remains object.*" But
> when the subject enters *Sunyata* and becomes identical with it, the
> subject itself is *Sunyata*, namely void. And when the void is really void,
> there is not even a cognizing subject in it. The subject has vanished and
> there cannot be a consciousness of this fact, because there is nothing left
> any more. There can also be no memory of it, because there was
> nothing....
> I want to know what there is to be known, but I don't want to make
> assumptions about things of which I know that one cannot know them.
> Thus it is absolutely impossible to know what I would experience when
> that "I" which could experience didn't exist any more. One calls this a
> *contradictio in adjecto*. To experience *Sunyata* is therefore an impossible
> experience by definition, as I explained above, and it is also impossible to
> experience consciousness in a field of which I know nothing. (*Letters*, Vol.
> 1, p. 263, letter to W. Y. Evans-Wentz dated 9 February 1939)

It would seem that Jung's comment that the introvert mystical
experience is "impossible by definition" needs qualification. For although
we can argue with the mystic about the meaning of his experience and how
it should be interpreted, we are less open to question that he had an
experience. Thus, Jung is opposed to one of the ways in which mystics
most commonly characterize their experience, the characterization of it as
a oneness in a consciousness devoid of all multiplicity. For in terms of
Jung's own framework of understanding, what happens in the mystical
experience is that there is a lowering of the threshold of consciousness
that allows an experience of the unconscious:

> It is psychologically correct to say that "At-one-ment" is attained by
> withdrawal from the world of consciousness. In the stratosphere of the
> unconscious there are no more thunderstorms, because nothing is
> differentiated enough to produce tensions and conflicts. (Vol. 11, pp.
> 498–499)

> Now if consciousness is emptied as far as possible of its contents, they
> will fall into a state of unconsciousness, at least for the time being. In Zen,
> this displacement usually results from the energy being withdrawn from
> conscious contents and transferred either to the conception of "empti-
> ness" or to the koan. As both of these must be static, the succession of
> images is abolished and with it the energy which maintains the kinetics of
> consciousness. The energy thus saved goes over to the unconscious and
> reinforces its natural charge to bursting point. (Vol. 11, p. 551)

Since Jung understands the mystical experience as analogous to other
more familiar types of experience of the unconscious (e.g., dreams or
visions), he then wants to say that the feeling that the bounds of the ego
have been dissolved and that the experiencer has become merged with the
oneness he experiences cannot be what it seems to be. For since all
experience of the unconscious is possible only through its relation to the
ego, the mystical experience must also involve the ego:[15]

If the Indians would call sublime psychic experience "psyche" or something equivalent to it, I would agree with them, but to call it consciousness cannot be substantiated by any evidence. If the highest psychic condition is *Sunyata*, then it cannot be consciousness, because consciousness is by definition the relationship between the subject and a representation. One is conscious *of* something. As long as you are conscious of *Sunyata* it is not *Sunyata*, because there is still a subject that is conscious of something. (*Letters*, Vol. 1, pp. 249-250, letter to W. Y. Evans-Wentz dated 8 December 1938)

As Jung understands the mystical experience, then, it involves only a relativizing of the ego perspective of consciousness rather than a complete elimination of it.

In addition, Jung's standpoint also amounts to a denial of the mystic's claim that his experience is of something outside himself, that is of something objectively real. It is not a direct experience of the essence of reality that the mystic enjoys, but only an insight into the unknown depths of himself. Of course from the psychological point of view, Jung is trying to restrict himself to the phenomena and avoid metaphysical assertions. However, the force of Jung's objections to the mystic's way of construing his experience as seen in the above quotations seems to be the argument that the psychological interpretation of mysticism in terms analogous to other more common experiences of the unconscious is at least consistent with psychological common sense, whereas the mystic's characterization of it is not. It is clearly evident, then, that Jung's understanding of mystical experience is one that is expressed in terms which conflict with the mystic's own way of interpreting his experience.

However, in spite of the fact that Jung disputes some of the claims the mystic makes for his experience on psychological grounds, he nonetheless considers the mystic experience as one of considerable value and significance. This is not really surprising since Jung understands mysticism as an experience of the unconscious. Consequently the value of the mystical experience is due to the positive effects of the expansion of consciousness that a direct insight into the unconscious makes possible. The experience affords an opportunity to realize the limitations of the perspective of ego consciousness and thus helps to bring about the process of individuation, the goal of which is an integration of the conscious and unconscious aspects of the personality.

The occurrence of satori[16] is interpreted and formulated as a *breakthrough*, by a consciousness limited to the ego-form, into the non-ego-like self. (Vol. 11, p. 543)

So far as Western mysticism is concerned, its texts are full of instructions as to how man can and must release himself from the "I-ness" of his consciousness, so that through knowledge of his own nature he may rise above it and attain the inner (godlike) man. (Vol. 11, p. 545)

> Satori corresponds in the Christian sphere to an experience of religious transformation. (Vol. 11, p. 547)

From our discussion of the relation between mysticism and Jung's views as a whole, we can conclude, then, that Jung does not appeal to a mystical framework of understanding in advocating his theory of archetypes since, rather than understanding the archetypes from a mystical point of view, he understands mysticism in terms of his ideas of the unconscious.

But if we have established that Jung does not defend his theory of archetypes by explicit appeal to a mystical perspective, there is yet an aspect of uncertainty about mysticism in relation to Jung's archetypes. For even if we can clearly show that Jung does not intend his theory to be understood as an expression of an essentially mystical viewpoint, the question remains as to the extent to which there is in fact a similarity between aspects of mysticism and the theory of archetypes. For example, what we have said about the numinosity of archetypal experience (page 44) agrees well with the mystical characteristic of "feeling that what is apprehended is holy, or sacred, or divine."

Concerning the mystical quality of "alleged ineffability," it is more difficult to make comparisons. For it is not clear what sense it makes to talk about degrees or kinds of ineffability. In any case, the mystical ineffability is related to the quality of paradoxicality in that paradoxical descriptions that violate basic laws of logic seem appropriate for its description. This way of talking about the mystic experience is then another way of stating the inability of language and logic to adequately express the inexpressible.

> The language which he finds himself compelled to use is, when at its best, the literal truth about his experience, but it is contradictory. *This is the root of his feeling of embarrassment with language.*[17]

But even though Jung does not follow the mystic in an explicit appeal to the transcendental domain of the ineffable, it might well be argued that there is, nonetheless, some similarity between the description of a mystical experience as ineffable and the ascription of numinosity to characterize archetypal experience. The point needs to be made, then, that although presumably all allegedly ineffable experience would be numinous, that is, charged with a great deal of emotional energy, Jung does not claim that the numinous experience of archetypes is ineffable. In this regard we need to examine what Jung says about the paradoxical and also consider to what degree the indeterminate nature of symbols, that is, the fact that they refer beyond themselves to an indeterminable extent, constitutes a kind of ineffability. These questions which serve to bring to focus the issue of the rationality of the archetypal theory will be discussed in a later section (see pages 110-119).[18] For the present it is sufficient to remark that there is a certain family resemblance between mysticism in the strict sense and some of the things Jung says about the archetypes. However, there seems to be no point in talking in terms of a weak or loose definition of mysticism. For the claim that Jung's theory is quasi-mystical must, in any case, be examined on the basis of the individual reasons for such a contention; and, to the understanding of the several relevant questions involved, the quasi-mystical label contributes nothing. Having established that Jung is not attempting to propound an expression of mystical views, the relevant question is then not the extent to which his theory is a mystical one, but whether in the absence of an explicit appeal to a mystical viewpoint, the theory is nonetheless an instance of a paradigmatically unscientific approach, that is, one opposed in principle to an attitude necessary for science or one that employs an unscientific methodology.

Jung's Attitude Toward Science

Introduction

We turn now to the question of Jung's scientific attitude. With regard to his theory of archetypes, we need to ask whether Jung holds views incompatible with an attitude necessary for science. The objection could be raised at this point that this question is an *ad hominem* type of consideration. For regardless of what beliefs an investigator holds concerning the nature of the scientific endeavor, the issue of whether his theories constitute good science must in any case be resolved in terms of what the theories can do in relation to acceptable scientific standards. However, in Jung's case the relationship he envisions between science and his archetypes is a very crucial concern. On the one hand, it is not always clear that Jung intended his theory of the archetypes to be understood as a scientific theory. In the following passage, for example, Jung seems to be very close to the position we have outlined as James Hillman's viewpoint where the logos is seen as a subset of the mythos:

> Psychology, as one of the many expressions of psychic life, operates with ideas which in their turn are derived from archetypal structures and thus generate a somewhat more abstract kind of myth. Psychology therefore translates the archaic speech of myth into a modern mythologem—not yet, of course, recognized as such—which constitutes one element of the myth "science." (Vol. 9-A, p. 179)

Looking at archetypes from this perspective then leads us to ask: Is the systematic study of archetypes to be understood as one branch of science, or is science merely one manifestation of archetypes? For if the latter should prove to be the case, we could not expect a scientific evaluation of the theory to be the most appropriate way to determine its validity.

On the other hand, even if Jung does want to see archetypes as falling within the scientific domain, the question remains as to the extent to which he really succeeded in being scientific as opposed to merely claiming an empirical basis for what is essentially a speculative mythological view, thereby confusing the mythological with the scientific.[19] Jung seems particularly vulnerable to this charge since he claims to be studying myths scientifically and to be doing so phenomenologically, that is, taking into account the phenomena in their totality.

As we have emphasized in the introduction, Jung's goal is to do justice to the mythos while maintaining an accountability to the logos perspective, thus respecting both mythos and logos and not seeking to subsume one totally to the other. Undeterred by the irrational nature of the subject matter, Jung wanted to achieve an empirically grounded and scientifically defensible theory of archetypes.[20] For example he says: "I saw that so much fantasy needed firm ground underfoot, and that I must first return wholly to reality. For me, reality meant scientific comprehension. I had to draw concrete conclusions from the insights the unconscious had given me—and that task was to become a life work." (*Memories, Dreams, Reflections*, p. 188)

However, in addition to a detached, objective study of archetypal events, Jung also advocated for therapy and was personally involved in efforts to interpret the meaning of the archetypal images from philosophical and religious viewpoints. Thus, Jung's attention is engaged at both the meta-level of archetypal events, theorizing about archetypal phenomena, and at the object-level in the direct experience of the archetypal images. In his clinical work, Jung endeavored to have his patients directly experience the archetypes and work through to a personal philosophy of life and religious outlook. Although it would be an exaggeration to say that Jung always succeeds in sharply distinguishing these levels of discourse—all too often he takes the distinction for granted, thus leading to many confusions—the point to be made is that Jung sees the distinction as an essential one that can preserve the scientific character of an archetypal theory independently of particular interpretations of the significance of the archetypal images. Thus, we must not be mislead by passages, such as the one quoted above, where Jung talks about the scientific myth. For Jung recognizes the pervasiveness of the mythical element in all experience, and the sense in which it can be said that all aspects of life are reflections of the archetypes, as well as seeing the particular value in the scientific method in offering a critical counterpoint and rational container for the fascination and power of the archetypal images.

We find, then, some cases where Jung defends the practical and therapeutic value of a metaphysical-religious outlook against an attempt to eliminate it entirely in favor of a world-view dominated by the findings of science and other places where Jung defends the necessity of a metaphysically neutral approach for science:

No science will ever replace myth, and a myth cannot be made out of any science. For it is not that "God" is a myth, but that myth is the revelation of a divine life in man. It is not we who invent myth, rather it speaks to us as a Word of God. (*Memories, Dreams, Reflections*, p. 340)

There is, however, a strong empirical reason why we should cultivate thoughts that can never be proved. It is that they are known to be useful. Man positively needs general ideas and convictions that will give a meaning to his life and enable him to find a place for himself in the universe. (*Man and His Symbols*, p. 76)

My subjective attitude is that I hold every religious position in high esteem but draw an inexorable dividing line between the content of belief and the requirements of science. (*Letters*, Vol. 1, p. 125, letter to Paul Maag dated 12 June 1933)

As a scientist I have to guard against believing that I am in possession of a final truth. (*Letters*, Vol. 1, p. 346, letter to H. Irminger dated 22 September 1944)

The Scientific and the Therapeutic

The close interrelation between the scientific level of discourse and the level of personally meaningful interpretation that we observe in Jung's writings is, as previously mentioned, a direct result of Jung's therapeutic involvements. For Jung is sensitive to the practical, therapeutic as well as the strictly theoretical, scientific aspects of his work. In order to make Jung's views on the nature of science intelligible, then, we need to more fully explore the basis for the particular tensions we find in Jung's views between what he sees as theoretical scientific knowledge on the one hand versus subjective, therapeutically relevant understanding on the other.

On this account what is necessary is to show how, on the one hand, when one goes from the scientific perspective of theoretical knowledge about archetypes to the therapeutic perspective one in effect makes a move not only from theoretical to practical knowledge, but also from the scientific to the religious and philosophical. On the other hand, we need to determine to what extent Jung understands the tension between the two levels of discourse about archetypes as due to an incommensurability between theory and practice, between scientific versus therapeutic aims, and to what extent Jung is trying to argue for an idiographic versus nomothetic type of distinction within the realm of theoretical knowledge itself.[21]

Now if we address ourselves to what Jung sees as an incommensurability in principle between his scientific theory and the practical work of therapy, it is not at all clear why this sort of incommensurable relationship must exist. For after all, it would seem that scientific knowledge about psychological matters would prove in the long run to be therapeutic. We can easily imagine paradigm cases of "unscientific" therapy such as a witch doctor treating a case of hysteria by trying to cast out the demon responsible. Even if the witch doctor succeeds and produces a cure, our scientific mentality assumes that suggestion or some such mechanism must be at work for which there exists a scientific explanation which, if known, would prove eventually to be therapeutically valuable. From the scientific point of view, then, we assume that there are discoverable principles at work in human psychology, which if we knew them, would greatly decrease the gap between our theoretical knowledge and what can be accomplished in terms of practical applications to therapy. From this point of view, it is simply the immaturity of science that leads to an incommensurability between theory and practice.

But this is not the sort of incommensurability between theory and practice that Jung principally has in mind. For parenthesizing for the moment idiographic considerations in terms of applicability of a theoretical knowledge for understanding the individual, it must be emphasized that Jung sees theoretical, scientific knowledge as necessary but never sufficient for accomplishing the work of psychotherapy. For it is characteristic of Jung's conception of therapy that it is necessary for the therapist to enable the patient to reorganize his philosophical and religious viewpoint. Therefore, for Jung, it is not that science is rejected in doing therapy, but that objective scientific knowledge about psychology must be complemented with a subjectively meaningful reorientation of the world-view. The Jungian therapist has to have competence, then, from both the mythos as well as the logos perspective.[22]

> The intellect is the sovereign of the scientific realm. But it is another matter when science steps over into the realm of its practical application. The intellect, which was formerly king, is now merely a minister—a scientifically refined instrument it is true, but still only a tool; no longer an end in itself, but merely a precondition. (Vol. 6, p. 57)

> ... sooner or later it was bound to become clear that one cannot treat the psyche without touching on man and life as a whole, including the ultimate and deepest issues, any more than one can treat the sick body without regard to the totality of its functions ... (Vol. 16, p. 76)

> I can hardly draw a veil over the fact that we psychotherapists ought really to be philosophers or philosophic doctors—or rather that we already are so, ... We could also call it religion *in statu nascendi*, for in the vast confusion that reigns at the roots of life there is no line of division between philosophy and religion. (Vol. 16, p. 79)

> The most healing, and psychologically the most necessary, experiences are a "treasure hard to attain," and its acquisition demands something out of the common from the common man.
> As we know, this something out of the common proves, in practical work with the patient, to be an invasion by archetypal contents. (Vol. 16, p. 82)

The statement that Jung sees scientific knowledge and psychotherapy as incommensurable irrespective of the state of the completeness of scientific knowledge amounts then to the claim that Jung believes that science cannot serve as a substitute for the religious and metaphysical needs of humankind in terms of which the Jungian therapy is primarily oriented. For the mythos and logos each have their own functions to fulfill and cannot be collapsed into each other.

When Jung talks about what he calls "psychological truth," he is emphasizing this subjective aspect of the therapeutic process for which the term scientific is not appropriate precisely because of the philosophical and/or religious nature of the questions involved. Psychological truth is that which as a matter of fact proves to be meaningful to the individual.

> Considered from the standpoint of realism, the symbol is not of course an external truth, but it is psychologically true,...
> Psychological truth by no means excludes metaphysical truth,... (Vol. 5, p. 231)

> Is there, as a matter of fact, any better truth about the ultimate things than the one that helps you to live? (Vol. 11, p. 105)

> When an idea is so old and so generally believed, it must be true in some way, by which I mean that it is *psychologically true*. (Vol. 5, p. 7)

In his *Ego and Archetype*, Edward Edinger furnishes an illuminating example of essentially what Jung has in mind by emphasizing the subjective nature of psychological truth, that is, its grounding in the perspective of the mythos:

> These are abstract, objective meanings conveyed by signs. However, there is another kind of meaning, namely, subjective, living meaning which does not refer to abstract knowledge but rather to a psychological state which can affirm life. It is this sense of the word we use when we describe a deeply moving experience as something meaningful.... It is the failure to separate these two different usages of the word "meaning" which leads one to ask the unanswerable question, "What is the meaning of life?" The question cannot be answered in this form because it confuses objective, abstract meaning with subjective, living meaning. If we rephrase the question to make it more subjective and ask, "What is the meaning of *my* life," it then begins to have the possibility of an answer....
> ... "Who am I?" The latter question is clearly a subjective one. An adequate answer can come only from within. Thus we can say: Meaning is found in subjectivity.[23]

This example from Edinger amply shows the subjective and essentially philosophical emphasis in Jungian therapy. But this subjective therapeutic emphasis should not mislead us into overlooking the possibility of a valid scientific level of understanding. Jung, for example, does attack the question of the meaning of life in general. His answer in terms of a theory of individuation purports to be an objectively valid account of the psychology of the various stages leading to a fulfillment of the personality and self-realization.

We must be careful, then, to distinguish between subjective, psychologically true statements and scientifically valid statements about psychological truth. Whereas in the first case we have what is found by the individual to be subjectively full of meaning, in the second case we have generalized statements concerning what has, as a matter of fact, been found to be meaningful.

> When psychology speaks, for instance, of the motif of the virgin birth, it is only concerned with the fact that there is such an idea, but it is not concerned with the question whether such an idea is true or false in any other sense. The idea is psychologically true inasmuch as it exists. (Vol. 11, p. 6)

But whereas from the scientific, theoretical point of view, psychological truth is the object of study; in the actual therapeutic situation, we are no longer on a meta-level of psychological truth, so to speak, but on the object-level working directly with the patient's "myth," that is, his life outlook. Moreover, it is just when the scientist-therapist moves from the objective scientific level of discourse about the unconscious to the level of personal psychological truth that Jung emphasizes the importance of taking what prove to be essentially idiographic considerations into account. In the practical therapeutic situation, we must, in Jung's view, be prepared to set aside our theoretical psychological knowledge to a large extent so that we can gain an understanding of the individual who may deviate from the scientific ideal case to a greater or lesser degree:

> Theories in psychology are the very devil. It is true that we need certain points of view for their orienting and heuristic value; but they should always be regarded as mere auxiliary concepts that can be laid aside at any time. (Vol. 17, p. 7)

> He [the therapist] should remember that the patient is there to be treated and not to verify a theory. For that matter, there is no single theory in the whole field of practical psychology that cannot on occasion prove basically wrong. (Vol. 16, p. 115)

Thus, Jung likes to emphasize that science is nomothetic in nature being concerned with the lawlike behavior of classes of particulars, whereas in therapy it is just the idiographic particularities of the individual that need to be understood. Instead of a nomothetic/ideographic terminology, Jung talks in terms of knowledge versus understanding:

> Every theory of complex psychic processes presupposes a uniform human psychology, just as scientific theories in general presuppose that nature is fundamentally one and the same. (Vol. 6, p. 490)

Hence it is not the universal and the regular that characterize the individual, but rather the unique.... At the same time man, as member of a species, can and must be described as a statistical unit; otherwise nothing general could be said about him.... This results in a universally valid anthropology or psychology, as the case may be, with an abstract picture of man as an average unit from which all individual features have been removed. But it is precisely these features which are of paramount importance for *understanding* man.... I can only approach the task of *understanding* with a free and open mind, whereas *knowledge* of man, or insight into human character, presupposes all sorts of knowledge about mankind in general. (Vol. 10, p. 250)

And if the psychologist happens to be a doctor who wants not only to classify his patient scientifically but also to understand him as a human being, he is threatened with a conflict of duties between the two diametrically opposed and mutually exclusive attitudes of knowledge on the one hand and understanding on the other. This conflict cannot be solved by an either/or but only by a kind of two-way thinking: doing one thing while not losing sight of the other.

In view of the fact that, in principle, the positive advantages of *knowledge* work specifically to the disadvantage of *understanding*, the judgment resulting therefrom is likely to be something of a paradox. Judged scientifically, the individual is nothing but a unit which repeats itself *ad infinitum* and could just as well be designated with a letter of the alphabet. For understanding, on the other hand, it is just the unique individual human being who, when stripped of all those conformities and regularities so dear to the heart of the scientist, is the supreme and only real object of investigation. (Vol. 10, p. 251)

Thus, we can see how Jung emphasizes the different aims of science and of therapy on two accounts. As already discussed, Jung understands theoretical psychology and his type of therapy as finally leading to different types of understanding: theoretical psychology to the objective scientific knowledge of the logos and therapy to the subjectively meaningful self-knowledge of the mythos. On the other hand, when Jung contrasts knowledge and understanding, this emphasizes what he sees as the limitations of a general scientific knowledge in its application to the particular individual.

But whereas if therapy eventually leads to a subjectively meaningful "psychological truth," we can readily agree that the therapist is involved in an enterprise with the individual patient for which the term scientific is not entirely appropriate; it is less clear that the mere particularity of the individual makes his understanding something beyond the range of science. In his discussion of knowledge and understanding, Jung seems to overlook the possibility of any idiographic scientific methods,[24] and seems on the whole to understand science in too narrow a way as only a study of universals.

In fairness to Jung, however, the essential point of the distinction between knowledge and understanding is to avoid the therapeutic attitude of seeing the patient only as a scientific problem. Moreover, the validity of this point would seem to hold independently of the question of nomothetic versus idiographic scientific methods. For Jung's "understanding" is not so much a question of seeing to what degree the individual's behavior conforms to lawlike scientific expectations or is idiosyncratic, but rather of establishing the right therapeutic relationship with the patient.

But, at any rate, it is evident that what Jung is saying about the incommensurability between the theoretical and practical aspects of psychology can often seem to be simply the adoption of an antiscientific attitude as in this example:

> Yet this is still "psychology" although no longer science; it is psychology in the wider meaning of the word, a psychological activity of a creative nature, in which creative fantasy is given prior place. (Vol. 6, p. 57)

Jung is open here to the criticism of giving the false impression of holding to a dichotomous division between theoretical and practical psychology; whereas, in reality, there is in fact a close interdependence and interrelation between the two aspects of his psychological outlook. For the distinctive aspects of Jung's therapy are a direct product of his theoretical understanding (compare Jung's emphasis on the religious and metaphysical needs of humankind with Freud's), and, on the other hand, Jung's psychological system is to a large extent the end result of his experiences in working with patients.

We can conclude, then, that there is a real basis in Jung's viewpoint for distinguishing a scientific level of discourse about archetypes from a level of personally meaningful interpretation. However, we must be aware of the danger of understanding this distinction between the two levels of discourse as a dichotomy between theoretical and practical knowledge about archetypes, implying that what is learned in theory does not have real application to the practical therapeutic needs of the individual, that therapy goes on completely independently of theoretical knowledge.[25] On the other hand, to abandon the distinction altogether is tantamount to giving up the scientific perspective of objectivity with respect to the study of archetypes.

Jung and the Scientific Attitude: Part 2

7

The Question of a Science of Archetypes

Introduction

OUR discussion of Jung's scientific attitude, the manner in which he understands his theory of archetypes to be scientific in principle, has led us to consider a distinction between two kinds of discourse: one appropriate for scientific statements about archetypes and one appropriate for statements on a personal, subjective level of meaning involving in many cases metaphysical and/or religious interpretations of archetypal experience. It is clear that Jung understands the distinction in terms of theoretical versus practical knowledge, as he is involved on both levels as scientist and therapist. Thus, sometimes Jung talks about his scientific views, and at other times he gives us practical, therapeutic advice or relates his personal, subjective understanding of the philosophical and religious implications of the archetypes.

With some slight changes, we can accept Jung's distinction as a way of separating scientific from extrascientific discourse about archetypes. We would phrase the distinction as one between the facts of archetypal experience versus attitudes one takes toward these facts, how they are to be interpreted and assimilated to other frameworks of experience. This way of phrasing the distinction contrasts the scientific perspective on archetypes with the philosophical/religious interpretations of archetypal experience that often result from the exploration of individual archetypal images.[1] By means of this distinction we can show how considerations from the scientific point of view need not be concerned with everything Jung says about archetypes.

But if we can now begin to see how the claim of the archetypal theory to be a scientifically credible one is not invalidated by the different kinds of discourse we find in Jung's writings about archetypes, our task of examining Jung's scientific attitude in relation to the question of the possibility of a scientifically defensible archetypal theory is far from complete. For in order to show how the archetypal theory avoids being an instance of a paradigmatically unscientific approach, we have still to discuss the problem of rationality in relation to the theory. This is the question of how the archetypal theory can be shown to satisfy acceptable criteria of rationality for a scientific theory, the extent to which the theory can be shown to adequately reflect the logos perspective.

The Question of Rationality

It will be recalled that the question of rationality in relation to the archetypal theory was originally raised in relation to the issue of mysticism (page 100). Although it was concluded that Jung's theory did not make an explicit appeal to a mystical framework of understanding, there was nonetheless a question as to the nature of a similarity between Jung's theory and a mystical approach. The question of such likeness was focused on the apparent similarity between the qualities of ineffability and paradoxicality that were said to characterize mystical experience and what Jung says about the paradoxical nature of archetypal experience and its symbolic character which "is never precisely defined or fully explained." (*Man and His Symbols*, p. 4)

But before proceeding to a discussion of the questions that came to light in the discussion of mysticism, it would be well to consider the question of rationality from a broader perspective. For irrespective of any similarity that the archetypal theory may have with mysticism, the issue of rationality is a pivotal one in determining the scientific viability of an archetypal theory. For in view of the apparent difficulty in maintaining an objective, theoretical discourse about archetypes—evidenced by the mixture of theoretical statements about archetypes and statements of an interpretive character concerning how we should relate to archetypal experience that we find in Jung's writings—we might well ask: Is a science of archetypes possible at all? One of Jung's followers, Gerhard Adler echoes the concern with this question in the following passage:

> Jung himself fought against the reproach of being a philosopher or metaphysician or even a mystic. He fought against this criticism because he felt that he had elevated his approach to the status of true science; but perhaps, also, he was still caught in the idealisation of the scientist's image, represented by natural science, so rampant in the first half of the century. There *are* vast philosophical, metaphysical, and even mystical aspects and implication in Jung's scientific researches and results,...[2]

Even Jung himself had moments of skepticism and doubt concerning whether irrational phenomena like archetypes and dreams were proper subject matter for science:

> Indeed, I am persuaded that, in view of the tremendous irrationality and individuality of dreams, it may be altogether outside the bounds of possibility to construct a popular theory. Why should we believe that everything without exception is a fit subject for science?... It might be better to look upon dreams as being more in the nature of works of art

instead of mere observational data for the scientist. (Vol. 17, pp. 163-164)

Of course, scientific is a characteristic of a method of study rather than a subject matter per se. But in this regard we would naturally expect that some subjects lend themselves more easily to the methods of science than do others. Certainly psychology is one of the most difficult subject matters to study in a rigorous scientific way. Moreover, within psychology itself Jung's interests can be easily identified as subjects that are at least at the very frontier of scientific endeavor, subjects that have either just begun to attract scientific attention or else have been given no previous scientific consideration at all. Such subjects as astrology, alchemy, UFO's, I Ching, and ESP are among Jung's professional interests in addition to investigations into the delusional systems of the insane and the worldwide literature of mysticism, mythology, and religions of all sorts. We might even chance a sweeping generalization and say that Jung's chief area of investigation is the irrational in all of its multiform manifestations. Although such a generalization perhaps stands in need of some qualification, it is easy to see how as an approximate truth this fact of Jung's professional interest in the occult and the irrational could lead to the conclusion that there is a similarity between the subject matter and its investigator. Jung addresses this problem in the following passage:

> If you call me an occultist because I am seriously investigating *religious, mythological, folkloristic and philosophical fantasies* in modern individuals and ancient texts, then you are bound to diagnose *Freud as a sexual pervert* since he is doing likewise with sexual fantasies, and a psychologically inclined criminologist must needs be a gaol-bird.... It is not my responsibility that alchemy is occult and mystical, and I am just as little guilty of the mystical delusions of the insane or the peculiar creeds of mankind. (*Letters*, Vol. 2, p. 186, letter to Calvin S. Hall dated 6 October 1954)

Although this sort of identification between a subject matter and its investigator is easily exposed as an error if taken as a necessary or universal type of relationship, it nonetheless contains an element of truth with respect to some individuals. For we wonder if there is not, as a matter of fact, some relationship between Freud's professional preoccupation with sex and his own sexual problems, between his theory of the Oedipus complex and the facts of his own family history. As an analogous case, Jung had an abundance of first hand experience with the irrational that was the source for at least part of the motivation for his researches as he confesses below:

> I was particularly satisfied with the fact that you clearly understand that I am not a mystic but an empiricist. It is true however that a vivid interest in religion and religious truth has guided my research. (*Letters*, Vol. 1, p. 237, letter to Norbert Drewitt dated 25 September 1937)

When we consider, then, the fact of Jung's interest in the irrational in regard to the question of the possibility in principle of a science of archetypes, we can conclude on the one hand that the irrationality of a subject matter should not disqualify it as legitimate subject matter for scientific study, since a scientific statement about the irrational need not itself be an irrational statement. But, on the other hand, we must acknowledge certain practical problems for scientific study that arise due to the irrational nature of archetypes. In this regard a major practical problem seems to be the difficulty of maintaining a suitable scientific attitude of objectivity and detachment. This is reflected in the problem of the two kinds of discourse as we saw how Jung frequently shifts from an objective, scientific discourse to a subjective, personally meaningful type. This problem is also exemplified in the very close relationship that exists between Jung's life and work. For it seems to be the case that archetypal experience does not produce only objective scientific knowledge, but also a personal involvement. One does not only assimilate the archetypes to one's scientific understanding, but in a sense one's overall outlook becomes modified by the archetypes. One not only gains a scientific concept of the irrational, there is, at least in the ideal case, a coming to terms with the irrational forces inside oneself.

From the therapeutic perspective, then, Jung can be seen to advocate the necessity for direct involvement with the irrational forces experienced in the unconscious. Especially in regard to this perspective, we need to determine the theoretical justification for what Jung says about the irrational. Thus, we need to know whether what Jung says about the irrational can itself be justified by rational means. In this respect it is essential to understand what theoretical claims Jung is trying to defend in relation to the irrational and in particular what he understands by this term.

Jung's Treatment of the Irrational

We find, then, that Jung closely associates the irrational with unconscious processes, whereas for him rationality is a correlate of consciousness:

> No matter how beautiful and perfect man may believe his reason to be, he can always be certain that it is only one of the possible mental functions, and covers only that one side of the phenomenal world which corresponds to it. But the irrational, that which is not agreeable to reason, rings it about on all sides. And the irrational is likewise a psychological function—in a word, it is the collective unconscious; whereas the rational is essentially tied to the conscious mind. (Vol. 7, p. 71)

To a large extent, then, the statements that Jung makes about the limits of reason and the intellect for comprehending the totality of experience can be seen to be the result of his view that consciousness has a necessarily incomplete comprehension of the totality of the unconscious.

There are several related reasons that Jung gives for the limitations of consciousness to fully comprehend the unconscious. The first has to do with the fact that knowledge of the unconscious necessarily is the product of its interaction with consciousness. Since consciousness always mediates the experience of the unconscious, Jung argues that there is a sense in which we never know the unconscious itself, but only as it interacts with the more or less interfering medium of consciousness:

> Between the conscious and the unconscious there is a kind of "uncertainty relationship," because the observer is inseparable from the observed and always disturbs it by the act of observation. (Vol. 9-B, p. 226)

In the concluding chapter of *Man and His Symbols*, Marie-Louise von Franz elaborates this same argument:

> Each new content that comes up from the unconscious is altered in its basic nature by being partly integrated into the conscious mind of the observer. Even dream contents (if noticed at all) are in that way semi-conscious. And each enlargement of the observer's consciousness caused by dream interpretation has again an immeasurable repercussion and influence on the unconscious.[3]

As we have previously remarked on other occasions (see page 56), Jung likes to think about the archetype per se in terms of Kant's concept of the thing-in-itself. Thus, he frequently makes the move from asserting that there exists an uncertainty relationship between conscious and unconscious to the statement that the ultimate nature of the archetype per se is unknowable in principle as a thing-in-itself:

> In *Mysterium Coniunctionis* my psychology was at last given its place in reality and established upon its historical foundations.... The moment I touched bottom, I reached the bounds of scientific understanding, the transcendental, the nature of the archetype per se, concerning which no further scientific statements can be made. (*Memories, Dreams, Reflections*, p. 221)

A third reason for asserting the limitations of consciousness to completely comprehend the unconscious is derived from the consideration that, as a matter of fact, consciousness is limited and finite in potential capacity, whereas the unconscious, although not infinite, contains a much larger relative store of content. Since consciousness is only possible through a restriction of attention, this narrower scope of consciousness means, then, that consciousness cannot be aware of all aspects of the unconscious. Although this line of reasoning strictly shows that consciousness is limited only at any one time to what it can be aware of, it is Jung's claim that the overall potential capacity for consciousness is limited. Thus, our attempts to make our actions and endeavors completely articulate and transparent to consciousness will always fail, and the unconscious in all its manifestations can never be completely assimilated to a conscious awareness.

> ... even the most matter-of-fact contents of consciousness have a penumbra of uncertainty around them. Even the most carefully defined philosophical or mathematical concept, which we are sure does not contain more than we have put into it, is nevertheless more than we assume. (*Man and His Symbols*, p. 29)

> ... Since we do not know everything, practically every experience, fact, or object contains something unknown. Hence, if we speak of the totality of an experience, the word "totality" can refer only to the conscious part of it. (Vol. 11, p. 41)

The fact that the unconscious is never completely assimilated to consciousness means then that for Jung human existence always consists to a large extent of essentially irrational aspects, and that consciousness and rationality are always circumscribed by the irrational and unconscious; the mythos element of experience can never by completely expunged:

> ... the rational is counterbalanced by the irrational, and what is planned and purposed by what *is*. (Vol. 9-A, p. 94)

> That is, I do not believe that reason can be the supreme law of human behaviour, if only because experience shows that in decisive moments behaviour is precisely *not* guided by reason but rather by overpowering unconscious impulses. (*Letters*, Vol. 1, p. 402, letter to Pastor H. Wegmann dated 12 December 1945)

> We have on the contrary good grounds for supposing that they [life and fate] are irrational, or rather that in the last resort they are grounded beyond human reason. (Vol. 7, p. 49)

But from the fact that Jung holds that human existence and reason do not mirror each other perfectly, can we then conclude that at least certain aspects of experience lie beyond the grasp of reason altogether? Jung apparently thinks that this is the case. For he says that "... there is a certain incommensurability between the mystery of existence and human understanding." (Vol. 12, p. 212)

Of course, it is just the archetypes of the collective unconscious that Jung has in mind as regards this "mystery":

> In these words Freud was expressing his conviction that the unconscious still harboured many things that might lend themselves to "occult" interpretation, as is in fact the case. These "archaic vestiges," or archetypal forms grounded on the instincts and giving expression to

them, have a numinous quality that sometimes arouses fear. They are ineradicable, for they represent the ultimate foundations of the psyche itself. *They cannot be grasped intellectually,* [italics mine] and when one has destroyed one manifestation of them, they reappear in altered form. (Vol. 10, p. 272)

In order to determine Jung's position on the irrational, then, we need to get clear about precisely what he means by "incommensurability" and "cannot be grasped intellectually." Although it may seem that in this regard what Jung says about the archetypes is very similar to mystical utterances, there is one sense in which what he means is very mundane. For in pointing to an incommensurability between archetypal experience and the understanding, part of what Jung wants to emphasize is the particular quality of the lived experience of archetypes that is not adequately captured by concepts.

However, many experiences of an emotional nature have in common with archetypes this feature of relative ineffability, that is, the feature of the relative inadequacy of concepts to express their lived quality. The particular emotive quality of a beautiful sunset, for example, is best expressed by a poem or a painting rather than by a concept. Because of the numinosity of the archetypes, then, a concept of archetypes does not adequately convey their essential nature as experienced.

However, considerations about the relationship between the experience of archetypes and the formulation of a theoretical understanding are not particularly crucial in regard to the question of the rationality of the archetypal theory. For Jung does not maintain that an intuitive knowledge of archetypes based on their immediate experience is the only sort of understanding of them which is possible. Rather he maintains on the whole that intuition is not sufficient for intellectual knowledge:

The safe basis of real intellectual knowledge and moral understanding gets lost if one is content with the vague satisfaction of having understood by "hunch." One can explain and know only if one has reduced intuitions to an exact knowledge of facts and their logical connections. (*Man and His Symbols*, p. 82)

On the other hand, Jung frequently points out the inadequacy of an intellectual understanding as a substitute for the experience of confronting the unconscious and the archetypes in a therapeutic context:

It is precisely our experiences in psychology which demonstrate as plainly as could be wished that the intellectual "grasp" of a psychological fact produces no more than a concept of it, and that a concept is no more than a name, a *flatus vocis*. (Vol. 9-B, p. 32)

We can understand, then, that from the therapeutic perspective it is just the emotive qualities of archetypes and the particular problems of value and purpose in relation to the individual's life as brought into focus by archetypal experience that are of utmost importance. Thus, much of what Jung has to say against reason must be understood in a therapeutic context. In this respect it is a misuse of reason rather than reason itself which is the object of vilification:

> ... a relativation of rationalism is needed, but not an abandonment of reason, for the reasonable thing for us is to turn to the inner man and his vital needs. (*Letters*, Vol. 2, p. 286, letter to Eugen Böhler dated 8 January 1956)

> The great difficulty seems to consist in the fact that on the one hand we must defend the sanity and logic of the human mind, and on the other hand we have to accept and to welcome the existence of illogical and irrational factors transcending our comprehension. (*Letters*, Vol. 2, p. 53, letter to Father Victor White dated 9 April 1952)

It would seem evident that if all Jung has in mind by his "cannot be grasped by the intellect" is to emphasize the practical therapeutic aspects of working with the archetypes on an experiential level, then the question of rationality need not be considered as a serious problem. However, in addition to the practical problems of assimilating archetypes into one's experience on a personal basis, Jung apparently feels that the archetypes also pose particular problems for theoretical understanding. This point is well exemplified in regard to the symbolic manifestations of archetypes:

> To the scientific mind, such phenomena as symbolic ideas are a nuisance because they cannot be formulated in a way that is satisfactory to intellect and logic. (*Man and His Symbols*, p. 80)

> It [symbol] has a wider "unconscious" aspect that is never precisely defined or fully explained. Nor can one hope to define or explain it. As the mind explores the symbol, it is led to ideas that lie beyond the grasp of reason. (*Man and His Symbols*, p. 4)

This metaphorical way of talking about what lies beyond the grasp of reason can be made clearer as well as more plausible if instead of talking about what cannot be grasped or understood, we say that archetypal experience cannot be completely rationalized. That is, the archetypes have a sort of cognitive autonomy that eludes attempts to completely reduce them to an unambiguous rational formulation. An example using the familiar phenomenon of dreams helps clarify this point.

When we try to rationally understand a dream, we attempt an interpretation that translates the pictographic images of the dream into words. We encounter difficulties, however, because the dream images frequently fail to conform to rational expectations of order and logic. Moreover, even with the most in-depth interpretation, we somehow feel that something is lost in the transition from the dream images to words. In addition to the emotive content that is difficult to convey in words, it seems that the dream has its own way of cognitive expression which an interpretation does not completely capture. The dream images thus represent a certain gestalt of meaning that often resists translation into a linear sequence of ideas. We might say, then, that any logos of the dream, any interpretive scheme, can never completely substitute for the mythos perspective that the dream itself offers.

Moreover, when we say that a dream or other manifestation of the unconscious cannot be rationalized, what we previously discussed in terms of the inability of consciousness to completely assimilate the unconscious must be borne in mind. Excepting Jung's appeal to the Kantian doctrine of the thing-in-itself, then, the arguments we mentioned there are additional reasons in support of this view.

Our way of talking in terms of the inability of the unconscious to be completely rationalized might seem to amount to the claim that a complete conscious reduction of unconscious experiences is inadvisable. And the objection could be raised at the point that if this is what our claim amounts to, then it is not so much relevant to the question of theoretical knowledge as to the problem of how best to deal with unconscious experience in a therapeutically beneficial way. From the theoretical perspective, it would seem that it is just our task to try to make unconscious experience intelligible, that is, to rationalize it.

However, in spite of Jung's unfortunate way of expressing himself in terms of what lies beyond the grasp of reason, what he has in mind does apply to the theoretical knowledge of archetypes. For it is his contention that we must make our theoretical statements about the archetypes reflect the actual nature of the phenomena. What we need to avoid in the problem of rationalizing the unconscious, then, is the reading in of more order and logic than is really there. If we think of dreams in terms of their being only informational static or noise in the brain, for example, an explanation satisfactory to the rational need to account for such disturbing phenomena in a theoretically elegant way, we not only fail to derive practical benefit from them, but we also miss the distinguishing feature of the phenomena, the fact that their cognitive content constitutes a meaningful message that can be shown to compensate the conscious attitude. Thus, Jung wants to argue that a conscious reduction of unconscious experiences is inadvisable, not only in terms of the practical situation of the individual dreamer, but also from the standpoint of scientific methodology.

The problem of the rational reduction of unconscious processes must also be kept in mind when we try to understand Jung's attitude toward the paradoxical. In regard to the paradoxical, then, we often find Jung associating the paradoxical and the metaphysical. For he says that metaphysical assertions can only be adequately formulated in an antinomian way:

> Every metaphysical judgment is *necessarily antinomian*, since it tran-
> scends experience and must therefore be complemented by its counter-
> position. (*Letters*, Vol. 2, p. 254, letter to Pastor Jakob Amstutz dated 23
> May 1955)

Thus, when we state a metaphysical truth in a paradoxical way, we
express what Jung sees as its quality of unknowability:

> Paradox is a characteristic of the Gnostic writings. It does more justice
> to the *unknowable* than clarity can do, for uniformity of meaning robs the
> mystery of its darkness and sets it up as something that is *known*. (Vol.
> 11, p. 275)

> Paradox is a characteristic of all transcendental situations because it
> alone gives adequate expression to their indescribable nature. (Vol. 9-B,
> p. 70)

This use of paradoxical links the paradoxical with a metaphysical way
of interpreting archetypal experience. In this regard there is a real
similarity with the way in which mystical experience is commonly
interpreted. But irrespective of Jung's Kantian views on the appropriate-
ness of an antinomian expression for the metaphysical, it seems that there
is no problem with rationality here since to say that archetypal experience
is frequently described in paradoxical terms is itself not a paradoxical
statement.

However, Jung also means not only that the ascription of paradoxical
qualities to archetypal experiences applies to the interpretation of the
experience in metaphysical terms, but also that it applies to a metaphysically neutral description. But in the latter regard when we say that
archetypal experience is paradoxical, this amounts to a restatement of the
considerations about the problem of rational reduction of archetypal
experience. For rather than an assertion that the experience cannot be
described except by contradictory predicates, this weak sense of paradoxical implies only that we cannot pin down the experience and make it
unambiguous, that is, it is open to different interpretations. This use of
paradoxical is then not an assertion that the experience transcends logic
altogether (the mystical sense of paradoxical), but only that it is
inherently ambiguous. For example, the frequent archetypal symbol of the
snake combines both negative and positive qualities: "Hence it is an
excellent symbol for the two aspects of the unconscious: its cold and
ruthless instinctuality, and its Sophia quality or natural wisdom, which is
embodied in the archetypes." (Vol. 13, p. 333)

Moreover, this ambiguity of the manifestations of the unconscious
reflects for Jung the tension between the conscious and the unconscious
attitudes. For symbols from the unconscious change their form in
response to the conscious attitude (see page 59). The symbols are a
reflection of this dynamic relationship between conscious and uncon-

scious and thus often represent a synthesis of opposites; they are a bridge between mythos and logos:

> And since the symbol derives as much from the conscious as from the unconscious, it is able to unite them both, reconciling their conceptual polarity through its form and their emotional polarity through its numinosity. (Vol. 9-B, p. 180)

What can we say then about the rationality of Jung's treatment of the archetypes? In the first place, it is obvious that Jung's sage statements about the unknowable are not satisfactory; that is, we want to know on what grounds he can talk meaningfully of what is unknowable. This sort of talk seems to imply a transhuman perspective from which the relationship between our ways of knowing and the world can be determined. However, as has been pointed out on other occasions, there is no necessity to follow Jung's Kantian line in order to rationally reconstruct the archetypal theory. And when we no longer think of the archetype per se as a thing-in-itself, many of Jung's least rationally sounding statements need no longer concern us. For if we disregard Jung's Kantian views on the unknowable, what Jung says about the irrational seems to be both reasonable and defensible on empirical grounds.

If there is a genuine similarity here between mysticism and Jung's ideas, it is that both concur in the discovery of genuinely irrational aspects of experience. However, whereas the mystic says that we have to accept this irrational given and abandon efforts to understand it rationally, it is always Jung's position that we must try to assimilate the irrational with our rational understanding as best we can. And although Jung's view that the rationality of consciousness as a matter of fact cannot completely assimilate and rationalize the unconscious may seem at first sight to be the very repudiation of the methodology of science, it is Jung's claim that far from deserting science his phenomenological method of approach to the archetypes provides the key for a valid objective understanding of them as a logos that can fully acknowledge the reality of the mythos.

We need to examine this phenomenological method in order to see whether it in fact qualifies as a valid and adequate scientific method.

Jung's Methodology

Introduction

In discussing the issue of Jung's methodology, it is important to understand what substantive issues are at stake. In the first place, we are attempting to get clear about the methodological grounds for Jung's claim that his study of archetypes is a scientific enterprise. This question, moreover, must be considered in the context of the discussion of the last section where the problem of the rationality of the archetypal theory was taken up. There it was emphasized that, although scientific statements about the irrational need not themselves be irrational, there are nonetheless special problems involved in studying archetypes which from the theoretical perspective we described by talking of the difficulty of accomplishing a rational reduction of archetypal experience, that is, the need to allow for a certain inherent ambiguity in the phenomena in order to characterize them properly. We need to discover, then, what actual consequences for the study of archetypes these considerations of the problem of the rational reduction produce.

The Problem of Subjectivity

If we inquire how Jung understands what he is doing, we discover that he asserts that his psychological views fall within the domain of natural science, although science with certain special limitations. "Analytical psychology is fundamentally a natural science, but it is subject far more than any other science to the personal bias of the observer." (*Memories, Dreams, Reflections*, p. 200)

The problem of subjectivity thus enters into psychology at the theoretical level. Jung likes to emphasize that this is due to the fact that in psychology we have no extrapsychological point of view from which to view the phenomena since all observations are themselves psychological processes: "... in contrast to any other scientific theory, the object of psychological explanation is consubstantial with the subject: one psychological process has to explain another." (Vol. 6, p. 494)

Moreover, this difficulty with objectivity is, as previously discussed, especially relevant with regard to the observation of unconscious processes. Jung quotes the physicist Wolfgang Pauli on this point: " '... this uncontrollable reactive effect of the observing subject on the unconscious limits the objective character of the latter's reality and lends it at the same time a certain subjectivity.' " (Vol. 8, p. 229, note 130, no Pauli source given)

For Jung this dilemma of subjectivity in psychology necessitates the toleration of a plurality of viewpoints. We must realize, then, that a psychological theory mirrors the psychology of its formulator. "The assumption that only *one* psychology exists or only *one* fundamental psychological principle is an intolerable tyranny, a pseudo-scientific prejudice of the common man." (Vol. 6, p. 41)

This point of the plurality of theories in psychology is developed in the context of Jung's theory of types.[4] He sometimes argues, therefore, that the necessity of considering a plurality of theories must be taken to the extent of admitting one "true" theory for each type:

> I believe that other equally "true" explanations of the psychic process can still be put forward, just as many in fact as there are types. (Vol. 6, p. 493)

For, besides his own theory, he would have to regard seven other theories of the same process as equally true, or, if that is saying too much, at least grant a second theory a value equal to his own.

I am quite convinced that a natural process which is very largely independent of human psychology, and can therefore be viewed only as an object, can have but one true explanation. But I am equally convinced that the explanation of a complex psychic process which cannot be objectively registered by any apparatus must necessarily be only the one which that subjective process itself produces. (Vol. 6, pp. 490-491)

In addition to the problem of the typological bias of an investigator making a truth claim in psychology, Jung also states that we must be prepared to see these truth claims as relative rather than absolute since, due to the polaristic nature of the psyche (conscious and unconscious attitudes do not coincide), we must be prepared to admit the reverse of our claim as also valid:

Because psychology basically depends upon balanced opposites, no judgment can be considered to be final in which its reversability has not been taken into account. (*Man and His Symbols*, p. 47)

... we must observe the rule that a psychological proposition can only lay claim to significance if the obverse of its meaning can also be accepted as true. (Vol. 16, p. 115)

Now if the above considerations are the sorts of things Jung has in mind as a way of remedying the special problems with subjectivity in psychology, we might well wonder if the solutions are not as problematic as the difficulties for which they are to be the corrective. However, Jung's statements about the relativity of truth in psychology and the necessity for admitting the validity of a plurality of theories remain more or less theoretical, methodological ideals for Jung rather than actual practices he observes.

In any case, these sorts of considerations are actually more relevant to problems of practical applications of theoretical reasoning in therapy than they are problems of theory itself. For example, in practicing therapy Jung emphasizes that the therapist must never put the desire for theoretical confirmation of his pet theory above the need to understand the patient as an individual. Moreover, it is just in therapy that the potential conflict of personalities as a result of differing personality types is most keenly relevant. Then, the need to consider questions from the standpoint of both the conscious and the unconscious attitudes comes to focus most clearly in regard to the working out of the individual's personal problems.

To generalize, as Jung sometimes does on these points, from what is useful in therapy to what is necessary for a theoretical psychological understanding in general is at best a questionable move. It is always open to us, however, to accept the psychological facts of subjectivity that Jung points to without drawing the same conclusions for theoretical understanding in psychology. That is, we can admit that there is a real problem with subjectivity without having to concede that truth claims in psychology can only be considered valid relative to individual personalities.[5]

We may consider the question of subjectivity in psychology, then, as a generalization of the problem of the rational reduction of archetypal experience.

Jung's Phenomenological Method

In regard to questions of methodology, if we can satisfactorily determine the allegedly scientific method by which Jung studies archetypes, we need thus not be unduly concerned if some of the things that Jung says about psychological methodology in general seem to be problematic.

We discover, then, that Jung recommends a phenomenological technique for the scientific study of archetypes. Here it is essential to understand what he means by phenomenology. The term connotes for him a theoretically unbiased observation of phenomena. It is clear, moreover, that the Freudian technique of dream interpretation (see page 75) is the sort of unphenomenological, theory-biased construing of unconscious phenomena to which Jung is opposed:

> Nevertheless, it cannot be maintained that the phenomenological point of view has made much headway. Theory still plays far too great a role, instead of being included in phenomenology as it should. Even Freud, whose empirical attitude is beyond doubt, coupled his theory as a *sine qua non* with his method, as if psychic phenomena had to be viewed in a certain light in order to mean something. (Vol. 9-A, pp. 54-55)

> Here the interpretation must guard against making use of any other viewpoints that those manifestly given by the content itself. If someone dreams of a lion, the correct interpretation can only lie in the direction of the lion;... (Vol. 17, p. 88)

What this phenomenological method entails for Jung becomes more evident in the following where, in response to a challenge that his study of archetypes is not grounded in a scientific method, Jung states his understanding of that method:

> I can entirely subscribe to your statement... "Its (the scientific method's) tool is the objective observation of phenomena. Then comes the classification of the phenomena and lastly the deriving of mutual relations and sequences between the observed data, thereby making it possible to predict future occurrences, which, in turn, must be tested by observation and experiment," if, I must add, the experiment is possible. (*Letters*, Vol. 2, p. 567, letter to E. A. Bennet dated 23 June 1960)

As may be expected, Jung's method of studying the archetypes does not employ an experimental technique:

> Every science is descriptive at the point where it can no longer proceed
> experimentally, without on that account ceasing to be scientific. (Vol.
> 9-A, pp. 55-56)

> Analytical psychology differs from experimental psychology in that it
> does not attempt to isolate individual functions (sense functions,
> emotional phenomena, thought-processes, etc.) and then subject them
> to experimental conditions for purposes of investigation. It is far more
> concerned with the total manifestation of the psyche as a natural
> phenomenon—a highly complex structure, ... (Vol. 17, pp. 91-92)

Jung justifies his nonexperimental method of study by pointing out that
as a medical psychologist he has to investigate the phenomena as they
appear in his patients without being able to institute controls and manipu-
late variables. In Maslow's terms, Jung's psychology is problem-centered
rather than method-centered:[6]

> ... academic psychology ... prefers to avoid complex situations by asking
> ever simpler questions, which it can do with impunity. It has full freedom
> in the choice of questions it will put to Nature.
> Medical psychology, on the other hand, is very far from being in this
> more or less enviable position. Here the object puts the question and not
> the experimenter. The analyst is confronted with facts which are not of
> his choosing and which he probably never *would* choose if he were a free
> agent. (Vol. 10, p. 272)

> The difference between this and all earlier psychologies is that
> analytical psychology does not hesitate to tackle even the most difficult
> and complicated processes. Another difference lies in our method of
> procedure. ... Our laboratory is the world. Our tests are concerned with
> the actual, day-to-day happenings of human life, and the test-subjects are
> our patients, relatives, friends, and, last but not least, ourselves. (Vol. 17,
> p. 92)

But, if it is clear that the primary context of discovery for the archetypes is the clinical situation, it must not then be concluded that this is also
the only context of validation. For when Jung uses the term phenomenological for his method of study, this should not be understood to mean that
it is entirely dependent upon introspective techniques. The other term
"empirical" that Jung employs for his method of study is then in some
respects more descriptive.

Thus, Jung emphasizes the necessity of supplementing the findings
derived from work with patients by examining the manifestations of archetypes in a cross-cultural context. For when the same sorts of phenomena
as appear in the clinical situation can be seen as exemplified in the art,
literature, mythology, and religion of many different cultures, this gives the
archetypes an extraclinical and publicly observable dimension. Jung
therefore likes to compare his method of study of archetypes to that of
comparative anatomy: "My scientific methodology is nothing out of the

ordinary, it proceeds exactly like comparative anatomy, only it describes and compares psychic figures." (*Letters*, Vol. 1, p. 360, letter to Pastor Max Frischknecht dated 7 April 1945)

> The psychologist must depend therefore in the highest degree upon historical and literary parallels if he wishes to exclude at least the crudest errors in judgment. (*Memories, Dreams, Reflections*, p. 200)

> Symbolism has today assumed the proportions of a science and can no longer make do with more or less fanciful sexual interpretations. Elsewhere I have attempted to put symbolism on the only possible scientific foundation, namely that of comparative research. (Vol. 17, p. 106)

The Problem of Ambiguity

In our discussion of Jung's scientific methodology, one chief question remains to be explored. This question has to do with what Jung sees as the appropriate method of characterizing archetypes. For if we understand that the phenomenological method tries to produce an accurate description of the archetypal phenomena that is as theoretically unbiased as possible, it seems evident Jung takes this to imply that his descriptions of the archetypes must mirror the phenomena described in the sense that they are themselves ambiguous descriptions:

> I don't know whether I ought to be glad that my desperate attempts to do justice to the reality of the psyche are accounted "ingenious ambiguity." At least it acknowledges my efforts to reflect, as best I can, the "ingenious ambiguity" of the psyche....
> The language I speak must be ambiguous, must have two meanings, in order to do justice to the dual aspect of our psychic nature. I strive quite consciously and deliberately for ambiguity of expression, because it is superior to unequivocalness and reflects the nature of life. (*Letters*, Vol. 2, pp. 69-70, letter to R. J. Zwi Werblowsky dated 17 June 1952)

We must, however, distinguish here between two senses of ambiguous description. On the one hand, there are empirically accurate descriptions of ambiguity, and on the other hand, there are ambiguous descriptions of ambiguous phenomena.

But if Jung is all too often guilty of the latter type of ambiguity, this should not prejudice our attitude toward the genuine problem posed by the rational reduction. For irrespective of Jung's individual style of talking about archetypes, a plausible case can still be made for the necessity of having our descriptions of the archetypes take into account their inherent ambiguity.

The Study of Archetypes as a Scientific Discipline

8

Introduction

IN the previous two chapters we have considered the question of whether Jung holds views incompatible with those necessary for science, and also looked at the methodological basis upon which he claims that his study of archetypes is scientific. From these discussions what can be concluded concerning Jung's scientific views?

In the first instance, it must be remarked that Jung's writings do not conform to any expectations we may have had concerning what constitutes ideal scientific writing. Moreover, this is due principally to the fact that the works are not uniformly scientific in character. In this regard we have suggested that be separating the theoretical claims Jung makes for the archetypes from statements where Jung discusses attitudes towards archetypal experience, we could examine the question of scientific status independently of what Jung says of a philosophical and religious nature in his exploration of the significance of individual archetypes. But if such a distinction is successful in isolating the question of scientific status, this is not to say that we have then purified the theory or arrived at its meaningful core, as if to imply that Jung should have done this himself at the very beginning. Such an attitude only confuses the logic of reconstruction and the process of discovery. For if we admit that the extrascientific aspects of Jung's personality may at times dominate his writings as a whole, this is not in the end to the disadvantage of scientific knowledge. For it is only through the wholeness of Jung's personality that we have such a theory that can then be examined in terms of scientific criteria, that is to say, it is only through Jung's interest in and involvement with the irrational aspects of experience, both as an individual and a therapist.

In regard to Jung's scientific views, then, our arguments so far have endeavored to show how Jung in fact did attempt to construct a theory compatible with scientific understanding. Considering the highly irrational nature of the phenomena that are the objects of such a theory, success in such an enterprise would most certainly entitle Jung to be regarded as a truly great scientific pioneer and investigator.

But did Jung succeed in formulating a theory that can be construed as a genuinely scientific one? Instead of attempting to discuss necessary and sufficient criteria of what is scientific in general, our approach to this question has been to examine possible reasons on the basis of which the scientific label could be withheld from Jung's theory. Rather than attempting to show that Jung's theory is scientific because of its similarity to paradigmatic models of science such as physics and chemistry, we have attempted to establish that it is not unscientific. This sort of approach allows for a liberal understanding of what constitutes a scientific theory. For rather than establishing a priori standards of what science must be, we instead examine the putative scientific theory in regard to what it can accomplish toward a rigorous understanding of its subject matter.

But the sort of considerations we have discussed in regard to showing that Jung's theory is not unscientific do not suffice to establish the scientific status of it. For if we have successfully shown, for example, that the theory can be understood as a rational theory, and that religious and philosophical utterances often associated with it are not a necessary part of the theory itself, these are, for the most part, special problems of the archetypal hypothesis. The resolution of these problems is thus necessary but not sufficient to show that the archetypal theory is not unscientific. There are other considerations that must be examined before the scientific critic will rest content. For we still need to discuss the problem of falsifiability. In addition we need to show what sorts of predictions the theory can make and what explanations result from it. Then we need to look at the nature of the evidence claimed in support of the theory.

With the examination of these remaining questions, the basis upon which we will advocate scientific status for the archetypal theory will not be so liberal as to admit other disciplines such as astrology and numerology from which we would wish to withhold the scientific label. For these questions are just the sort of questions that any discipline must be capable of answering in a satisfactory way if it is to be included in the domain of science.

Falsifiability

A preliminary topic that must be discussed in confronting the issue of falsifiability is the problem of specifying the basis on which we claim that an archetype is present. The question at stake here is brought into focus by the difficulties encountered by the non-Jungian in determining what observational states of affairs count as evidence for the presence of an archetype:

> The existence and working of the Jungian archetypes seems more difficult to demonstrate operationally: one can define objectively particular stimulus features or combinations of these, and can say whether or

not they are present; but the Jungian archetypes have no clearly defined essential features by which their presence may be unequivocally established, and so many specific features are included as possible manifestations of one or another archetype that it is always possible to claim one is present.[1]

Moreover, Jungians themselves sometimes make statements that seem to indicate that they see archetypes in everything. The following statement from Jolande Jacobi indicates an attitude insensitive to the problem of falsifiability:

And since all psychic life is absolutely grounded in archetypes, and since we can speak not only of archetypes, but equally well of archetypal situations, experiences, actions, feelings, insights, etc., any hidebound limitation of the concept would only detract from its richness of meaning and implication.[2]

Thus, in order to show that claims involving archetypes cannot be made compatible with all possible observational states of affairs, we must clearly indicate the observational basis for the presence of archetypes.

A clue to how we can go about meeting this difficulty is provided by further reflection on the problem of the individuation of archetypes. This is the problem of how to tell one archetype from another. This problem is one manifestation of what we have called the "problem of the rational reduction." For it seems that the archetypal phenomena do not readily lend themselves to classification into unambiguous types:

These unconscious nuclei are the archetypes and they can, up to a point, be classified and enumerated through special images—the myth-ologems—but these have a tendency to, as it were, dissolve into each other so that they seem at one time to be numerous and at others to be a single entity.[3]

When we speak of a problem of rational reduction, this is to indicate that the ambiguity is inherent to the phenomena rather than being a result of the inadequacy of the classificational criteria. In this regard it is helpful to consider the analogous problem of individuating species or other biological groups such as phyla. When we consider, then, on what basis it is decided that in this instance you have two species whereas in another instance only one, we do not expect from our taxonomist a definite decision procedure that can be applied in all problematic cases. Rather the classification of species turns in the end not so much on a priori criteria of speciation as on the reasonable judgment of the professional taxonomist, subject to its acceptance by the professional taxonomic community.

The point of this analogy is to indicate that, when dealing with naturally occurring complex phenomena, precise operational definitions cannot be expected in regard to the classification of the basic entities. Thus, there are no simple answers to the question of where to draw the line between one archetype and another. But although it is unreasonable to expect a definitive decision procedure for distinguishing archetypes, nonetheless discriminations can be carried out by the experienced Jungian practitioner; although on analogy with biological speciation, this will not eliminate the element of conventionality and thus professional controversy concerning the specification of particular archetypes.[4]

If we now consider the more general problem of the recognition of archetypes in regard to the difficulty of the non-Jungian in deciding what to call an archetype, the sort of answer we give is one couched in terms of lack of experience with the theory:

> To understand the peculiar phenomenon of the archetype one needs a lot of practical experience, f.i. the numinous quality, so indispensable to the recognition of an archetype, is an indefinable imponderable like the expression of the human eye, which is indubitable yet indescribable. (*Letters*, Vol. 2, p. 490, letter to Stephen I. Abrams dated 5 March 1959)

But, of course, the claim that difficulties with the empirical interpretation of the theory are due to lack of knowledge of the theory or lack of experience in applying it in specific cases can easily be construed as a possible defense against all criticism of the theory. For to say that only the person experienced with application of the theory really knows whether or not it applies in any specific case seems to work against the possibility of there being critique of the theory from standpoints that do not already assume it:

> In order to understand Jung, it has been said, one must experience his findings at first hand—his work must be "at least partially lived through and validated existentially, before it can be thoroughly grasped on a conscious level." [Ira Progoff, *Jung's Psychology and Its Social Meaning* (New York: Julian Press, 1953), p. ix] From the academic side, by contrast, comes the argument that a considerable amount of direct contact is likely to diminish objectivity. This, of course, is the old dilemma often set forth for depth psychology in general—either one remains outside and therefore insufficiently acquainted with the facts, or one moves inside and is cured of the desire to criticize.[5]

However, although the practical difficulties with knowing how to apply the theory do seem in fact to lead to a situation in which only experts in the theory can determine for certain how it applies in a specific case, this does not have the consequence of making the theory unfalsifiable or immune from the possibility of criticism. In order to demonstrate this point, it will be necessary to recapitulate the observational grounds for asserting the presence of archetypes.

Recalling the discussion of this topic from chapter 3 (pages 57-58), it was stated that the chief difficulty in establishing the presence of archetypes was the fact that, although archetypes were postulated to be part of the collective unconscious, the form of their manifestation in the individual always reflects the cultural and personal experiences of the individual. The problem of identifying the presence of archetypes, then, is one of distinguishing the personal and collective contents. Moreover, what was distinctive of the collective, archetypal contents was their alien character, that is, the fact that they appear in consciousness without the individual being able to account for them solely on the basis of his or her previous, personal experience. But these are introspective and subjective features, and if the claim that there are archetypes just rested on these types of claims, the critic would be justified in pointing out the difficulties of establishing validation of introspective reports. This difficulty would be accentuated by the fact that the reports are usually made by patients in Jungian therapy. However, in addition to the subjective, introspective reports of archetypal experience, Jung points to the presence of the same motifs in the mythology, religion, art, and literature of widely divergent cultures. A knowledge of cross-cultural symbology is then brought to bear on the symbolic manifestations in the individual. The claim is that these cultural parallels help to explain the meaning and implications of particular symbolic manifestations in the individual in ways that cannot be satisfactorily accounted for solely by appeal to the person's individual development or previous experiences. An example of how this method is used to elucidate the meaning of symbols by appeal to cultural parallels helps clarify this point:

> I can remember many cases of people who have consulted me because they were baffled by their own dreams or by their children's. They were at a complete loss to understand the terms of the dreams. The reason was that the dreams contained images that they could not relate to anything they could remember or could have passed on to their children.…
> I vividly recall the case of a professor who had had a sudden vision and thought he was insane. He came to see me in a state of complete panic. I simply took a 400-year-old book from the shelf and showed him an old woodcut depicting his very vision. "There's no reason for you to believe that you're insane," I said to him. "They knew about your vision 400 years ago." Whereupon he sat down entirely deflated, but once more normal.
> (*Man and His Symbols*, p. 58)

It should be evident, then, where the difficulty is encountered in knowing how to apply the theory. For if the non-Jungian has access to the same data as the Jungian practitioner, he can be shown that there were nuministic symbolic images with cross-cultural parallels, and that in this sense there were archetypes, but he would be at a loss to say what archetypes he had been shown or what was their full meaning. In order to deal with the latter problems and employ the theory in a meaningful way, it is necessary to gain a working knowledge of cross-cultural symbologies. This will entail, for example, a knowledge of the motifs of worldwide mythologies and religions. From the standpoint of its empirical basis, then, it is easy to understand why the archetypal theory is frequently not given much serious consideration. For the archetypal skeptic often lacks either extensive experience with unconscious phenomena or else is unacquainted with the sort of cross-cultural parallels that Jungians claim as validation for the theory.[6]

But although confirmation of the archetypal theory would entail a certain amount of erudition, the validational basis of the theory, the cross-cultural parallels, is nonetheless part of the public domain. Moreover, these de facto considerations concerning the practical difficulty of gaining a working knowledge of the employment of the theory do not mean that the validity of the theory cannot be evaluated by the non-Jungian. For although to understand how the theory works in a practical way involves specialized knowledge, the theory claims certain states of affairs that can be checked independently of a detailed knowledge of the manifestations of individual archetypes.

For example, the theory claims that archetypal manifestations can be demonstrated in all races and civilizations of people without exception. What then will count as showing that archetypes are not present in a group of humans? In this regard the ideal test case would be a tribe that has not had previous cultural contact with other human groups. This is to guard against the possibility of the group having taken over symbols through contact with other cultures. To gather evidence against the archetypal theory, we have to show that the group had no indigenous religious or mythological symbols. This would in effect involve showing that the group had no indigenous religious or mythological beliefs.

Other consequences that follow from the archetypal theory include the postulation of biological parallels to the archetypes in lower organisms. For since the archetypes are assumed to arise through the course of evolution, they must be prefigured in the other animals. Moreover, due to the close relationship that is postulated between the archetypes and the instincts, this is an especially critical point since we would expect whatever instinctual aspects there are in humankind to have homologies in the animal kingdom (see pages 45-48). If the efforts of the ethological school of animal behavior to demonstrate the existence of innate patterns of behavior can be shown to be misguided, then this will count against the archetypal theory.

A third consequence that follows from the archetypal theory is the assertion that archetypes will be manifested in altered states of consciousness.[7] Although this seems to be a very vague claim, what it rules out is the situation where archetypes appear only in patients undergoing Jungian therapy or in individuals who have read Jung. In this regard experimental results can be brought to bear for or against the theory. If experimental techniques designed to produce altered states of consciousness uniformly do not produce any sort of subject reports that describe phenomena similar to the Jungian description of archetypal experience, then this will be damning evidence against the theory.

These three examples indicate what sort of evidence would count against the theory and thus what sorts of states of affairs are incompatible with it.[8]

Explanation

Although we cannot enter here into all aspects of the question of archetypal explanation,[9] one principal problem with explanation in the archetypal theory is that it does not seem possible in principle to predict when an archetype will be manifested nor what its appearance will be like except within broad outlines:

> Although in human beings the archetype represents a collective and almost universal mode of action and reaction, its activity cannot as a rule be predicted; one never knows when an archetype will react, and which archetype it will be. (Vol. 18, pp. 657-658)

> As has been stressed in this book, there are no laws governing the specific form in which an archetype might appear. There are only "tendencies" ... that, again, enable us to say only that such-and-such is likely to happen in certain psychological situations.[10]

However, it is not reasonable to expect laws depicting the relationship between the archetype per se and the archetypal image. For the questions of when an archetype appears, and what its manifestation will be like are answered in terms of the interaction between the innate archetype per se and the environment. The archetypal image is then always a product of these two factors interacting with each other in a dynamic way.

This often leads to a state of affairs in which we explain a situation by appeal to the archetypal theory that we could not have predicted. For example, Jung attempted to explain the phenomenon of National Socialism on the basis of the activation of specific archetypes in the German people.[11] However, previous to the rise of Hitler and shortly thereafter, Jung was uncertain of what outcome would ensue from the possession of the German people by these archetypes.

In regard to explanation, then, the archetypal theory is more like evolution theory then Newtonian mechanics. For prediction on the basis of the principles of evolution, such as the prediction that the fittest populations of organisms will survive, is always subject to unforseeable environmental circumstances. For example, what species survives might be due, as a matter of fact, to some environmental accident such as location proximate to the eruption of a volcano, which has no relation to the organisms' adaptation to the environment.[12] Thus, the course of evolution cannot be predicted with certainty, although this does not mean that the theory of evolution is not explanatory.

In the archetypal theory, on the other hand, what is unforseeable that prohibits reliable prediction of the outcome of behavior of individuals or groups due to the activation of archetypes is exactly how a new archetypal manifestation will interrelate with the existing cultural matrix. For example, we can explain the appeal of the cult of Guru Maharaj Ji, a teenage Indian who was celebrated as the Messiah by the Divine Light Mission in India and the United States, on the basis of the projection of the Archetype of the Divine Child.[13] When we attempt to determine why this particular archetype is manifested in this particular form at this particular time in history, the answers we give are in terms of the loss of numinosity of the traditional religious symbols and the consequent appeal of symbolic forms from a non-Western culture that are different enough to seem new and alive, yet similar enough to the old symbols to be easily assimilated to the existing culture. However, due to the uniqueness and complexity of the factors that are involved in any particular time in history, this explanation of the appearance of a new manifestation of the archetype of the Divine Child is not sufficient for us to make lawlike generalizations from which we could then expect exact predictions.

If we consider the situation in the individual rather than talking from a cultural perspective, the uncertainty that prohibits our knowing exactly when an archetype will appear and what its manifestation will be like is again due to the indeterminancy of the relationship between the innate archetype per se and environment. For the appearance of archetypes is conditioned by one's overall knowledge and experience.[14]

Moreover, whereas from the cultural perspective the difficulty with predicting archetypal manifestations is primarily due to the complexity and uniqueness of the relevant factors (here archetypal theory shares the same problems with historical explanation and prediction); with regard to the individual, there is the additional factor of an ethical issue. For in order to be able to separate the variables at work in determining how environment conditions the appearance of archetypes in the individual, we would need to perform an isolation experiment on a human being lasting several years.[15]

In addition to the ethical problems with the isolation experiment, another reason that complicates the problems with determining the appearance and manifestation of archetypes is the effect of the conscious attitude. For the degree to which the individual works with the archetypes and attempts to understand their relationship to his personality affects how and when they appear to the individual. Moreover, it is evident that Jung's work in attempting to trace this relationship between the phenomenology of archetypes and the development of personality as encompassed by his theory of individuation is very much pioneer work and that much additional study on this matter still needs to be done.

With regard to explanation and prediction with the archetypal theory, then, we must conclude that two principal factors prohibit the theory from being able to accomplish feats of explanation and prediction similar to those of the physical sciences. On the one hand, it is evident that the archetypal theory is an immature theory in the sense that its full empirical implications have yet to be worked out. Moreover, in many respects the theoretical foundations of the theory are still far from adequate.[16] To mention one example, the relationship which Jung has in mind between archetypes and instincts needs to be more precisely specified. It has been one of the goals of this study to attempt to make some progress in the direction of clarifying foundational questions, but it must be acknowledged that a great deal of further work in this direction needs to be done before we could expect its acceptance and widespread employment in such obviously applicable areas as anthropology.

But, on the other hand, if we admit that the theory is an immature theory, this is not to say that the theory is not scientifically defensible or that its methods are inadequate for what they attempt to accomplish. For the complex nature of the subject matter imposes certain definite limitations on what we could expect from even a foundationally impeccable archetypal theory whose empirical implications had been thoroughly worked out. Especially with regard to explanation and prediction, then, we can hardly expect perfect knowledge in principle from an archetypal theory.[17]

Evidence

The archetypal image is postulated to be the end result of the interaction between the innate archetype per se and the environment. But from the discussion in the last section, we saw that the archetypal theory does not attempt to specify precisely how these two factors interrelate to produce the archetypal image. Thus, in the absence of any archetypal laws specifying how these two factors interact to produce the archetypal images, the question arises as to how the innateness of the archetype per se is to be established. For if we are not in fact able to separate these two factors through some type of isolation experiment, it might well seem that the claim that the archetypes are innate, rather than acquired as a result of experiences in individual development, would be on very weak ground. Moreover, if we cannot substantiate the innate nature of the archetype per se, then the theory as a whole will lack a credible basis.

In this regard it is instructive to consider in general the sort of evidence Jung gives in support of his theory. In particular we need to examine how he attempts to establish that the archetypal images are due to innate factors.

Jung argues, then, that the archetypal images are due to innate factors primarily on the basis of paradigm cases in which it can be reasonably ascertained that the persons involved had had no previous exposure to the sort of motifs that appear in the dreams or visions. Although from an ethical point of view, we cannot isolate the human subject from the possibility of cultural influences; in some actual cases it is nevertheless possible to determine that the subject could not have learned of the motifs. Naturally in most cases of alleged archetypal manifestations, this degree of control will not be possible. For when individuals report that they cannot trace a specific image to something they have acquired through learning, they may be either lying or mistaken. In the latter case the possibility of cryptomnesia must always be kept in mind, that is, the possibility that the persons have forgotten what they had previously learned which now appears as an alien content of consciousness without apparent connection with antecedent experience, when in fact this connection has been simply forgotten. A third complicating factor is the element of suggestion, where, instead of the images being spontaneously produced, their appearance is due to the suggestive influence of the investigator.

Moreover, in order to establish that the content of the dream or vision is an archetype, in addition to establishing that it has not been acquired through previous experience, we must also show that it has cultural parallels. However, in this regard the sort of correlation that we need to establish between spontaneous products without previous experiential antecedents and similar manifestations in cultural symbology is not one between images but rather one between motifs. By emphasizing the similarity between motifs rather than symbols per se, we rule out the possibility that the similarity between symbols is due to chance or is a similarity with no significance. For in order to establish that a symbol is a manifestation of an archetypal motif, rather than simply comparing the similarity of isolated symbols, we must examine how the symbols function in relation to their context:

> It does not, of course, suffice simply to connect a dream about a snake with the mythological occurrence of snakes, for who is to guarantee that the functional meaning of the snake in the dream is the same as in the mythological setting? In order to draw a valid parallel, it is necessary to know the functional meaning of the individual symbol, and then to find out whether the apparently parallel mythological symbol has a similar context and therefore the same functional meaning. (Vol. 9-A, p. 50)

Thus, if we can show that a given content is not due to previous learning and has the required cultural parallels, this is the sort of evidence that Jung gives in support of his theory of archetypes. Moreover, it is evident here that it is the first factor, the demonstration that the spontaneous content had not been learned, that will be the most difficult aspect of the task of evidentially substantiating the archetypes.

A paradigm case to which Jung refers most often in the latter regard involves the vision of a schizophrenic patient which Jung noted in 1906:

One day I found the patient standing at the window, wagging his head and blinking into the sun. He told me to do the same, for then I would see something very interesting. When I asked him what he saw, he was astonished that I could see nothing, and said: "Surely you see the sun's penis—when I move my head to and fro, it moves too, and that is where the wind comes from." (Vol. 9-A, pp. 50-51)

Jung, who at the time was not well-acquainted with the literature of mythology, did not know what to make of the vision. However, four years later in a text describing a rite of Mithras he discovered an account that depicted the same motif:

Draw breath from the rays, draw in three times as strongly as you can and you will feel yourself raised up and walking towards the height, and you will seem to be in the middle of the aerial region.... The path of the visible gods will appear through the disc of the sun, who is God my father. Likewise the so-called tube, the origin of the ministering wind. For you will see hanging down from the disc of the sun something that looks like a tube. And towards the regions westward it is as though there were an infinite east wind. But if the other wind should prevail towards the regions of the east, you will in like manner see the vision veering in that direction. (Quoted from Albrecht Dieterich, *Eine Mithrasliturgie* [Leipzig, 1903], pp. 6ff.; Vol. 9-A, p. 51)

The possibility of the patient having previously learned of this archetypal motif, "the idea of a wind-tube connected with God or the sun," (Vol. 9-A, p. 52) is largely negated by the fact that the passage that Jung cites as a parallel was only published in 1903, which was after the patient had been committed. Moreover, other incidences of this rare motif as depicted in medieval paintings were not in the local gallery in Zurich where the patient had lived his whole life. (Vol. 9-A, p. 52)

Another example cited by Jung in *Man and His Symbols* involves archetypal dream motifs reported by a ten-year-old girl:

"The evil animal," a snakelike monster with many horns, kills and devours all other animals. But God comes from the four corners, being in fact four separate gods, and gives rebirth to all the dead animals....

A small mouse is penetrated by worms, snakes, fishes, and human beings. Thus the mouse becomes human. This portrays the four stages of the origin of mankind.

A drop of water is seen, as it appears when looked at through a microscope. The girl sees that the drop if full of tree branches. This portrays the origin of the world. (*Man and His Symbols*, p. 59)

The first citation contains the motif of divine restitution, *Apokatastasis*, as well as the motif of a divine quaternity. The second and third citations illustrate the cosmogonic myth depicting the origin of the world and human beings. (*Man and His Symbols*, pp. 60-61)

The problem with this sort of evidence is that it has the character of a selected demonstration of a limited number of individual cases. Moreover, it is never possible with absolute certainty to rule out the possibility of deception and/or cryptomnesia, and Jung's assurance is just about all the basis we have for judging the reliability of his subjects and determining their lack of previous exposure to symbols from cultural sources.

But within the context of his method of investigation, which is phenomenological rather than experimental, it is difficult to see how we could go beyond the sort of evidence Jung presents. With this type of approach, the best we could manage would seem to be a larger collection of similar paradigm cases. In regard to numbers of cases, Jung often says that he could easily multiply his examples, but hesitates to do so since each case requires lengthy discussion in order to make clear the context out of which the symbols are taken for comparison:

> Establishing such facts not only requires lengthy and wearisome researches, but is also an ungrateful subject for demonstration. As the symbols must not be torn out of their context, one has to launch forth into exhaustive descriptions, personal as well as symbological, and this is practically impossible in the framework of a lecture. (Vol. 9-A, p. 50)

In order to make clear what is meant by an archetypal motif, then, rather than giving a summary of its essential features, the best approach is to give examples of the motif within its various contexts of manifestation. This is illustrated when we try to give a list of archetypes. For without actual examples of how these archetypes function in a given context, such a list produces only a very superficial understanding of what an archetypal motif involves. Moreover, in any case archetypal motifs are not easily divided into unambiguous, discrete types. These sorts of considerations, then, are reasons why Jung adheres to a descriptive, phenomenological method of investigation that yields evidence of an essentially nonquantitative nature.

However, the archetypal theory would rest on a very suspect empirical basis if the only evidence we had for the theory is the sorts of cases just discussed, which for the most part arise out of the context of therapeutic work done by Jungians. In order for the theory to be credible at all, it must be shown to have consequences that are manifested outside of the Jungian therapeutic context.

In this regard we can appeal to the commonality of symbolic motifs in cultures throughout the world widely separated in space and time. However, although this type of evidence is of an extraclinical and publicly observable nature, it has definite limitations so far as constituting compelling evidence for the archetypal theory is concerned. For it is even more difficult to establish the spontaneous origin of symbolic motifs in cultures than it is in individuals, since the history and influences on the former are more uncertain than for an individual. Moreover, appeal to cross-cultural similarities will not have much probative strength independently of the ability to demonstrate the emergence of these same archetypal motifs in individuals.

Although we might expect that, irrespective of the difficulty of substantiating the spontaneous origin of symbolic motifs in various cultures, anthropological evidence would nonetheless prove to be very helpful in establishing the credibility of the theory, this expectation has not been fulfilled for the most part. Due to the difficult nature of the theory in its practical application, anthropologists tend either to accept the theory and to interpret their data from a Jungian perspective or else reject the theory from an unknowledgeable standpoint. In the latter case, it is difficult to determine the degree to which their findings support the theory, since for the most part they are not sensitive to what consititutes an archetype and are unaware of the diverse phenomenology of the various archetypal motifs.[18]

Due to the difficulties of evaluating the evidence for the archetypal theory independently of a Jungian framework of understanding, we earlier suggested that reports from experiments designed to induce altered states of consciousness be studied in order to see whether anything similar to descriptions of archetypal motifs were reported. If none were reported, then this would be strong evidence against the theory. On the other hand, however, the claim that there are such similar descriptions that constitute confirming evidence for the archetypal theory is rendered problematic by the fact that many of the investigators are influenced by Jung's work and thus readily assume his theoretical viewpoint in interpreting their data. Moreover, in many of the studies involving drugs, the element of suggestion was a relevant variable not controlled. (Both of these considerations apply to the Masters and Houston study discussed below.)

But it is clear that this sort of research offers the promise of a solution to the problem of extending the validational basis of the theory beyond the sort of evidence to which Jung originally appealed. For if no additional support for the theory is forthcoming besides the sort of data for which it was originally designed to explain, we would then have to conclude that the theory has very weak empirical support.

One example of such evidence from altered states of consciousness research is reported by R. E. L. Masters and Jean Houston in *Varieties of Psychedelic Experience*. It involved work with the chemical substances LSD-25 and peyote and covers a period of more than fifteen years. A total of 206 drug sessions were involved.[19]

The investigators reported that the perception of the guides in the experiment was frequently distorted in such a way that they were apparently seen as archetypal figures:

> In a fairly common distortion the guide may be perceived by the subject as one or more of a variety of archetypal figures. For example, a

female guide may be seen as a goddess, as a priestess, or as the personification of wisdom or truth or beauty. Descriptions of some of these "archetypal" perceptions have included seeing the guide's features as "glowing with a luminous pallor" and her gestures as being "cosmic, yet classical."[20]

Moreover, in the course of the experiments, mythological and religious symbolic imagery was frequently encountered:

> In the psychedelic drug-state mythologies abound. The guide often may feel that he is bearing witness to a multi-layered complex of mythological systems as they arise out of their latency in the mind of the subject.[21]

The most frequently recurring mythic themes were summarized as follows:

> Myths of the Child-Hero, Myths of Creation, Myths of the Eternal Return (Cycles of Nature), Myths of Paradise and the Fall, Hero Myths, Goddess Myths, Myths of Incest and Parricide (Oedipus, Electra, etc.), Myths of Polarity (Light and Darkness, Order and Chaos), Myths of the Androgyne (Male-Female Synthesis), Myths of the Sacred Quest, Prometheus-Faust Myths (Myths of the Trickster).[22]

Religious images of some kind were reported in ninety-six percent of the 206 subjects. These included images of religious figures: Christ, Buddha, saints, godly figures, William Blake-type figures (fifty-eight percent); devils and demons (forty-nine percent); and angels (seven percent).[23]

Despite the factors of the influence of Jung's work and the problem of suggestion, these results seem to constitute convincing evidence for the archetypal theory.

Stanislav Grof, whose work involved LSD research conducted in Prague, Czechoslovakia, obtained results that support the Masters-Houston research. For example, he states:

> An important group of transpersonal experiences in LSD sessions are phenomena for which C. G. Jung has used the terms primordial images, dominants of the collective unconscious, or archetypes. They repeatedly occur in sessions of both those subjects familiar with this concept and naïve individuals without any previous exposure to Jungian ideas.[24]

Archetypes and Evolution Theory

In considering the scientific status of the archetypal theory, it has been our concern to demonstrate that the theory as reconstructed is compatible in principle with a contemporary scientific understanding. In this regard, it is essential to establish that the theory is not logically tied to an evolutionary theory that has been repudiated by modern biologists, namely, one involving appeal to the inheritance of acquired characteristics.

As we saw in chapter 3 (page 52), there was one point in Jung's career where he postulated that the archetypes were inherited by means of such a mechanism and that archetypes were the deposits of repeated experiences. (Vol. 7, p. 69) However, Jung retracted this view and thereafter did not attempt to explain the evolutionary mechanism by which archetypes become part of the innate structure of the psyche except to say that the archetypes were inherited as part of the structure of the brain and hence evolved as humankind evolved.

It is clear how the latter position can be construed as in principle compatible with Darwinian mechanisms of evolutionary change. However, although we can see how this sort of origin of archetypes through evolution is possible in principle, we might still question whether the inheritance of such dispositions to produce symbolic images is plausible from the standpoint of modern evolutionary theory. In other words, is there any reasoning from the biological point of view that can support the hypothesis that such dispositions are in fact inherited?

In this regard, the recent work of Edward O. Wilson and Charles Lumsden offers some interesting research that seems to support the Jungian view. For Wilson argues that there is a coevolutionary link between mind and culture in which genetically transmitted epigenetic rules influence the direction in which culture develops.[25] Culture itself then acts as a selective pressure increasing the prevalence of the epigenetic factors.

The main import of Wilson's work consists in working out the genetic mechanisms by which complex social behavior patterns are influenced by hereditary factors. In his view this influence is generally manifested as an innately determined preference for the development of certain cultural forms over others. For example, there is a strong universal cultural bias against incest. Moreover, the deepest moral feelings are said to originate from epigenetically determined sources.[26]

Wilson's views are similar to Noam Chomsky's arguments for the existence of an innate language capacity that functions as an innate grammatical guide facilitating the acquisition of language by children.[27] However, Wilson envisions a more general influence in which many other forms of cultural activity are shaped by genetic factors. Although Wilson makes no references to Jung's view, when he states that " ... most or all forms of perception and thinking are biased by processes in the brain that are genetically programed,"[28] this falls right in line with the archetypal theory.

Even if Wilson's work is open to question and we could not precisely specify the sort of genetic mechanisms that were responsible for the inheritance of the kind of dispositions what Jung postulates, this lack of knowledge would not by itself cast doubts on the theory, since the genetic mechanisms that are responsible for many aspects of human nature are as yet, to say the least, imperfectly understood.

But if it can be shown how a structure enables an individual to be better adapted to the environment in such a manner as to produce relatively more progeny than another individual lacking the structure, then it is reasonable to suppose from the standpoint of modern evolutionary theory that whatever genes are responsible for the structure will tend to increase in the overall population of the species. Showing that dispositions to produce numinous symbolic images have probably been inherited is then reducible to the problem of showing the basis in terms of which it is reasonable to believe that these dispositions did in fact confer a selective advantage on those humans or predecessors of humans who happened to have the necessary genes to produce them.

In this regard we point to the fact that humankind is not a solitary species but evolved as a social animal. Thus, it is not difficult to see how the survival of humankind as a species has been enhanced by mechanisms that facilitate social cooperation such as the development of a shared culture. Moreover, it is easy to understand how the religious or mythological heritage of a human society gives it unity and stability and how "The integration of the social group, its cohesion, is maintained by the direction of certain sentiments toward a symbolic center."[29]

If we admit that religious and mythological symbolic systems have survival value in that they enhance social cooperation within the human community, the likelihood that dispositions that tend to produce symbolic manifestations will be selected for in the course of evolution would seem to be very great. The perspective of modern evolution theory is thus one which supports the prospect of there being innate dispositions to produce numinous symbolic images such as the archetypal theory assumes.[30]

Notes

Introduction

1.   "Psychic events are observable facts and can be dealt with in a
'scientific' way. Nobody has ever shown me in how far my
method has not been scientific. One was satisfied with shouting
'unscientific.' Under these circumstances I do make the claim
of being 'scientific' because I do exactly what you describe as
the 'scientific method.' I observe, I classify, I establish relations
and sequences between the observed data, and I even show
the possibility of prediction."

C. G. Jung, *Letters*, ed. Gerhard Adler and Aniela Jaffé, trans. R. F. C. Hull, Vol.
1: *1906-1950*, Vol. 2: *1951-1961* (Princeton; Princeton University Press, Vol. 1, 1973;
Vol 2, 1975); *Letters*, Vol. 2, p. 567, letter to E. A. Bennet dated 23 June 1960.
Hereafter cited as *Letters* Vol. 1 or Vol. 2.

In the following we have for convenience sake sometimes referred to Jung's
theory of the collective unconscious as the "theory of archetypes." The collective
unconscious, however, is postulated to contain both instincts as well as
archetypes. See page 30.

2.   C. G. Jung, *The Collected Works of C. G. Jung*, ed. Sir Herbert Read, Michael
Fordham, Gerhard Adler, William McGuire, trans. R. F. C. Hull (Princeton: Princeton
University Press, 1953-1979), Vol. 18, pp. 467, 489. Quotations are from the
following editions: Vol. 1: *Psychiatric Studies*, 2d ed., 1970; Vol. 2: *Experimental
Researches*, trans. Leopold Stein and Diana Riviere, 1973; Vol. 3: *The Psychogenesis
of Mental Disease*, 1960; Vol. 4: *Freud and Psychoanalysis*, 1961; Vol. 5: *Symbols of
Transformation*, 2d ed., 1967; Vol. 6: *Psychological Types*, 1971; Vol. 7: *Two Essays
on Analytical Psychology*, 2d ed., 1966; Vol. 8: *The Structure and Dynamics of the
Psyche*, 2d ed., 1969; Vol. 9: Part 1: *The Archetypes and the Collective Unconscious*,
2d ed., 1968 (hereafter cited as Vol. 9-A); Vol. 9: Part 2: *Aion: Researches into the
Phenomenology of the Self*, 2d ed., 1968 (hereafter cited as Vol. 9-B); Vol. 10:
Civilization in Transition, 2d ed., 1970; Vol. 11: *Psychology and Religion: West and
East*, 2d ed., 1969; Vol. 12: *Psychology and Alchemy*, 2d ed., 1968; Vol. 13: *Alchemical
Studies*, 1968; Vol. 14: *Mysterium Coniunctionis*, 2d ed., 1970; Vol. 15: *The Spirit in
Man, Art, and Literature*, 1966; Vol. 16: *The Practice of Psychotherapy*, 2d ed., 1966;
Vol. 17: *The Development of Personality*, 1954; Vol. 18: *The Symbolic Life*, 1976; Vol.
19: *Bibliography*, 1979; Vol. 20: *General Index*, 1979. Hereafter cited by volume
number.

3.   The justification for each of these reconstruction moves is further discussed in the text. Synchronicity as an aspect of the archetypal theory is discussed on pages 64-66. The possibility of subsistent archetypes is treated on pages 33-34. See also the quotation from Jung on this point in note 17. The archetype per se understood as a hypothetical construct is discussed on pages 55-57.

4.   Edinger makes this same point in a helpful way: "Jung considers his own psychological theories as an attempt to provide a new mythology or vessel for the archetypes which will be acceptable to the modern scientific mind." Edward Edinger, "The Collective Unconscious as Manifested in Psychosis," *American Journal of Psychotherapy* 9 (October 1955): 625.

5.   Ernst Cassirer, *Philosophy of Symbolic Forms*, trans. Ralph Manheim, Vol. 2: *Mythical Thought* (New Haven: Yale University Press, 1955), p. 25.

6.   Ibid., p. xiii.

7.   Ernest Cassirer, *The Myth of the State* (New Haven: Yale University Press, 1946), pp. 297-298.

8.   Ibid., p. 60.

9.   In some ways Cassirer could be seen as thinking out of a perspective that does appreciate the mythos. What he takes to be the role of imagination in structuring experience would be an example. Moreover, the whole focus on myth as one of the basic forms of symbolic expression, albeit a primitive one, is a way of acknowledging its cultural value and importance.

10.   C. G. Jung, ed., *Man and His Symbols* (New York: Dell, 1964), p. 29. Hereafter cited as *Man and His Symbols*.

11.   See chapter 5 for a fuller discussion of James Hillman's views.

12.   James Hillman, *The Myth of Analysis: Three Essays in Archetypal Psychology* (New York: Harper and Row, 1972), p. 179.

13.   James Hillman, *Re-Visioning Psychology* (New York: Harper and Row, 1975), p. 169.

14.   Ibid., p. xii.

15.   Ibid., p. 169.

16.   On this point see Vol. 18, p. 662.

17.   "But since, as I showed in the introduction, the archetypes in question are not mere objects of the mind, but are also autonomous factors, i.e., living subjects, the differentiation of consciousness can be understood as the effect of the intervention of transcendentally conditioned dynamisms. In this case it would be the archetypes that accomplish the primary transformation.... Therefore the question as to whether the process is initiated by consciousness or by the archetype can never be answered;..." (Vol. 11, pp. 469-470)
See also the passage quoted on page 55 from Vol. 10, pp. 69-70.

18.   We distinguish the philosophical and religious viewpoints on archetypes, which often accompany the exploration of individual archetypal images, from the scientific perspective in terms of a distinction between scientific discourse and personally meaningful interpretations of archetypal experience. See pages 102-103.

19.   David Bohm, *Wholeness and the Implicate Order* (London: Routledge and Kegan Paul, 1980). Bohm postulates the existence of an order of undivided wholeness called the "implicate order" that lies beyond space and time as ordinarily understood. The world of ordinary phenomena, the explicit order, unfolds out of the implicate order to produce the discrete and separate elements of our everyday experience.

20.   Rupert Sheldrake, *A New Science of Life: The Hypothesis of Formative Causation* (London: Blond and Briggs, 1981). Sheldrake proposes that in addition to the material and energetic processes that science studies, physical and biological systems are also in part regulated by invisible organizing fields lacking mass and energy called "morphogenetic fields." These fields are patterns reinforced by repetition of events over time. Whenever an animal learns a new behavior, for example, this alters the morphogenetic field that helps regulate the behavior of that animal. If sufficient animals learn the behavior, then learning in new animals takes progressively less time. Thus, Sheldrake's morphogenetic field hypothesis supports the thesis of the existence of a real collective memory within species.

21.   Jung interprets the mystical experience as an experience of the unconscious, for example. See pages 97-100.

22.   Thomas S. Kuhn, *The Structure of Scientific Revolutions* (Chicago: University of Chicago Press, 1962).

23.   Although Jung did deal with what he took to be parapsychological aspects of archetypal experience, such as in his theory of synchronicity, the archetypal phenomena for the most part are not as anomalous in relationship to conventional frameworks of knowledge as are psychic phenomena.

1. Jung's Mental Constructs

1.   As will become evident as our exposition proceeds, Jung means psyche to be richer in connotation than the term mind in its ordinary usage. Moreover, it is just the features of the collective unconscious which contribute this additional meaning to the psyche.

2.   The term "libido" is used extensively in Jung's earlier work and reflects the influence of Freud. Jung did not employ the term much in his later writings (from 1935 onward) although his psychology continued to view the psyche on the model of energetic processes and to speak of psychic energy.

3.   We do not mean to imply here that reductionism can be compatible only with a version of the identity theory or vitalism only with substantial dualism. However, identity theory and substantial dualism seem to be the mind-body positions most obviously compatible with reductionism and vitalism respectively.

4.   It is not in the passage where he speaks of Bergson that this is made clear but in the essay "On Psychic Energy," Vol. 8, pp. 3-66 where the implications of the libido theory with respect to the problem of the mind-body relation are discussed in detail.

5.   By double aspect theory is meant the view that the mental and physical are different aspects of some third entity that is itself neither mental nor physical. By panpsychism is understood the view that the mental and physical are related in such a way that these attributes always occur as integral parts of each other rather than there being matter completely devoid of mind or completely immaterial mind.

6.   See pages 25-27 for more discussion of psychoid processes. The theory of synchronicity is discussed on pages 64-66. The so-called synchronistic events discussed below involve meaningful but acausal coincidences between psychic contents and physical events. For example, a clock stops at the moment of the owner's death.

7.   Perhaps it can yet be shown how the occurrences of synchronicity, ESP, out-of-body experiences, and even survival of bodily death can be explained within the interactionist—panpsychist double aspect view that we have claimed as Jung's basic theory of mind. For as we have previously remarked, Jung's theoretical model of the psyche is capable of being able to accommodate in principle at least some of these extraordinary phenomena. However, the point is that Jung in trying to account for these events did not always do so within the context of the theory of mind he employs in the great majority of his writing. For he at times talks of parallelism and implies a position of substantial dualism that would require a radically different theory of mind than that upon which his psychology as a whole is based.

8.   Strictly speaking, the archetypes are completely incapable of being made conscious in the sense that what appears in consciousness is never the archetype per se but only an archetypal image. This distinction between the archetype per se and the archetypal image is further discussed on pages 55-57.
     When archetypes come into consciousness, they limit the will by means of their numinosity, a sort of fascination (see pages 43-44). Thus, the individual's will is often caught up in the spell of the archetype so that, for example, the man in love becomes enthralled by the archetype of the anima as embodied in his object of affection.

9.   See Ira Progoff's *The Death and Rebirth of Psychology* (New York: McGraw-Hill, 1956), pp. 173-177 for an insightful discussion of the psychoid from the evolutionary point of view.

10.   In addition to being a bridge between the psychic and the physiological, the psychoid elements in their spiritual aspect, that is, the archetypes, are also postulated to constitute an interface between psyche and matter in the context of the theory of synchronicity where parallel events are hypothesized in physical nature and in psychological meaning (see pages 20-21 and 65). However, since in line with our program of naturalistic reconstruction we are setting apart the synchronicity hypothesis from the archetypal theory as we reconstruct it, we will consider the psychoid elements only from the point of view of the physiological

interface, not as indication of the possibility of the psyche operating in physical nature.

11.   Concerning the two quotes that seem to indicate racial, ethnic, and geographic differentiations in the collective unconscious, Jung states that he wrote the first in 1927. (Vol. 10, p. 544) The second was apparently written in 1916 as it appears in the 1916 version of the "Structure of the Unconscious." (Vol. 7, p. 275) Both of these passages are, however, retained in the version of *Two Essays on Analytical Psychology* revised in 1942.

12.   Jung sometimes carries his argument for the existence of essential psychological differences in distinct racial, ethnic, and geographic groups to what would seem to be indefensible extremes. For example he writes in 1934: "I must confess my total inability to understand why it should be a crime to speak of 'Jewish' psychology." (Vol. 10, p. 541)

Jung also states that Eastern yoga should not be practiced by Westerners since it cannot be assumed that the Westerner's psyche can assimilate without possible harm a practice that evolved out of the cultural tradition of the East:

> "In the East, where these ideas and practices originated, and where an uninterrupted tradition extending over some four thousand years has created the necessary spiritual conditions, yoga is, as I can readily believe, the perfect and appropriate method of fusing body and mind together so that they form a unity that can hardly be doubted....
>
> He [the European] will infallibly make a wrong use of yoga because his psychic disposition is quite different from that of the Oriental. I say to whomsoever I can: 'Study yoga—you will learn an infinte amount from it—but do not try to apply it, for we Europeans are not so constituted that we apply these methods correctly, just like that.'" (Vol. 11, pp. 533-534)

Jung's social and political views have been the subject of widespread misunderstanding due in no small measure to Jung's notorious political ineptness. For an unbiased account of Jung's social-political views and his unfortunate adventures in public affairs, see Aniela Jaffé's *From the Life and Work of C. G. Jung,* trans. R. F. C. Hull (New York: Harper and Row, 1971).

13.   The issue of whether or not the collective unconscious is a superindividual entity seems to be dependent to some extent on whether it is considered from a mythos or a logos point of view. From the mythos perspective there is only one collective unconscious and it is everywhere and timeless. But from the standpoint of consciousness, from which science and the logos have to proceed, there are manifestations of the collective unconscious in every person. From the logos perspective the idea that the collective unconscious is a superindividual entity is a hypostatization, it is only a theoretical construct rather than being an actual thing in its own right. Jung's facile passage from a logos to a mythos discourse about archetypes easily confuses the issue here. It is clear, however, that in his later work, from about 1940 onward, Jung came to suspect that there might be some literal oneness to the collective unconscious as evidenced by various parapsychological events of which he was attempting to take cognizance in his psychological views. The rationale for taking the naturalistic reconstructive tack of separating these

speculations from the main body of Jung's theory is that it saves the archetypal theory from speculative and metaphysical implications that unnecessarily cloud the main empirical grounds on which the theory as a whole is based.

2. Theory of Archetypes: Part 1

1.   This dream was provided by a friend, George Clough.

2.   "Dismemberment is a practically universal motif of primitive shamanistic psychology. It forms the main experience in the initiation of a shaman." (Vol. 13, p. 70, note 4) "Dismemberment can be understood psychologically as a transformative process which divides up an original unconscious content for purposes of conscious assimilation. Or, put another way, it is original unity submitting to dispersal and multiplicity for the sake of realization in spatio-temporal existence." (Edward F. Edinger, *Ego and Archetype: Individuation and the Religious Function of the Psyche* [Baltimore: Penguin, 1972], p. 140.)

3.   In calling the archetypes "dispositions" we do not mean to imply that they are intervening variables rather than hypothetical constructs. (Compare Kenneth MacCorquodale and Paul E. Meehl, "On a Distinction Between Hypothetical Constructs and Intervening Variables," *Psychological Review* 55 [March 1948]: 95-107). That is, the archetype per se is meant to designate an entity rather than being simply a convenient term to describe a precisely specified set of observational statements.

The sense of disposition connected with the notion of the archetype per se is that archetypes as archetypal images cannot be said to be inherited, it being rather the possibility to form such images that is innate. Jung emphasizes this dispositional quality of the archetype per se in order to counter the misconception that his archetypal theory implies a concept of inherited ideas or inherited images. When we later call the archetypes organizing and structuring principles (pages 56-57), we mean to refer to this same dispositional quality of the archetype per se.

4.   The fact that Kant had a strong influence on the development of Jung's ideas is amply evidenced by the many explicit references to Kant scattered throughout Jung's works. Moreover, when Jung talks of the philosophers who had been important to his intellectual development, we again find him acknowledging the influence of Kant: "The philosophical influence that has prevailed in my education dates from Plato, Kant, Schopenhauer, Ed. v. Hartmann, and Nietzsche. These names at least characterize my main studies in philosophy." (*Letters*, Vol. 2, pp. 500-501, letter to Joseph F. Rychlak dated 27 April 1959)

In his autobiography Jung describes an interest in Kantian philosophy that was part of a "philosophical development" that "extended from my seventeenth year until well into the period of my medical studies." (C. G. Jung, *Memories, Dreams, Reflections*, recorded and ed. Aniela Jaffé, trans. Richard and Clara Winston [New York: Random House, 1963], p. 70. Hereafter cited as *Memories, Dreams, Reflections*.) The extent of that interest is revealed when Jung relates that while a medical student "The clinical semesters that followed kept me so busy that scarcely any time remained for my forays into outlying fields. I was able to study Kant only on Sundays." (*Memories, Dreams, Reflections*, p. 101)

5.   Jolande Jacobi, *Complex/Archetype/Symbol in the Psychology of C. G. Jung*, trans. Ralph Manheim (Princeton: Princeton University Press, 1959), p. 52.

6.   Carl G. Hempel, *Philosophy of Natural Science* (Englewood Cliffs, New Jersey: Prentice-Hall, 1966), p. 16.

7.   By the transpersonal nature of the archetype is meant that the experience seems to refer to something beyond the individual's own ego and personal boundaries, and that the experience is not completely explicable by reference to the individual's past experience or development.

3.   *Theory of Archetypes: Part 2*

1.   As will become apparent as we proceed, this hope will not be fulfilled. It is only in Jung's earlier writing that he attempts to explain how archetypes originate through ideas about the origins of myths. However, due to the fact that Jung's views on this matter become implicated with ideas about the inheritance of acquired characteristics, this earlier view merits full discussion.

Also, at least one commentator on Jung has advanced the idea that the origin of myths and archetypes are causally interrelated. In *Jung, Gods, and Modern Man* Antonio Moreno states:

> "In spite of Jung's explanation, the relation of myth and archetypes is not yet clear. It is the myth which forms the archetype, and at the same time, it is the archetype which produces mythical ideas. Is it a vicious circle? Not likely, because for Jung, the subjective fantasies of myths are the causes of archetypes. But once the archetype is formed, it is endowed with a kind of readiness to arouse the same mythical ideas which were the cause of its formation, a familiar psychological process. Habits and dispositions are formed in the same way; repetition of acts forms the habit, but once the habit exists it is inclined to produce the very acts that were the cause of its existence: ..." (Antonio Moreno, *Jung, Gods, and Modern Man* [Notre Dame: University of Notre Dame Press, 1970], p. 19.)

2.   In the above we have not distinguished the spiritual from the religious, as in the previous discussion of the spiritual when the latter term referred to the archetypal manifestation and "religious" to the product of collective consciousness. Jung does not always use these terms in a consistent way, although from the context it is usually clear whether he is referring to the individual or the collective manifestation.

3.   However, it is easy to fall into the opposite error of seeing alchemy solely as a philosophico-religious enterprise and thus fail to appreciate the important role that alchemical work has played in the history of chemistry. Jung, in his work with the psychological significance of alchemical symbols, is particularly open to the criticism that he has overemphasized the psychological aspect of alchemy while failing to give due credit to the naturalistic and practical aspects of the art.

4.   The term "mechanicomorphize" is taken from Joseph F. Rychlak, *A*

Philosophy of Science for Personality Theory (Boston: Houghton Mifflin, 1968), p. 57. "It is also possible to take the opposite approach, [to anthropomorphism] and assign non-human characteristics to human organisms. Some psychologists feel that the behaviorist does this when he 'mechanicomorphizes' man (Allport, 1940)."

5.   Richard Semon, *The Mneme*, trans. Louis Simon (New York: MacMillan, 1921), pp. 11-12.

6.   Ibid., p. 12.

7.   In addition to natural phenomena, Jung also discusses psychological and physiological processes as causative factors in the generation of myths. (Vol. 8, pp. 155-156)
      The change in Jung's position concerning the origin of archetypes occurred sometime around the year 1930.

8.   Issues surrounding the relationship between evolution theory and archetypes are further discussed on pages 66-68 and 138-140.

9.   James Hillman's perspective on archetypes rejects the archetype per se/ archetypal image distinction. Hillman takes the image as ultimate and is not interested in theoretical points of view that seek to explain the multiform archetypal images in terms of any underlying causes. See chapter 5 for a full discussion of the Hillman position on archetypes.

10.   The problem of the individuation of archetypes is further discussed on pages 63 and 127-128. Here the issue is briefly taken up in the context of the problem of the relation between archetype per se and archetypal image. On page 63 the question is considered from the perspective of a discussion of the phenomenology of the chief archetypes. On pages 127-128 the question of the individuation of archetypes is discussed with the intent of showing how in the absence of a definite decision procedure for individuating archetypes, such questions as what to count as an archetype and how to talk in a meaningful way about different archetypes, can nonetheless be operationally decided by those sufficiently acquainted with the theory.

11.   Ira Progoff, *Jung, Synchronicity, and Human Destiny: Noncausal Dimensions of Human Experience* (New York: Julian Press, 1973), p. 156.

12.   The application of the Kantian phenomena/noumena distinction to the problem of archetype per se versus archetypal image is not unproblematic. For the appeal to the archetype per se as the principle responsible for the archetypal image would seem to imply the attribution of qualities to the thing-in-itself, that is, that the latter was real and had certain effects. Thus, if we take the archetype per se as strictly analogous to the thing-in-itself, we end up attributing properties to that, which from Kant's viewpoint, we are not supposed to be able to attribute anything at all. See Edward Casey's article "Toward An Archetypal Imagination," *Spring* (1974): 29, note 9.

13.   We are using the work "extraspection" in the sense ascribed to it by Joseph F. Rychlak in *A Philosophy of Science for Personality Theory*, p. 27: "If the theorist

takes an extraspective perspective or frame of reference, he defines his abstractions from his vantage point as observer, regardless of the point of view of the object of study."

14.   In this portion of a dream of Jung's, for example, the shadow archetype appears as "Dr. Y. and his son." Moreover, the image of Jung's father also plays an archetypal role in the dream. In contrast to the relationship Jung had with his real father, this symbolic father acts as a guide to the mysteries of the unconscious:

> "It started with my paying a visit to my long-deceased father. He was living in the country—I did not know where. I saw a house in the style of the eighteenth century, very roomy, with several rather large outbuildings.... My father guarded these as custodian.
>
> He was, as I soon discovered, not only the custodian but also a distinguished scholar in his own right—which he had never been in his lifetime. I met him in his study, and, oddly enough, Dr. Y.—who was about my age—and his son, both psychiatrists, were also present. I do not know whether I had asked a question or whether my father wanted to explain something of his own accord, but in any case he fetched a big Bible down from a shelf, a heavy folio volume like the Merian Bible in my library. The Bible my father held was bound in shiny fishskin. He opened it at the Old Testament—I guessed that he turned to the Pentateuch—and began interpreting a certain passage. He did this so swiftly and so learnedly that I could not follow him. I noted only that what he said betrayed a vast amount of variegated knowledge, the significance of which I dimly apprehended but could not properly judge or grasp. I saw that Dr. Y. understood nothing at all, and his son began to laugh. They thought that my father was going off the deep end and what he said was simply senile prattle....
>
> The two psychiatrists represented a limited medical point of view which, of course, also infects me as a physician. They represent my shadow—first and second editions of the shadow, father and son." (*Memories, Dreams, Reflections*, pp. 217-218)

15.   In talking in this way about the insight of a universal perspective, there is a temptation to speak in terms of the "wisdom" of the unconscious. In regard to collective compensation, then, we must be careful to avoid the misunderstanding that this type of language implies that the unconscious is a sort of higher consciousness that purposively guides the personality to its destination. For the sort of "guidance" which the unconscious provides is that which results from the working of a natural process that itself has no end in view. Jung makes this point in a discussion concerning compensation by the unconscious:

> "Yet it would, in my view, be wrong to suppose that in such cases the unconscious is working to a deliberate and concerted plan and is striving to realize certain definite ends. I have found nothing to support this assumption. The driving force, so far as it is possible for us to grasp it, seems to be in essence only an urge towards self-realization. If it were a matter of some general

> teleological plan, then all individuals who enjoy a surplus of unconsciousness would necessarily be driven towards higher consciousness by an irresistible urge." (Vol. 7, p. 184)

16.   The anima is in part a man's inner image of women. See page 62-63 for further characterization of the anima archetype.

17.   Although the content of all the archetypes is conditioned by the individual's personal experience, the shadow and the anima/animus differ from the other archetypes in the fact that their content is more directly related to the individual's personal situation than the other archetypes. In terms of the analogy of depth, then, these archetypes occupy a position intermediate between consciousness and the personal unconscious and the other aspects of the collective unconscious.

18.   See Ira Progoff, *Jung, Synchronicity, and Human Destiny*, p. 106.
> Since causation has been ruled out, the question might well be raised how the "influence" of the archetype can then be made intelligible. It would seem that some sort of lawlike ordering principle must be postulated not involving a cause and effect relationship between the objective event and the correlated internal state of expectancy. Making clear how the archetype is supposed to function as this ordering principle is one of the major conceptual ambiguities that must be resolved in order to make synchronicity into a truly explanatory hypothesis.

19.   Since the position taken here is that a rational reconstruction of the archetypal theory is not committed to the task of a rational reconstruction of synchronicity, we will not attempt a critical assessment of synchronicity in this study. In order to carry out that task, several key questions would have to be considered. In addition to the problem of making archetypal "influence" intelligible, additional clarification is needed concerning how the crucial distinction between coincidence and meaningful coincidence can be made operationally sound.

20.   Stevens speculates that the archetypes are located in the midbrain and brain stem:
> "Moreover, there is now good reason to suppose that the 'command neurones' subserving archetypal systems may be situated in the phylogenetically ancient cerebral regions of the midbrain and brain stem, ... " (Anthony Stevens, *Archetypes: A Natural History of the Self* [New York: Quill, 1982]: p. 274.)

Even if Rupert Sheldrake is correct in his theory of morphic resonance (see page 143, note 20), this would not mean that new archetypes suddenly spring into being with new learning. For the archetypes would still be subject to the sort of genetic stability demonstrated in the basic genetic structure of species that breed true for generations in spite of new environmental conditions. For example, finches trapped on the Galapagos Islands and sent to California showed innate fear responses to hawks they saw in California even though there had been no predator birds on the islands, and the finches had thus not been exposed to the sight of a predator bird for hundreds of thousands of years since this innate response first evolved. (Stevens, p. 48)

21.   Wilson's and Lumsden's research is further described on page 139. Charles J.

Lumsden and Edward O. Wilson, *Promethean Fire: Reflections on the Origin of Mind* (Cambridge: Harvard University Press, 1983).

22. Compare June Singer: "Archetypes: Eternal or Evolving," public seminar sponsored by C. G. Jung Society of San Francisco given in San Francisco November 6, 1982.

23. Lumsden and Wilson, p. 15.

24. Compare Samuels:
> "Archetypal metaphors do change with the passing of each generation; this does not imply change in the archetype as such. New metaphors do receive cultural acknowledgment and each subsequent generation has a different store of images on which to draw." (Andrew Samuels, *Jung and the Post-Jungians* [London: Routledge and Kegan Paul, 1985], p. 74)

4. Critiques of the Theory of Archetypes

1. As the interpretation of Jung's archetypes as occult or supernatural agencies is not attributed to any particular author in the following, it should be mentioned that this line of interpretation is one which is very popular with uncritical Jungian enthusiasts who are eager to embrace doctrines which, from their point of view, represent sensationalistic alternatives to a scientific world-view.

2. Jung's analytical inclinations and abilities at times fail to keep pace with the flood of insights and ideas from the unconscious. His expositions frequently become so involved with lengthy examples and parenthetical elaborations that the main thread of discussion is lost. Vol. 5 of the *Collected Works*, *Symbols of Transformation*, is a good example of this overdetermination of content at the expense of form.

3. Gerhard Adler, Letter to the Editor, *Horizon* 19 (June 1949): 454.

4. See Philip Rieff, *The Triumph of the Therapeutic: Uses of Faith After Freud* (New York: Harper and Row, 1966), p. 41 where this terminology is used.

5. Philip Rieff, "C. G. Jung's Confession: Psychology as a Language of Faith," *Encounter* 22 (May 1964): 49.

6. Edward Glover, *Freud or Jung?* (Cleveland: Meridian, 1956), p. 33.

7. As might be expected, what we have called "criticisms based on misunderstanding" could also conceivably be fitted into this second category of systematically biased critiques. Although it is not clear what ideological motives Rieff may have, Glover is obviously a Freudian defending the faith. But as many of Glover's criticisms cannot be understood solely in terms of a Freudian interpretation of the psychological phenomena, they have no value for determining whether an alternative hypothesis can account for the objects of Jungian theoretical interest. Thus some, but not all, of Glover's objections to Jung's ideas can be relegated to the first category.

The examples of systematically biased critiques to be discussed below are from psychoanalysis and Judeo-Christian theology.

8.   One could conceivably criticize Jung's archetypal hypothesis from other standpoints than those mentioned here. One could well imagine a behaviorist critique, for example. However, an examination of such a critique would not shed much light on archetypal theory. A more fruitful discussion would be one drawn from the standpoint of an existentialist critique. Although the phenomenologists and existentialists do not for the most part address themselves to Jung's concept of the collective unconscious, it might well be thought that their attempt to frame their ideas without appeal to a concept of an unconscious would constitute a strong implicit repudiation of Jung's viewpoint. But such thinkers as Husserl, Heidegger, Sartre, and Medard Boss, although they claim to describe human experience without the need for an unconscious, have in actuality smuggled it back into their views with functionally equivalent concepts. For example, in Heidegger's work the concepts of "horizon" and "thrownness" seem to be functionally equivalent to what Jung means by the unconscious.

9.   Glover, p. 35.

10.   Ibid., p. 38.

11.   Nandor Fodor, *Freud, Jung, and Occultism* (New Hyde Park, New York: University Books, 1971), p. 177.

12.   Ibid., p. 180.

13.   Ibid., p. 182.

14.   Anthony Storr, *C. G. Jung* (New York: The Viking Press, 1973), p. 38.

15.   Ibid., p. 37.

16.   Paula Heimann, "Some Notes on the Psycho-analytic Concept of Introjected Objects," *British Journal of Medical Psychology* 22 (1949): 14.

17.   Storr, p. 39.

18.   Ibid., p. 68.

19.   Glover, p. 160.

20.   In saying that the question of the value of imputing a spiritual dimension to experience cannot be resolved only through argumentation, the point being made is not that the importance of such a dimension cannot be argued for at all, but that the final justification of an image of humankind based upon the belief in the value of such a dimension will be how well it enables us to understand and effectively deal with the human situation in the long run.

21.   " ... *archetypes of transformation.* They are not personalities, but are typical situations, places, ways and means, that symbolize the kind of transformation in question." (Vol. 9-A, p. 38)

22.   Fodor, p. 176.

23. Ibid., p. 177.

24. The emergence of a group of Jungians interested in developmental issues has the effect of blurring somewhat the sharp contrast between the Freudian and Jungian images of humankind as sketched here. These developmentally oriented Jungians include such writers as Michael Fordham, Kenneth Lambert, Alfred Plaut, Joseph W. T. Redfearn, and Andrew Samuels. See Samuels' *Jung and the Post-Jungians* where he describes what he calls the Developmental School of Jungians as contrasted with the Classical School and Hillman's Archetypal School.

25. Josef Goldbrunner, *Individuation: A Study of the Depth Psychology of Carl Gustav Jung* (Notre Dame: University of Notre Dame Press, 1964), p. 172.

26. Martin Buber, *Eclipse of God: Studies in the Relation between Religion and Philosophy* (New York: Harper and Row, 1952), pp. 83-84.

27. Ibid., pp. 135-136.

28. William McGuire and R. F. C. Hull, eds., *C. G. Jung Speaking: Interviews and Encounters* (Princeton: Princeton University Press, 1977), p. 251.

29. Moreno, p. 111.

30. The editors of Jung's *Letters*, Gerhard Adler and Aniela Jaffé, give the following explanation of this commonly used expression of Jung's:
> "A term frequently used by Jung to denote the common habit of explaining something unknown by reducing it to something apparently known and thereby devaluing it. It is borrowed from William James, *Pragmatism* (1907), p. 16: 'What is higher is explained by what is lower and treated for ever as a case of "nothing but"—nothing but something else of a quite inferior sort.' " (*Letters*, Vol. 1, p. 142, note 1)

31. From the Kantian point of view, it might be objected that a Kantian interpretation of the archetypes is still possible even if we do not identify the archetype per se with the thing-in-itself. For it is possible to think of both the archetypal image and the archetype per se as part of the phenomenal realm and as distinct from the noumenal archetypal referent. In keeping with the intent of Jung's line of reasoning on this matter, we could then state that what is said about the God archetype does not necessarily implicate us with claims about God as noumena.

32. Compare James Hillman's "Why 'Archetypal' Psychology?" *Spring* (1970): 216 where he opts for the latter view.

5. *The Challenge of James Hillman's Archetypal Psychology*

1. James Hillman, *Archetypal Psychology: A Brief Account* (Dallas: Spring Publications, 1983), p. 3.

2. Ibid., p. 6.

3. James Hillman, *Loose Ends: Primary Papers in Archetypal Psychology* (Dallas: Spring Publications, 1975), pp. 161-162, note 3.

4.   What is referred to as the "positivistic position" is a view taken by some contemporary psychologists who hold that dreams are really nonsense. According to Robert W. McCarley and J. Allen Hobson of Harvard University, for example, dreams are just random images in the brain. J. Allan Hobson and Robert W. McCarley, "The Brain as a Dream State Generator: An Activation-Synthesis Hypothesis of the Dream Process," *American Journal of Psychiatry* 134 (December 1977): 1335-1348.

5.   James Hillman, *The Dream and the Underworld* (New York: Harper and Row, 1979), p. 112.

6.   Ibid., p. 95.

7.   Hillman, *Re-Visioning Psychology*, p. 208.

8.   Ibid., p. 132.

9.   Ibid., pp. 132-133.

10.   James Hillman, "Peaks and Vales: The Soul/Spirit Distinction as Basis for the Differences between Psychotherapy and Spiritual Discipline," in *On the Way to Self-Knowledge*, ed. Jacob Needleman and Dennis Lewis (New York: Knopf, 1976), p. 118.

11.   Hillman, *Re-Visioning Psychology*, p. 209.

12.   Ibid., p. 156.

13.   Ibid., p. 127.

14.   Ibid., p. xii.

15.   Ibid., p. 150.

16.   Ibid., p. 160.

17.   Hillman, *The Dream and the Underworld*, p. 199.

18.   Hillman, *Re-Visioning Psychology*, p. 133.

19.   Ibid., p. 130.

20.   Ibid., p. 131.

21.   Hillman, *The Myth of Analysis*, p. 179.

22.   Hillman, *Re-Visioning Psychology*, p. 150.

23.   Ibid., p. 152.

24.   Ibid., p. xiii.

25.   Ibid., p. 134.

26.   Ibid., p. 228.

27.   Ibid., p. 227.

28. Ibid., p. 169.

29. Ibid., p. 219.

30. Ibid., p. 191.

6. *Jung and the Scientific Attitude: Part 1*

1. It might seem that the issue of methodology should be included in the question of Jung's scientific attitude if the latter is understood as the way Jung understands his theory of archetypes to be scientific in principle. However, for the sake of maintaining the continuity of our discussion, we have treated the question of what methodology Jung employs in his study of archetypes separately from the issues grouped under the heading of Jung's scientific attitude.

2. Edward M. L. Burchard, "Mystical and Scientific Aspects of the Psychoanalytic Theories of Freud, Adler, and Jung," *American Journal of Psychotherapy* 14 (April 1960): 306.

3. Paul Friedman and Jacob Goldstein, "Some Comments on the Psychology of C. G. Jung," *Psychoanalytic Quarterly* 33 (April 1964): 196.

4. Rieff, "Jung's Confession," p. 47.

5. Rieff, *Triumph of the Therapeutic*, p. 114.

6. Compare Campbell: "The denotation of this neologism [mysticism] in the polemical literature of the social sciences, where it is employed as a term of abuse, is obscure. It seems to mean, roughly, 'unscientific.' " Joseph Campbell, "Bios and Mythos," in *Psychoanalysis and Culture*, ed. George B. Wilbur and Warner Muensterberger (New York: International Universities Press, 1951), p. 331, note 10.

7. Walter T. Stace, *Mysticism and Philosophy* (Philadelphia: J. B. Lippincott, 1960), p. 79.

8. Ibid., p. 110.

9. Ibid., p. 79.

10. The absence of personal mystical experience, on the other hand, would naturally not be sufficient to establish that Jung does not understand his archetypal theory from an essentially mystical point of view.

11. For out-of-body experience see *Memories, Dreams, Reflections*, p. 289. For examples of some paranormal psychic experiences see *Memories, Dreams, Reflections*, pp. 137 and 155. Jung tells of conversing with a ghostly guru on p. 183. For visions see pp. 179 and 284. An instance of hearing voices is related on p. 191 of the autobiography.

12. Stace, p. 47.

13. Ibid., p. 49.

14.   Sunyata, the Void, is the term used in Mahayana Buddhism for the introverted mystical state. See Stace, p. 107.

15.   This feeling of loss of individuality and being merged with the One, which occurs during mystical experience, would be a consequence of the experience of an empty consciousness, if it were possible. For a consciousness devoid of multiplicity could not distinguish subject and object. See Stace, p. 111.

16.   Satori is the experience of enlightenment in Zen Buddhism. It can be considered a paradigm type of mystical state.

17.   Stace, pp. 304-305.

18.   We have deferred the discussion of these questions concerning the issue of rationality until the next chapter in order to first explore the question of the relation between scientific and extrascientific discourse about archetypes.

19.   Erich Neumann seems to doing this is his book *The Origins and History of Consciousness*, trans. R. F. C. Hull (Princeton: Princeton University Press, 1954) where he is apparently engaging in speculative mythology while giving the appearance of an empirical study. See Wolfgang Giegerich's critique of Neumann's work where he aptly demonstrates this point. Wolfgang Giegerich, "Ontogeny = Phylogeny?" *Spring* (1975): 110-129.

20.   The present section is only a preview of the full argument we want to make in support of the idea that Jung did view his theory of archetypes in a perspective appropriate for the designation of the label "scientific." The rest of the present chapter and chapter 7 support this position.

21.   We are using these terms in the sense in which Rychlak characterizes them: "Nomothetic study essentially presumes that a theoretical abstraction can be made which has general applicability for several members of a given class (i.e., distribution). Idiographic study, on the other hand, emphasizes the uniqueness of personality manifestation." (Rychlak, p. 24)
      Thus, there are two distinct issues involved in discussing the basis for the tension betwen a scientific level of discourse about archetypes versus a personal, therapeutic level. The issue of an incommensurability in principle between theory and practice, and the issue of nomothetic versus idiographic methods for understanding the individual. As will become clear, Jung does not really distinguish between these two questions, but equates idiographic with the therapeutic and extrascientific. We intend to show how Jung's distinction between the two levels of discourse is defensible on the basis of the first issue. With respect to the second issue, we do not intend to fully explore the question of the relative merits of nomothetic versus idiographic methods for studying the individual. However, it can be reasonably maintained that an idiographic scientific study is possible outside the context of therapy. Thus, although what Jung says about the value of an idiographic approach to the individual makes sense within the therapeutic context, Jung fails to point out how the idiographic approach does not have to be identified with the aims of practical psychology, but can also be defended as a legitimate scientific method in its own right.

22.   The Jungian therapist does not advocate that the patient adopt any *specific* metaphysical or religious point of view.

23.   Edinger, *Ego and Archetype*, p. 108.

24.   What we have in mind by idiographic scientific method is the sort of study recommended by Gordon Allport who suggests, for example, that the psychologist learn from biography and literature the merit of such things as the in-depth study of individual cases of personality. Gordon W. Allport, *Personality and Social Encounter* (Boston: Beacon Press, 1960), p. 12.

It seems that in this regard we have a discrepancy between what Jung says and what he actually does. For the in-depth study of individual cases is in fact characteristic of his work. The massive volume *Symbols of Transformation* (Vol. 5) is primarily an extended commentary centered around the material of one schizophrenic individual. (The person was not a patient of Jung's.)

25.   Thus, when we distinguish a scientific level of discourse from a level of personally meaningful interpretation, questions can still be raised concerning the scientific justification of what is advocated for therapy. For we wish our theoretical knowledge to rule out some therapeutic practices even if we admit that scientific knowledge is not itself sufficient for therapeutic success as determined by the individual's gain in self-knowledge and self-realization.

7.   *Jung and the Scientific Attitude: Part 2*

1.   Jung's distinction between theoretical and practical knowledge of archetypes is one that is aptly expressed in terms of object and meta-levels of archetypal experience. However, often Jung can be seen to generalize from personal and therapeutic experience with archetypes and to relate his views on what is beneficial for man in general. In this way, a great deal of philosophizing does in fact appear in Jung's writings. Because of this philosophical perspective in Jung's work, our modified distinction will be in terms of kinds of discourse rather than levels.

2.   Gerhard Adler, "Analytical Psychology and the Principle of Complementarity," in *The Analytic Process: Aims, Analysis, Training: The Proceedings of the Fourth International Congress for Analytical Psychology*, ed. Joseph B. Wheelwright (New York: G. P. Putnam's Sons, 1971), p. 120.

3.   Marie-Louise von Franz, "Conclusion: Science and the Unconscious," in *Man and His Symbols*, ed. C. G. Jung (New York: Dell, 1964), pp. 382-383.

4.   Jung's typology works with two attitude types called "extrovert and introvert" that indicate the overall orientation of the individual with regard to objective or subject processes respectively. There are also four function types: intuition, thinking, feeling, and sensation. Together with the attitude types, this yields then eight basic types of personality: an extroverted intuitive, thinking, feeling, and sensing type and an introverted intuitive, thinking, feeling, and sensing type.

5.   In fairness to Jung, it must be pointed out that Jung is usually sensitive to a distinction between theoretical and practical knowledge as outlined in the section

on science and the individual. However, as exemplified in the passages cited here, Jung sometimes is guilty of not distinguishing between the practical requirements for applying a theory in therapy and requirements for the acceptance of a theoretical claim.

6.   "...many psychologists who choose to work as best they can with important problems (problem-centering) rather than restricting themselves to doing only that which they can do elegantly with the techniques already available (method-centering)." Abraham H. Maslow, *The Psychology of Science: A Reconnaissance* (New York: Harper and Row, 1966), p. 16.

8.   *The Study of Archetypes as a Scientific Discipline*

1.   John L. Fischer, "The Sociopsychological Analysis of Folktales," *Current Anthropology* 4 (June 1963): 256.

2.   Jacobi, p. 59.

3.   Michael Fordham, *New Developments in Analytical Psychology* (London: Routledge and Kegan Paul, 1957), p. 57. See also the Jung quotes on page 56 on this point.

4.   An aspect of disanalogy with biological speciation in the problem of individuating archetypes is that, whereas it is reasonable to expect that biological species delineate distinct entities, namely populations of similar organisms capable of interbreeding with each other, archetypes are better thought of as interpenetrating processes rather than as discrete entities.

5.   Avis M. Dry, *The Psychology of Jung: A Critical Interpretation* (New York: John Wiley and Sons, 1961), p. xiii.

6.   In regard to the operational difficulty of employing the archetypal theory, the work of H. Yehezkel Kluger has to be mentioned. Kluger developed a rating scale for discriminating between archetypal and nonarchetypal dreams. In order for a dream to be counted as archetypal, it must have three out of four of the following characteristics:
> "a) A parallel to a mythological motif (under which term are included also motifs from fairy-tales, folklore, and religious symbolism).
> b) Heightened affect.
> c) Remoteness from everyday experience.
> d) Non-rational imagery or behavior." (H. Yehezkel Kluger, "Archetypal Dreams and 'Everyday' Dreams: A Statistical Investigation into Jung's Theory of the Collective Unconscious," *Israel Annals of Psychiatry and Related Disciplines* 13 [March 1975]: 22)

The author has employed a modified form of this rating scale in an experiment conducted by Dr. Larry Gestenhaber (unpublished). Each of the four Kluger categories was given a number scale. For example, mythological parallels were rated to be distant, moderate, or loose. Irrationality was rated from rational-not unlikely, rational-possible, rational-unlikely, borderline-nonrational but comprehensible, irrational (impossible in reality), bizarre. There was a high correlation between the overall rating score indicating the presence of archetypal content in the author's rating and that of another rater.

7.   By experiments with altered states of consciousness, we have in mind such things as dream research, work with hypnosis, biofeedback, meditation, sensory deprivation, and psychedelic drugs.

We do not mean to imply here that archetypes can only be manifested in altered states of consciousness. Presumably the archetypes influence consciousness in all of its states. However, analogously to other aspects of the unconscious, the archetypes are most noticeable when consciousness is intefered with in some way, as under the influence of drugs, or if there is a relaxation of conscious attention, as in hypnosis or dreams.

8.   But this is not to say, of course, that there are no possible ad hoc modifications that would save the theory from contrary evidence in these cases. For in addition to the fact that we must not underestimate the ingenuity of theorists, theories are not in any case simply overthrown by single incidences of contrary evidence. However, in the cases cited, it is very difficult to see what sort of ad hoc modifications could be invoked that would not involve a radical revision of the theory itself.

9.   Thus, we will not discuss the explanatory role of the archetypes with regard to the therapeutic situation. Jung discusses many case histories showing how the archetypal theory helps explain what is happening to the individual in the course of therapy. See, for example, Vol. 7, pp. 132-138.

10.   Franz, p. 383.

11.   See Jung, Vol. 10, part 3 for a detailed discussion on this question.

12.   Michael Scriven, "Explanation and Prediction in Evolutionary Theory," in *Man and Nature: Philosophical Issues in Biology*, ed. Ronald Munson (New York: Dell, 1971), pp. 213-227.

13.   See Jung, "The Psychology of the Child Archetype," in Vol. 9-A. The sort of motif at work here is roughly the same as that which is involved in the story of the Christ child, that is, miraculous origins followed by heroic childhood deeds.

14.   This, then, is one reason why persons who have had experience with Jung's work dream Jungian dreams. The theoretical knowledge of Jung is an additional aspect of one's overall understanding in terms of which the appearance of the archetypal manifestations are conditioned:

> "There are people who can read my books and never have a dream of anything reminiscent of my writings, but it is true that if you understand what you have read, you get a frame of mind or a problematical outlook which you did not have before, and that, of course, influences your dreams." (*Letters*, Vol. 2, p. 187, letter to a young Greek girl dated 14 October 1954)

15.   The sort of experimental problems we have in mind with regard to an isolation experiment would be similar to those encountered in ethological studies

designed to investigate innate behavior patterns. See Konrad Lorenz, *Evolution and Modification of Behavior* (Chicago: University of Chicago Press, 1965).

With regard to archetypes, two separate questions are at stake. On the one hand, we would want to know whether archetypal images were manifested at all under conditions of isolation; and, on the other hand, we could investigate the relationship between selected environmental stimuli such as television or a particular literature and archetypal appearance.

16.   Jung is the first to admit that his work is of a pioneer nature and thus often without adequate theoretical foundations:

> "However, as you have rightly seen, I have landed myself in enormous difficulties by framing general formulations which are intended to explain the whole field of human experience. I had to keep to experiences that were directly accessible to me and compare them with data drawn from the whole history of the mind. This gives rise to some degree of inexactitude which makes my efforts appear provisional. It is perfectly clear to me that everything I do is pioneer work which has still to be followed by a real laying of foundations, but there are gratifying signs that others are beginning to make forays into this territory." (*Letters*, Vol. 1, pp. 231-232, letter to Rudolf Pannwitz dated 27 March 1937)

17.   By perfect knowledge is meant a situation in which a symmetry exists between explanation and prediction such that every adequate explanation is also a potential prediction. Compare Carl G. Hempel, *Aspects of Scientific Explanation: And Other Essays in the Philosophy of Science* (New York: Macmillan, 1965), p. 364.

18.   It might seem that these considerations indicate that one must assume the archetypal theory in order to be able to see what counts as data in favor of it. However, this difficulty of appraising the evidence for the archetypal theory from a non-Jungian perspective exemplifies the close interrelationship that exists between theory and evidence. That is to say, the theory determines which data are relevant as evidence and what is relevant as evidence from one theoretical perspective is irrelevant from another. The fact that Jung employs a phenomenological method of investigation does not of course mean that he does not select what is relevant for description from essentially theoretical considerations.

19.   R. E. L. Masters and Jean Houston, *The Varieties of Psychedelic Experience* (New York: Dell, 1966), p. 5

20.   Ibid., p. 92.

21.   Ibid., p. 224.

22.   Ibid., pp. 224-225.

23.   Ibid., p. 265.

24.   Stanislav Grof, *Realms of the Human Unconscious: Observations from LSD Research* (New York: Dutton, 1976), p. 198.

Other evidence involving work with altered states of consciousness includes the works of the following researchers: Phillip A. Faber, Graham S. Saayman, and Stephen W. Touyz, "Meditation and Archetypal Content of Nocturnal Dreams," *Journal of Analytical Psychology* 23 (January 1978): 1-22; Ann Faraday, *Dream Power* (New York: Berkley Publishing, 1972), pp. 120-126; Elmer Green and Alyce Green, *Beyond Biofeedback* (New York: Dell, 1977), p. 145; Kluger, "Archetypal Dreams and 'Everyday' Dreams"; Wolfgang Kretschmer, "Meditative Techniques in Psychotherapy" in *Altered States of Consciousness*, ed. Charles T. Tart (New York: John Wiley and Sons, 1969), pp. 223-224; Walter N. Pahnke and William A. Richards, "Implications of LSD and Experimental Mysticism" in *Altered States of Consciousness*, pp. 409-410; Charles T. Tart, *States of Consciousness* (New York: Dutton, 1975), pp. 113-114.

25.   Lumsden and Wilson, p. 19. The authors define epigenesis as " ... the sum of all the interactions between the genes and the environment that create the distinctive traits of an organism." (p. 71)

26.   Ibid., pp. 182-184.

27.   Ibid., p. 112.

28.   Ibid., p. 181.

29.   Bernard G. Campbell, *Human Evolution: An Introduction to Man's Adaptations* (Chicago: Aldine, 1966), p. 314.

30.   Of course, the archetypal theory is not the only possible explanation of how religious and mythological symbolic systems come into being. When the point about the survival value of religions and mythologies is admitted, this only entails the inheritance of dispositions to produce symbolic images rather than the full archetypal theory. One might wish to argue, for example, that all that was necessary for such systems to come into being is language and imagination. However, it would seem that the archetypal theory with its hypothesis of the innate archetypes offers a theory of dispositions to produce numinous images that goes a long way toward explaining the culturally universal similarity and emotional appeal of religious and mythological motifs, whereas this additional explanatory import is lacking with other ideas of how symbolic ideas might have originated.

Bibliography

Adler, Gerhard. "Analytical Psychology and the Principle of Complementarity." In *The Analytic Process: Aims, Analysis, Training: The Proceedings of the Fourth International Congress for Analytical Psychology*, pp. 110-121. Edited by Joseph B. Wheelwright. New York: G. P. Putnam's Sons, 1971.

_____. Letter to the Editor. *Horizon* 19 (June 1949): 454.

Allport, Gordon W. *Personality and Social Encounter*. Boston: Beacon Press, 1960.

Balmer, Heinrich H. *Die Archetypentheorie von C. G. Jung: Eine Kritik*. Berlin: Springer-Verlag, 1972.

Bär, Eugen. "Archetypes and Ideas: Jung and Kant." *Philosophy Today* 20 (Summer 1976): 114-123.

Barnes, Hazel E. "Neo-Platonism and Analytical Psychology." *Philosophical Review* 54 (November 1945): 558-577.

Barron, Frank. "Is Psychic Energy an Objective, Impersonal Force?" *Contemporary Psychology* 15 (May 1970): 348-350.

Boden, Margaret A. *Purposive Explanation in Psychology*. Cambridge: Harvard University Press, 1972.

Boer, Charles, and Kugler, Peter. "Archetypal Psychology is Mythical Realism." *Spring* (1977): 131-152.

Bohm, David. *Wholeness and the Implicate Order*. London: Routledge and Kegan Paul, 1980.

Bolen, Jean S. *The Tao of Psychology: Synchronicity and the Self*. San Francisco: Harper and Row, 1979.

Brome, Vincent. *Jung*. New York: Atheneum, 1978.

Buber, Martin. *Eclipse of God: Studies in the Relation Between Religion and Philosophy*. New York: Harper and Row, 1952.

Burchard, Edward M. L. "Mystical and Scientific Aspects of the Psychoanalytic Theories of Freud, Adler, and Jung." *American Journal of Psychotherapy* 14 (April 1960): 289-307.

Campbell, Bernard G. *Human Evolution: An Introduction to Man's Adaptations*. Chicago: Aldine, 1966.

Campbell, Joseph. "Bios and Mythos: Prolegomena to a Science of Mythology." In *Psychoanalysis and Culture*, pp. 329-343. Edited by George B. Wilbur and Warner Muensterberger. New York: International Universities Press, 1951.

Capra, Fritjof. *The Tao of Physics*. Berkeley: Shambhala, 1975.

Casey, Edward S. "Toward an Archetypal Imagination." *Spring* (1974): 1-32.

Cassirer, Ernst. *The Myth of the State*. New Haven: Yale University Press, 1946.

————. *The Philosophy of Symbolic Forms*. Translated by Ralph Manheim. Vol. 2: *Mythical Thought*. New Haven: Yale University Press, 1955.

Christou, Evangelos. *The Logos of the Soul*. Zürich: Spring Publications, 1976.

Cohen, Edmund D. *C. G. Jung and the Scientific Attitude*. New York: Philosophical Library, 1975.

Coward, Harold. *Jung and Eastern Thought*. Albany: State University of New York Press, 1985.

D'Aquili, Eugene. "The Influence of Jung on the Work of Claude Levi-Strauss." *Journal of the History of the Behavioral Sciences* 11 (January 1975): 41-48.

Demos, Raphael. "Jung's Thought and Influence." *Review of Metaphysics 9* (September 1955): 71-89.

Dilman, Ilham. "Is the Unconscious a Theoretical Construct?" *Monist* 56 (July 1972): 313-341.

Dodds, E. R. *The Greeks and the Irrational*. Berkeley: University of California Press, 1951.

Drake, Carlos C. "Jungian Psychology and Its Uses in Folklore." *Journal of American Folklore* 82 (April 1969): 122-131.

Dry, Avis M. *The Psychology of Jung: A Critical Interpretation*. New York: John Wiley and Sons, 1961.

Dudley, Guilford. "Jung and Eliade: A Difference of Opinion." *Psychological Perspectives* 10 (Spring 1979): 38-47.

Edinger, Edward F. "The Collective Unconscious as Manifested in Psychosis." *American Journal of Psychotherapy* 9 (October 1955): 624-629.

_____ . *Ego and Archetype: Individuation and the Religious Function of the Psyche.* Baltimore: Penguin, 1972.

Eliade, Mircea. *Myth and Reality.* Translated by Willard R. Trask. New York: Harper and Row, 1963.

Ellenberger, Henri F. *The Discovery of the Unconscious: The History and Evolution of Dynamic Psychiatry.* New York: Basic Books, 1970.

Faber, Phillip A.; Saayman, Graham, S.; and Touyz, Stephen W. "Meditation and Archetypal Content of Nocturnal Dreams." *Journal of Analytical Psychology* 23 (January 1978): 1-22.

Faraday, Ann. *Dream Power.* New York: Berkley Publishing, 1972.

Fiegl, Herbert and Scriven, Michael, eds. *Minnesota Studies in the Philosophy of Science.* Vol. 1. Minneapolis: University of Minnesota Press, 1956.

Fischer, John L. "The Sociopsychological Analysis of Folktales." *Current Anthropology* 4 (June 1963): 235-295.

Fodor, Nandor. *Freud, Jung, and Occultism.* New Hyde Park, New York: University Books, 1971.

Fordham, Freida. *An Introduction to Jung's Psychology.* Baltimore: Penguin, 1953.

Fordham, Michael. "Jungian Views of the Body-Mind Relationship." *Spring* (1974): 166-178.

_____ . *New Developments in Analytical Psychology.* London: Routledge and Kegan Paul, 1957.

_____ . *The Objective Psyche.* London: Routledge and Kegan Paul, 1958.

Franz, Marie-Louise von. *C. G. Jung: His Myth in Our Time.* Translated by William H. Kennedy. Boston: Little, Brown and Co., 1975.

_____ . "Conclusion: Science and the Unconscious." In *Man and His Symbols,* pp. 375-387. Edited by C. G. Jung. New York: Dell, 1964.

_____ . *Number and Time: Reflections Leading toward a Unification of Depth Psychology and Physics.* Translated by Andrea Dykes. Evanston: Northwestern University Press, 1974.

_____ . *On Divination and Synchronicity: The Psychology of Meaningful Chance.* Toronto: Inner City Books, 1980.

Friedman, Paul, and Goldstein, Jacob. "Some Comments on the Psychology of C. G. Jung." *Psychoanalytic Quarterly* 33 (April 1964): 194-225.

Giegerich, Wolfgang. "Ontogeny = Phylogeny? A Fundamental Critique of Erich Neumann's Analytical Psychology." *Spring* (1975): 110-129.

_____ . *"Die wissenschaftliche Psychologie als subjektivistische und zudeckende Psychologie."* *Analytische Psychologie* 8 (1977): 262-283.

Glover, Edward. *Freud or Jung?* Cleveland: Meridian, 1956.

Goldbrunner, Josef. *Individuation: A Study of the Depth Psychology of Carl Gustav Jung.* Notre Dame: University of Notre Dame Press, 1964.

Goldenberg, Naomi R. "Archetypal Theory After Jung." *Spring* (1975): 199-220.

Gras, Vernon W. "Myth and the Reconciliation of Opposites: Jung and Lévi-Strauss." *Journal of the History of Ideas* 42 (July 1981): 471-487.

Green, Elmer, and Green, Alyce. *Beyond Biofeedback.* New York: Dell, 1977.

Grim, Patrick, ed. *Philosophy of Science and the Occult.* Albany: State University of New York Press, 1982.

Grof, Stanislav. *Realms of the Human Unconscious: Observations from LSD Research.* New York: Dutton, 1976.

Hannah, Barbara. *Jung: His Life and Work: A Biographical Memoir.* New York: G. P. Putnam's Sons, 1976.

Heimann, Paula. "Some Notes on the Psycho-analytic Concept of Introjected Objects." *British Journal of Medical Psychology* 22 (1949): 8-15.

Heisig, James W. *Imago Dei: A Study of C. G. Jung's Psychology of Religion.* Lewisburg, Pa.: Bucknell University Press, 1979.

Hempel, Carl G. *Aspects of Scientific Explanation: And Other Essays in the Philosophy of Science.* New York: Macmillan, 1965.

_____ . *Philosophy of Natural Science.* Englewood Cliffs, New Jersey: Prentice-Hall, 1966.

Hillman, James. *Archetypal Psychology: A Brief Account.* Dallas: Spring Publications, 1983.

_____ . *The Dream and the Underworld.* New York: Harper and Row, 1979.

_____ . *Insearch: Psychology and Religion*. New York: Charles Scribner's Sons, 1967.

_____ . *Inter Views: Conversations with Laura Pozzo on Psychotherapy, Biography, Love, Soul, Dreams, Work, Imagination, and the State of the Culture*. New York: Harper and Row, 1983.

_____ . *Loose Ends: Primary Papers in Archetypal Psychology*. Dallas, Spring Publications, 1975.

_____ . *The Myth of Analysis: Three Essays in Archetypal Psychology*. New York: Harper and Row, 1972.

_____ . "On the Necessity of Abnormal Psychology." In *Facing the Gods*, pp. 1-38. Edited by James Hillman. Dallas: Spring Publications, 1980.

_____ . "Peaks and Vales: The Soul/Spirit Distinction as Basis for the Differences between Psychotherapy and Spiritual Discipline." In *On the Way to Self-Knowledge*, pp. 114-147. Edited by Jacob Needleman and Dennis Lewis. New York: Knopf, 1976.

_____ . *Re-Visioning Psychology*. New York: Harper and Row, 1975.

_____ . *Suicide and the Soul*. New York: Harper and Row, 1964.

_____ . "Why 'Archetypal' Psychology?" *Spring* (1970): 212-219.

Hobson, J. Allan, and McCarley, Robert W. "The Brain as a Dream State Generator: An Activation-Synthesis Hypothesis of the Dream Process." *American Journal of Psychiatry 134* (December 1977): 1335-1348.

Hobson, Robert F. Critical Notice. *Journal of Analytical Psychology* 6 (July 1961): 161-168.

Homans, Peter. *Jung in Context: Modernity and the Making of a Psychology*. Chicago: University of Chicago Press, 1979.

Hook, Sidney, ed. *Psychoanalysis, Scientific Method, and Philosophy*. New York: New York University Press, 1959.

Hyland, Drew A. *The Origins of Philosophy*. New York: G. P. Putnam's Sons, 1973.

Jacobi, Jolande. *Complex/Archetype/Symbol in the Psychology of C. G. Jung*. Translated by Ralph Manheim. Princeton: Princeton University Press, 1959.

_____ . *The Psychology of C. G. Jung*. Translated by Ralph Manheim. 8th ed. New Haven: Yale University Press, 1973.

Jaffé, Aniela. *From the Life and Work of C. G. Jung*. Translated by R. F. C. Hull. New York: Harper and Row, 1971.

———. *The Myth of Meaning: Jung and the Expansion of Consciousness.* Translated by R. F. C. Hull. New York: G. P. Putnam's Sons, 1971.

———, ed. *Word and Image.* Translated by Krishna Winston. Princeton: Princeton University Press, 1979.

Jung, C. G. *The Collected Works of C. G. Jung.* Edited by Sir Herbert Read, Michael Fordham, Gerhard Adler, and William McGuire. Translated by R. F. C. Hull (except for Vol. 2, translated by Leopold Stein and Diana Riviere). Vol. 1: *Psychiatric Studies,* 2d ed., 1970; Vol. 2: *Experimental Researches,* 1973; Vol. 3: *The Psychogenesis of Mental Disease,* 1960; Vol. 4: *Freud and Psychoanalysis,* 1961; Vol. 5: *Symbols of Transformation,* 2d ed., 1967; Vol. 6: *Psychological Types,* 1971; Vol. 7: *Two Essays on Analytical Psychology,* 2d ed., 1966; Vol. 8: *The Structure and Dynamics of the Psyche,* 2d ed., 1969; Vol. 9: Part 1: *The Archetypes and the Collective Unconscious,* 2d ed., 1968; Vol. 9: Part 2: *Aion: Researches into the Phenomenology of the Self,* 2d ed., 1968; Vol. 10: *Civilization in Transition,* 2d ed. 1970; Vol. 11: *Psychology and Religion: West and East,* 2d ed., 1969; Vol. 12: *Psychology and Alchemy,* 2d ed., 1968; Vol. 13: *Alchemical Studies,* 1968; Vol. 14: *Mysterium Coniunctionis,* 2d ed., 1970; Vol. 15: *The Spirit in Man, Art, and Literature,* 1966; Vol. 16: *The Practice of Psychotherapy,* 2d ed., 1966; Vol. 17: *The Development of Personality,* 1954; Vol. 18: *The Symbolic Life,* 1976; Vol. 19: *Bibliography,* 1979; Vol. 20: *General Index,* 1979. Princeton, Princeton University Press, 1953-1979.

———. *Letters.* Edited by Gerhard Adler and Aniela Jaffé. Translated by R. F. C. Hull. Vol. 1: *1906-1950;* Vol. 2: *1951-1961.* Princeton: Princeton University Press, Vol. 1, 1973; Vol. 2, 1975.

———. *Memories, Dreams, Reflections.* Recorded and edited by Aniela Jaffé. Translated by Richard and Clara Winston. New York: Random House, 1963.

———, ed. *Man and His Symbols.* New York: Dell, 1964.

Kamman, Robert J. "An Investigation into the Correspondence and Parallels Between Jung's Structure of the Psyche and Quantum Physics." Ph.D. dissertation, California School of Professional Psychology, 1977.

Keutzer, Carolin S. "Archetypes, Synchronicity and the Theory of Formative Causation." *Journal of Analytical Psychology* 27 (July 1982): 255-262.

Kluger, H. Yehezkel. "Archetypal Dreams and 'Everyday' Dreams: A Statistical Investigation into Jung's Theory of the Collective Unconscious." *Israel Annals of Psychiatry and Related Disciplines* 13 (March 1975): 6-47.

Kretschmer, Wolfgang. "Meditative Techniques in Psychotherapy." In *Altered States of Consciousness*, pp. 219-228. Edited by Charles T. Tart. New York: John Wiley and Sons, 1969.

Kuhn, Thomas S. *The Structure of Scientific Revolutions*. Chicago: University of Chicago Press, 1962.

Lakoff, George, and Johnson, Mark. *Metaphors We Live By*. Chicago: University of Chicago Press, 1980.

Lorenz, Konrad. *Evolution and Modification of Behavior*. Chicago: University of Chicago Press, 1965.

Lumsden, Charles J., and Wilson, Edward O. *Promethean Fire: Reflections on the Origin of Mind*. Cambridge: Harvard University Press, 1983.

MacCorquodale, Kenneth, and Meehl, Paul E. "On a Distinction Between Hypothetical Constructs and Intervening Variables." *Psychological Review* 55 (March 1948): 95-107.

Manicas, Peter T., and Secord, Paul F. "Implications for Psychology of the New Philosophy of Science." *American Psychologist* 38 (April 1983): 399-413.

Maslow, Abraham H. *The Psychology of Science: A Reconnaissance*. New York: Harper and Row, 1966.

Masters, R. E. L., and Houston, Jean. *The Varieties of Psychedelic Experience*. New York: Dell, 1966.

Mattoon, Mary Ann. *Jungian Psychology in Perspective*. New York: Macmillan, 1981.

McGuire, William and Hull, R. F. C., eds. *C. G. Jung Speaking: Interviews and Encounters*. Princeton: Princeton University Press, 1977.

Mitroff, Ian I. "The Mythology of Methodology: An Essay on the Nature of a Feeling Science." *Theory and Decision* 2 (March 1972): 274-290.

Mitroff, Ian I., and Kilmann, Ralph H. *Methodological Approaches to Social Science*. San Francisco: Jossey-Bass, 1978.

Moreno, Antonio. *Jung, Gods, and Modern Man*. Notre Dame: University of Notre Dame Press, 1970.

Neumann, Erich. *The Origins and History of Consciousness*. Translated by R. F. C. Hull. Princeton: Princeton University Press, 1954.

Odajnyk, Volodymyr W. *Jung and Politics: The Political and Social Ideas of C. G. Jung*. New York: New York University Press, 1976.

Olson, Alan M., ed. *Myth, Symbol, and Reality*. Notre Dame: University of Notre Dame Press, 1980.

Pahnke, Walter N., and Richards, William A. "Implications of LSD and Experimental Mysticism." In *Altered States of Consciousness*, pp. 399-428. Edited by Charles T. Tart. New York: John Wiley and Sons, 1969.

Pauson, Marian L. "C. G. Jung and the *A Priori*." *Tulane Studies in Philosophy* 18 (1969): 93-103.

Philipson, Morris. *Outline of a Jungian Aesthetics*. Evanston: Northwestern University Press, 1963.

Progoff, Ira. *The Death and Rebirth of Psychology*. New York: McGraw-Hill, 1956.

_____ . *Depth Psychology and Modern Man*. New York: McGraw-Hill, 1959.

_____ . *Jung's Psychology and Its Social Meaning*. New York: Julian Press, 1953.

_____ . *Jung, Synchronicity, and Human Destiny: Noncausal Dimensions of Human Experience*. New York: Julian Press, 1973.

Quispel, Gilles. "From Mythos to Logos." In *Eranos Jahrbuch* 39 *(1970) Man and Speech*, pp. 323-339. Edited by Adolf Portmann and Rudolf Ritsema. Leiden: E. J. Brill, 1973.

Rieff, Philip. "C. G. Jung's Confession: Psychology as a Language of Faith." *Encounter* 22 (May 1964): 45-50.

_____ . *The Triumph of the Therapeutic: Uses of Faith After Freud*. New York: Harper and Row, 1966.

Rossi, Ernest. "The Cerebral Hemispheres in Analytical Psychology." *Journal of Analytical Psychology* 22 (January 1977): 32-51.

Rychlak, Joseph F. *Introduction to Personality and Psychotherapy: A Theory-Construction Approach*. Boston: Houghton Mifflin, 1973.

_____ . *A Philosophy of Science for Personality Theory*. Boston: Houghton Mifflin, 1968.

Samuels, Andrew. *Jung and the Post-Jungians*. London: Routledge and Kegan Paul, 1985.

Sanford, John A. "Analytical Psychology: Science or Religion? An Exploration of the Epistemology of Analytical Psychology." In *The Well-Tended Tree: Essays into the Spirit of Our Time*, pp. 90-105. Edited by Hilde Kirsch. New York: G. P. Putnam's Sons, 1971.

Schwankl, Peter. "On the Phenomenology of the Unconscious." *Human Context* 5 (Summer, 1973): 318-330.

Scott, Charles E. "Archetypes and Consciousness." *Idealistic Studies* 7 (January 1977): 28-49.

Scriven, Michael. "Explanation and Prediction in Evolutionary Theory." In *Man and Nature: Philosophical Issues in Biology*, pp. 213-227. Edited by Ronald Munson. New York: Dell, 1971.

Sem-Jacobsen, Carl Wilhelm. *Depth-Electrographic Stimulation of the Human Brain and Behavior*. Springfield, Illinois: Thomas, 1968.

Semon, Richard. *The Mneme*. Translated by Lewis Simon. New York: Macmillan, 1921.

Shelburne, Walter A. "A Critique of James Hillman's Approach to the Dream." *Journal of Analytical Psychology* 29 (January 1984): 35-56.

———. "Synchronicity: A Rational Principle of Explanation." *Anima* 3 (Fall 1976): 58-66.

Sheldrake, Rupert. *A New Science of Life: The Hypothesis of Formative Causation*. London: Blond and Briggs, 1981.

Singer, June. "Archetypes: Eternal or Evolving." Public seminar sponsored by C. G. Jung Society of San Francisco and given in San Francisco November 6, 1982.

———. *Boundaries of the Soul: The Practice of Jung's Psychology*. New York: Doubleday, 1972.

Snell, Bruno. *The Discovery of the Mind: The Greek Origins of European Thought*. Cambridge: Harvard University Press, 1953.

Stace, Walter T. *Mysticism and Philosophy*. Philadelphia: J. B. Lippincott, 1960.

Staude, John-Raphael. *The Adult Development of C. G. Jung*. Boston and London: Routledge and Kegan Paul, 1981.

Stegmüller, Wolfgang. "Towards a Rational Reconstruction of Kant's Metaphysics of Experience." *Ratio* 9 (June 1967): 1-32.

Stein, Leopold. "Language and Archetypes." In *Contact with Jung: Essays on the Influence of His Work and Personality*, pp. 75-78. Edited by Michael Fordham. Philadelphia: Lippincott, 1963.

Stern, Paul J. *C. G. Jung: The Haunted Prophet*. New York: Dell, 1976.

Stevens, Anthony. *Archetypes: A Natural History of the Self*. New York: Quill, 1982.

Storr, Anthony. *C. G. Jung*. New York: The Viking Press, 1973.

Tart, Charles T. "Causality and Synchronicity: Steps Toward Clarification." *The Journal of the American Society for Psychical Research* 75 (April 1981): 121-141.

———. *States of Consciousness*. New York: Dutton, 1975.

———— , ed. *Altered States of Consciousness*. New York: John Wiley and Sons, 1969.

Toulmin, Stephen. *The Return to Cosmology: Postmodern Science and the Theology of Nature*. Berkeley: University of California Press, 1982.

Turner, Merle B. *Psychology and the Philosophy of Science*. New York: Meredith, 1968.

Valle, Ronald S., and Eckartsberg, Rolf von, eds. *The Metaphors of Consciousness*. New York: Plenum Press, 1981.

Van der Post, Laurens. *Jung and the Story of Our Time*. New York: Random House, 1975.

Wehr, Gerhard. *Portrait of Jung: An Illustrated Biography*. Translated by W. A. Hargreaves. New York: Herder and Herder, 1971.

Wheelwright, Philip E. *Metaphor and Reality*. Bloomington: Indiana University Press, 1962.

Index